A
forest
of
SIGNS

RICHARD BAIM

JUDITH BARRY

ERICKA BECKMAN

GRETCHEN BENDER

DARA BIRNBAUM

BARBARA BLOOM

TROY BRAUNTUCH

SARAH CHARLESWORTH

JACK GOLDSTEIN

JENNY HOLZER

LARRY JOHNSON

RONALD JONES

MIKE KELLEY

JEFF KOONS

BARBARA KRUGER

LOUISE LAWLER

THOMAS LAWSON

SHERRIE LEVINE

ROBERT LONGO

ALLAN MCCOLLUM

MATT MULLICAN

PETER NAGY

STEPHEN PRINA

RICHARD PRINCE

CINDY SHERMAN

LAURIE SIMMONS

HAIM STEINBACH

MITCHELL SYROP

JAMES WELLING

CHRISTOPHER WILLIAMS

A
forest
of
SIGNS

ART IN THE CRISIS OF REPRESENTATION

Exhibition Organized by Ann Goldstein and Mary Jane Jacob
Edited by Catherine Gudis

THE MUSEUM OF CONTEMPORARY ART, LOS ANGELES

THE MIT PRESS

CAMBRIDGE, MASSACHUSETTS

LONDON, ENGLAND

This publication accompanies the exhibition,
"A FOREST OF SIGNS: ART IN THE CRISIS OF REPRESENTATION,"
May 7 - August 13, 1989,
curated by Mary Jane Jacob and Ann Goldstein,
and organized by The Museum of Contemporary Art, Los Angeles.

"A FOREST OF SIGNS"
is made possible through a generous grant from Jay Chiat.
Additional support has been provided by Lilian and Albert Levinson;
the National Endowment for the Arts, a federal agency;
the California Arts Council, a state agency;
the Lannan Foundation; David Vena;
and Eileen & Peter Norton.

LIBRARY OF CONGRESS CATALOGING-IN-PUBLICATION DATA

A Forest of signs: art in the crisis of representation / [edited by Catherine Gudis].
p. cm.
"This publication accompanies the exhibition,
'A Forest of signs: art in the crisis of representation,' May 7-August 13, 1989,
curated by Mary Jane Jacob and Ann Goldstein,
and organized by the Museum of Contemporary Art, Los Angeles"
—T.p. verso.
"Texts by Ann Goldstein [and others]; foreword by Richard Koshalek" —P.
Includes index.
ISBN 0-262-07119-3 : $35.00
1. Figurative art, American—Exhibitions. I. Gudis, Catherine.
II. Jacob, Mary Jane. III. Goldstein, Ann. IV. Museum of Contemporary Art (Los Angeles, Calif.)
N6512.5.F5F67 1989
709'.73'074019494—dc19
89-3178
CIP

Endpapers: *Peter Nagy*
BELIEF IN STYLE, 1989 (detail)
Acrylic on canvas
72 x 72 in.
Collection of John L. Stewart, New York

Edited by Catherine Gudis
and Terry A. Neff, T.A. Neff Associates, Chicago
Designed by Lorraine Wild/AGENDA, Los Angeles
Typeset by Continental Typographics, Chatsworth, California
Printed by Donahue Printing Co., Inc., Los Angeles

This publication is dedicated to WILLIAM OLANDER (1950-1989),
Senior Curator at The New Museum of Contemporary Art in New York,
who was a friend and early champion of many of the artists represented here.
The creative world has been diminished by the loss of William Olander
and the many others whose lives have been claimed by AIDS.

LENDERS to the EXHIBITION

Consiline and Tony Antoville, *Rancho Palos Verdes, California*
Art & Knowledge Workshop, Inc., *Bronx, New York*
Josh Baer Gallery, *New York*
Neil and Barbara Bluhm, *Chicago*
Mary Boone Gallery, *New York*
Isabel Brones, *Los Angeles*
Nora Halpern Brougher and Kerry Brougher, *Los Angeles*
Linda Cathcart, *Venice, California*
Phoebe Chason, *Harrison, New York*
Alain Clairet, *New York*
Eileen and Matthew Cohen, *New York*
Douglas Crimp, *New York*
Galerie Crousel-Robelin, Bama, *Paris*
Dorit Cypis, *Minneapolis, Minnesota*
Gabriella de Ferrari, *New York*
Ellyn and Saul Dennison, *Bernardsville, New Jersey*
Hunter Drohojowska, *Venice, California*
William S. Ehrlich, *New York*
Joyce Eliason, *Los Angeles*
First Bank System, Incorporated, *Minneapolis, Minnesota*
Timothy and Suzette Flood, *Chicago*
Fried, Frank, Harris, Shriver and Jacobson Art Collection, *New York*
Shaunna and Joe Garlington, *La Crescenta, California*
Barbara Gladstone Gallery, *New York*
Jay Gorney Modern Art, *New York*
Doris and Robert Hillman, *New York*
Rhona Hoffman Gallery, *Chicago*
Max Holtzman Inc., *Rockville, Maryland*
Isabella Kacprzak, *Cologne, West Germany*
Lee Kaplan, *Los Angeles*
Kent Fine Art, *New York*
Michael Klein, Inc., *New York*
Alice and Marvin Kosmin, *New York*
Rosalind E. Krauss, *New York*

THE MUSEUM OF CONTEMPORARY ART is proud to present "A Forest of Signs: Art in the Crisis of Representation," a major exhibition that looks at the redefinition of art-making in America in the 1980s. The exhibition focuses on the central artistic issue or "crisis" of our time: the meaning of art in a media- and consumer-influenced era, and the meaning of representation within this art. The title of the exhibition refers to the "forest" of signs and symbols that define contemporary culture: the flow of images from films, billboards, bus benches, magazines, television, and art itself that are with us daily. These images have come to represent a new reality in their own right—a reality that we seek to enter and imitate in our own lives.

As life is increasingly filtered through the lens of television and film, and the message-laden pictures of advertising, the line between reality and fiction has become ambiguous. Art, like life today, has become subject to this same filtration process through its many presentations in exhibitions, books, and reproductions. Hence questions arise: What is the meaning of originality and the role of the artist as creator? Does the artist today function simply as a knowing producer and presenter of commodities for a burgeoning art market? And finally, what is the function of art today?

The works shown in "A Forest of Signs" perform double duty. They lament the loss of personal identity and singular, real experience. At the same time, they suggest that all art is yet another powerful set of images and narratives attempting to represent reality. They incorporate slogans, symbols, and stereotypes that pose questions about the social context in which words and images operate and manipulate us. Instead of documenting reality, they fabricate it anew.

It is a crucial role for MOCA to present and open up a forum for dialogue on recent art. For a contemporary museum, it is important not only to give historical viewpoints, but also to show history-in-the-making, even before "the verdict is in." Therefore, MOCA's exhibition program can provide definitive presentations of the past concurrent with "A Forest of Signs," such as the retrospectives of Man Ray ("Perpetual Motif: The Art of Man Ray," organized by the National Museum of American Art in Washington, D.C., and on view at MOCA's California Plaza facility March 19 through May 28)

and Marcel Broodthaers (organized by the Walker Art Center in Minneapolis and at California Plaza July 15 through October 22), artists who are sources for the artists of today. Along with these exhibitions, MOCA is providing a look at new ideas in art that have a briefer history, one that is not yet fully written, as with "A Forest of Signs."

This exhibition also provides an opportunity to assess the importance of Los Angeles as a major locus of activity (several of the artists studied at California Institute of the Arts, Valencia, and five live and work in Los Angeles) in the context of a New York dominated art world. Moreover, the expansive plan of the Temporary Contemporary—unique in the American museum world today—provides MOCA with the opportunity to undertake such an ambitious project, allowing each artist to present a sizable body of related work or a major installation.

"A Forest of Signs" could not have been realized without the enthusiasm and cooperation of the artists and the generosity of the lenders listed on the preceding pages. The exhibition's cocurators, Chief Curator Mary Jane Jacob and Assistant Curator Ann Goldstein, have worked on this project for over two years, and their contributions can be seen in the exhibition itself and in this catalogue. The guidance of Associate Director Sherri Geldin, who has overseen the myriad of organizational and financial issues related to the exhibition, and the skills of Director of Development Erica Clark in fund-raising activities, were crucial to the realization of the show.

This exhibition is made possible through a generous grant from Jay Chiat. Additional support has been provided by Lilian and Albert Levinson; the National Endowment for the Arts, a federal agency; the California Arts Council, a state agency; the Lannan Foundation; David Vena; and Eileen & Peter Norton. MOCA's staff and I would also like to express our gratitude to the Board of Trustees and its Program Committee for their continued support of the museum's programs and their affirmation of the museum's commitment to contemporary art.

RICHARD KOSHALEK
Director

INTRODUCTION and ACKNOWLEDGMENTS

"A FOREST OF SIGNS: ART IN THE CRISIS OF REPRESENTATION" aims to trace a tendency in American art as it has developed since the late 1970s. The title, taken from a line in the poem "Correspondences" in *Les Fleurs du Mal* by Charles Baudelaire (1821-1867) that refers to "des forêts de symboles," points to the current crisis of finding meaning in the multiplicity of signs that exist in today's culture. The sources for this work are the scores of cultural signs that represent the world—from the images and messages of the mass media, to architecture, language, cultural institutions, history, and art. The thirty artists included in "A Forest of Signs" attempt to examine how these representations function, questioning their authority in an effort to reveal how meaning is made. A network of issues has surfaced that connects the artists represented in this exhibition, including: the role of originality and authorship in the production of meaning; the impact of the mass media on the individual; the investigation of truth, reality, and fiction in representation; the position of art in the art market; and the artist as a self-conscious producer of commodities.

By about the mid-1970s artists were developing different strategies and approaches to art-making in order to address the issues that they saw affecting perceptions of art and contemporary life. The time frame for "A Forest of Signs" begins around 1977, coinciding with the "Pictures" exhibition (curated by Douglas Crimp for Artists Space in New York), the first group show to display and discuss this new tendency in American art. The present exhibition attempts to reassess the work of artists active since "Pictures," as well as to address the work of those artists who have emerged in the 1980s. The work of thirty artists has been included in this exhibition in order to provide an extensive, yet still manageable, look at this very significant and active area of artistic investigation that will continue to grow and change. Rather than surveying the history of each artist's work independently over this brief period of about twelve years, the exhibition features each artist through a single body of work, particular series, or major project, some specifically commissioned for this occasion.

An exhibition of this size and scope is the product of the efforts of many individuals, some of whom I would like to recognize and thank here on behalf of Mary Jane Jacob, cocurator of the exhibition, and myself. A major aspect of this exhibition is its accompanying catalogue. In addition to the introductory essay by Mary Jane Jacob and my discussions of each individual artist represented in the exhibition, this publication is greatly enhanced by the contributions of two guest authors: Anne Rorimer has thoughtfully provided a historical perspective on this recent American art, finding its sources in the generation of American and European conceptual artists of the prior decade. Howard Singerman, formerly MOCA's editor, played an essential role in the exhibition; his

knowledge and interest in this subject were key to its genesis during the early discussions in which he participated at MOCA. In addition to providing the exhibition's title, he has also contributed an illuminating essay on developments in critical theory that parallel the work of these artists. Since this exhibition documents a period in which artists have taken a more active role in the reading and distribution of their work, each was invited to make a contribution in the catalogue by designing a double-page spread for the artists' portfolio section.

The realization of this lengthy and richly illustrated publication would most certainly not have been possible without the continuing and tireless efforts of catalogue editor Catherine Gudis. She willingly assumed the monumental task of organizing every detail of this publication's editing and production. Terry A. Neff, T.A. Neff Associates, Chicago, edited the four essays herein and her expertise was particularly helpful for the scope of these texts. Curatorial Assistant Eric Freedman aided with manuscript production, in addition to his extraordinary efforts in all phases of the exhibition's preparation, loan procedures, and organization, being of essential assistance in keeping this extensive project on track. Vibeke Olson, research assistant, provided help at a critical time in the catalogue preparation, particularly in the compilation of the chronology of exhibitions that provides an analytical reference to the coincidence and proliferation of shows during this period. Finally, Lorraine Wild has thoughtfully and beautifully incorporated the ideas of the show into the design of this catalogue. This catalogue is the result of a joint venture with The MIT Press and the interest and support of Roger Conover, acquisition editor.

I wish to thank the entire museum staff for their involvement in this major exhibition at MOCA, and in addition to those individuals cited above, the following have been of particular help in this project. Director Richard Koshalek and Associate Director Sherri Geldin demonstrated unfailing support for this very ambitious project. The enthusiasm and counsel of Chief Curator Mary Jane Jacob enabled "A Forest of Signs" to develop to its fullest potential. The efforts of Mo Shannon, registrar, and her staff implemented the complicated logistics of the transportation of intricate works. John Bowsher, exhibition production manager, and his superb installation staff mounted a very difficult exhibition with great expertise and enthusiasm, and Brenda Mallory, preparator, worked tirelessly with the artists whose special installations needed particular attention. David Bradshaw, audiovisual technician, oversaw the production of several media-based projects, working closely with the artists to ensure the successful realization of these complicated installations. Coordinator of Touring Exhibitions Alma Ruiz saw through the details of the artists' contracts. Robin Hanson, grants officer, made great efforts that successfully resulted in significant grants, and Jack Wiant, controller, carefully oversaw the disposition of funds. Director of Education Vas Prabhu has organized a series of "Art Talks" to complement the exhibition, while Cynthia Campoy, assistant press officer; Sylvia Hohri, marketing and graphics manager; and Zoe Walrond, communications secretary, conveyed the content of this exhibition to the press. For their contributions, I also wish to thank Diana Schwab, assistant to the chief curator; Linda Hooper-Kawakami, curatorial secretary; Yvonne Carlson, membership and development coordinator; and former Research Assistant David Platzker and Curatorial Intern Kristin Lahmeyer who aided in the early stages of the exhibition's formation.

In the process of developing the concept of this exhibition, many individuals generously shared their thoughts, including Dan Cameron, Morgan Fisher, Hudson, William Olander, Brian Wallis, Helene Winer, as well as all of the artists. For their assistance and patience in assembling the works in the exhibition and providing information on the artists, I wish to thank the following galleries and their staff: in Los Angeles, Rosamund Felsen, Rosamund Felsen Gallery; Margo Leavin, Margo Leavin Gallery; and Daniel Weinberg, Daniel Weinberg Gallery; in New York, Josh Baer, Josh Baer Gallery; Mary Boone and Peter Opheim, Mary Boone Gallery; Barbara Gladstone, Richard Flood, and Sophie Hager Hume, Barbara Gladstone Gallery; Jay Gorney, Holly Hughes, and Caroline Roland-Lévy, Jay Gorney Modern Art; Douglas Walla and Susan Harris, Kent Fine Art, Inc.; Tracy Williams, Michael Klein, Inc.; Helene Winer, Janelle Reiring, and David Goldsmith, Metro Pictures; Peter Nagy, Nature Morte; Antonio Homem and Stefano Basilico, Sonnabend Gallery; Lisa Spellman and Tina Lyons, 303 Gallery; John Weber Gallery; in Paris, Chantal Crousel, Galerie Crousel-Robelin, Bama; and in Santa Monica, Richard Kuhlenschmidt, Jeff Beall, and Tony Green, Richard Kuhlenschmidt Gallery. Additional thanks are due to Suzanne Ghez, Liz Lambert, Thomas Lawson, Russell Lewis, Robbin Lockett, Karen Marta, Stephen Prina, Vincent Riggs, Joel Wachs, Thea Westreich, Christopher Williams, and Christopher Wool for their contributions and support during the research and organizational phases of this exhibition.

Finally, and most important, I would like to express my sincere gratitude to the artists in the exhibition. Without their tremendous personal involvement and commitment the major undertaking of this exhibition and publication could not have been realized. It is hoped that this exhibition will pay tribute to their efforts and to their art, which was its inspiration and its starting point.

ANN GOLDSTEIN
Assistant Curator

ART in the AGE of REAGAN: **1980–1988**

By Mary Jane Jacob

ARTISTS TODAY ARE COLLEGE-EDUCATED, most with advanced degrees. Unlike the training of earlier generations, theirs is focused around aesthetic theory, criticism, art history, and the pragmatics of the art world, rather than traditional art-school skills such as draftsmanship. All over America, college courses have been added to prepare artists for an MBA (masters of the business of art). Sometimes called "survival courses," these classes teach artists how to present their slides, how to talk about their work, how to get a gallery, how to read and write criticism, how to curate shows, and so on. The professionalization of the art student has led to the professionalization of the artist. The goal of artists is now to build a career, not just to make their art. Along with this, the scene has been set for a new art.

IN 1976 ALTERNATIVE SPACES were the mainstay of the young artist. Every artist hoped to and probably could be included in at least one show in one of these galleries. Artists themselves ran these spaces, aiming to gain control over the art world by presenting an alternative to the commercial gallery system that shut out young artists and were virtually closed to new, less salable forms of art (installation, Conceptual Art, performance, video, etc.). Alternative spaces were for artistic experimentation and dialogue. Housed in shabby quarters and making few sales, these modest institutions were crucial to keeping new art alive and providing many artists with their first means of encouragement along the hard road of gaining the necessary exposure that might someday, perhaps, lead to a big-time commercial gallery. In addition to alternative artists' spaces, key means of support for artists during this period were the traditional route of teaching and the new fellowship programs for artists, who, during this period, came to be called "emerging." Most prominent were the grants for visual artists from the National Endowment for the Arts (NEA), but there were also a host of other, newly created state- and city-funded programs. Artists knew it would be years, if ever, before they could live off sales of their art, but alternative spaces and an occasional grant and teaching job helped them to make it along the way.

In February 1979 an amazing event happened in the art world: a twenty-nine-year old artist named Julian Schnabel had his first one-person exhibition at the new Mary Boone Gallery in SoHo and was *instantaneously* a success. All of the paintings, priced between $2,500 and $3,000, were sold even before the show opened. With this one example it became possible for a young artist to rise from complete oblivion to cultural stardom. It became possible for a young artist to command high prices and to have a "retrospective" or major survey show within a few years of first appearing on the scene, an honor heretofore reserved only for artists in their fifties or sixties.

The work that began this turn of art economic events was mainly painting, a more collectable commodity. With this, painting took the lead again after a decade of Conceptual and Post-Minimal Art. At the same time, Europe reentered the American scene; there was considerable painting to be found there, most notably the three "Cs" from Italy (Enzo Cucchi, Francesco Clemente, Sandro Chia) and Neo-Expressionism from Germany (for example, Georg Baselitz, Anselm Kiefer, and A.R. Penck).

In 1985 Robert Hughes spoke of how the possibility for success at an early age, reinforced by sales and high prices, had led to a movement of careerism and the danger of the young artist being locked into an identifiable, salable style.[1] Moreover, he postulated that: "the moral economy of the art world has been

---

[1] Robert Hughes, "Careerism and Hype Amidst the Image Haze," *Time*, June 17, 1985, pp. 78-83.

so distorted by hype and premature careerism that the serious artist in New York must now face the same unreality and weightlessness as the serious actor in Los Angeles."[2] Nonetheless, for artists in the 1980s, the goal is to have secured a gallery by the time of graduation. And now that it has become possible for galleries to be successful with the work of young artists, dealers visit graduate studios and see MFA shows to make their "picks"; and with a well-schooled rap, student-artists make convincing statements about their graduate work.

IN THE 1970S FEW COLLECTORS purchased the work of unknown, young artists. There was support for a handful of local heroes or favorites by collectors as a sidelight to their more serious acquisitions, but major sales were by-and-large reserved for established figures.

In the 1980s, young artists are no longer "unknown." Not only did it become possible for them to be in private collections, but collectors had to "take a number" as the unprecedented phenomenon of the waiting list became commonplace. Artists and their dealers strategized about obtaining important collectors for their work. Whereas earlier only museums could lend real credibility, now it was possible, even preferable, to be in the "right" collections.

By the same token, collectors, so empowered, could make or hinder an artist's career. The most famous example is "the Saatchi Factor."[3] Adman par excellence, Saatchi has wielded an influence as tastemaker beyond that of any other single collector, critic, or curator. Like the best advertisement, others have followed him by purchasing the "brand names": the hot artists he designates. Or, as in the now famous instance of Saatchi's 1985 sale of six works by Chia, his influence can affect the market in an opposite way as well. Following the leads of Saatchi and a few other key collectors has given rise to another 1980s phenomenon: the sense that everyone has the *same* collection.

Coinciding with a shift in the economy from recession to rejuvenation through Reaganomics, art also underwent a "boom," as Calvin Tompkins called it in his article of the same name at the beginning of the decade. In it he stated: "The conjunction of this new audience and the latest crop of artists lends a febrile glow to the current scene—a nervous excitement that is good for business, if not necessarily for art."[4] Less than one year after Tompkin's statement, Grace Glueck wrote about the increased buying activity and excitement of the scene.[5] The continuation of this boom and where it has led is easily discernible by comparing Glueck's article of less than eight years ago to now. She quoted prices that today would seem a great bargain; among her examples are $1,500 for drawings and $7,000 - $15,000 for paintings by Anselm Kiefer—grouping Kiefer in the same price category as Markus Lupertz.[6] Not only do Kiefer's paintings today command one-half to one million dollars each, but he has left Lupertz well in his wake. One used to speak of buying art only if one liked it. But now, even for art lovers, cost is a factor. When one pays hundreds of thousands of dollars, or millions, for the work of a relatively young artist, one must ask: Will it retain its value? Is it a good investment?

[2]Ibid., p. 83.
[3]Richard W. Walker, "The Saatchi Factor," *ArtNews* 86, 1 (Jan. 1987): 117-121.
[4]Calvin Tompkins, "Boom," *The New Yorker*, Dec. 22, 1980, p. 78.
[5]Grace Glueck, "Fresh Talent and New Buyers Brighten the Artworld," *The New York Times*, Oct. 18, 1981, sec. 2, pp. 1-2.
[6]Ibid., p. 20.

In the 1970s emerging artists endeavored to find a critic to look at their work, write a review, and perhaps get it published in a national magazine. The artist at least hoped to get a review in one of the regional publications that were coming on the scene at that time (the West Coast's *Artweek*, Chicago's *New Art Examiner*, Ohio's *Dialogue*, Atlanta's *Art Papers*), that were providing more opportunities for the unknown or emerging artist.

Greater recognition and sales of the work of young artists have gone hand-in-hand in the 1980s. Reviews and articles have come to be used in unprecedented ways as art criticism has taken on the roles of publicity and advertising. In order for younger artists to make a place in today's market, reputations need to be made fast; we have come to speak of hyping the new. Now, in addition to the standard art press, popular and fashion magazines—*Time*, *Newsweek*, *People*, *Elle*, *Vanity Fair*, and *Vogue*, to name a few—regularly deal with art and often feature artists or collectors in glossy profiles. And so art and its stars (artists, dealers, critics, collectors, curators) have all become subjects for articles. The publicity surrounding art has changed. It is true that the lives of Picasso, Dali, Pollock, or Warhol have all been brought before the general public in this way. But today the number of art personalities and the immediacy of coverage have exploded. Today's artists (with perhaps the sole exception of Cindy Sherman), however, are not using the media in the way that Andy Warhol or Gilbert & George did, namely, keeping careful control over their images and making it part of their art. Rather, the artists are partially complicit. As Karen Benson pointed out in 1985 in an article in *ZG*, their "image is inescapable from their work even, though self-image is not the work's exclusive subject matter."[7] Lifestyle, an important catchword of the era, has become confused with art itself; we are familiar with images of the artists in their lofts, but also with images of the collectors in their lofts, and perhaps know these as well or better than we do the images of the works of art themselves. Whereas artists once struggled alone in their studios, today they have opened themselves up to the cameras, the collectors, and the tour groups. Just as this "opening up" helped to sell the art, so are the images of the artists, their art, or other art-world personalities used to sell products—from Absolut Vodka to Barney's men's clothing. Ads sell art and art sells a lifestyle.

In the mid-1970s, in order to increase the public funding base for art, a more democratic campaign inspired by the bicentennial spirit, was established to bring art to the people. NEA, city and state arts councils, and museums all developed new outreach programs, from exhibitions housed in trains and buses to artist-in-residency and school programs. Their common goal was to spread knowledge, understanding, and interest in the arts, and ultimately to increase the audience for art. In short, the goal was to promote art. Although the underlying spirit was evangelical, the techniques were those of marketing.

Art has become more popular, but perhaps not in this "art for the people" way. While art is more clearly valued today, it is unclear whether it is valued for aesthetic or monetary reasons. In 1985, with the opening of the third Whitney branch museum, Grace Glueck in *The New York Times* questioned why, for all the altruistic, do-gooder posturing of the Whitney, their branches were located solely in Manhattan and in a well-to-do suburb of Connecticut, rather than in truly needy, disadvantaged areas and other boroughs of the city—areas to which the Whitney was far more inaccessible.[8] From the museum point of view, one can read-

[7]Karen Benson, "Art Stars: Out of the Studios, into the Glossies," *ZG* 14 (Summer 1985): 4-6.

[8]Grace Glueck, "Are the Whitney's Satellite Museums on the Right Course?," *The New York Times*, June 9, 1985, pp. 31, 34.

ily understand that the audiences around the Philip Morris Building, Equitable Life Assurance Society, and Stamford, Connecticut, location (funded by Champion International) were logical places from which to attract and extend the museum's audience. The many exhibitions staged at these locations give people access to art on a daily basis—during their lunch hours—with the hope that on weekends they will come visit the Whitney itself. But Glueck intimated that such embellishments to corporate headquarters may be just another example of the kind of publicity, that is, favoritism, that corporate sponsors can buy.[9] Satellite branches—many museums, large and small, have them—can indeed be viewed as a 1980s manifestation of bringing art to the people, however, the manner in which the Whitney has undertaken this remains circumspect to some critics. A few months after Glueck's article, Calvin Tompkins echoed the same sentiments about the most recent branch of the Whitney at Equitable Center: "Lichtenstein, Chia, and Burton can help to sell real estate, it appears, as effectively as Cimabue and Giotto helped to sell Christianity."[10]

Another 1980s development that increases public exposure to art, at least on a limited basis, is the private collection museum. This is not a new phenomenon—in Los Angeles we have the J. Paul Getty and Norton Simon Museums, New York has the Frick Collection, and Boston is home to the Isabella Stewart Gardner Museum. However, with acquiring large numbers of contemporary work rapidly, within just a few years rather than collecting over a lifetime, many individuals soon feel they have established a worthy "collection." What to do with all these works, how to store them, how to access the works for themselves and others, how to benefit from tax breaks, were all reasons that led some to start their own museums or museumlike spaces.

Most prominent among the private collection projects proposed for this decade was Ed Broida's failed museum in New York. Conceived as a public institution, it was the great hope of arts professionals and the museum-going public to rectify New York's critical problem of space to accommodate major traveling exhibitions. The plan was to include a full complement of museum-organized exhibitions and education programs. With this proposal, private initiative seemed to be making the grand gesture of patronage to the public. But in 1986, after several years in the planning by a professional staff, the project proved to be too complex and difficult for funder-founder Broida, and he abandoned his plans. A project successfully undertaken has been Charles and Doris Saatchi's space for their collection that opened in London in 1985. Their clear and simple exhibition program consists of ongoing, rotating displays solely of their collection, without other programming and education. While it does not aim to be a museum, it has taken on certain guises of a museum, such as the publishing of a four-volume collection catalogue, *Art of Our Time*, that constitutes a contemporary version of H.W. Janson's *History of Art*.

CORPORATIONS ONCE STOOD OUTSIDE of the art world. In the 1970s perhaps a few works adorned the CEO's office or the board room. While the history of corporate collecting can be traced back to 1959 with Chase Manhattan Bank's establishment of an art-buying program, it is really a phenomenon of the 1980s.

In 1986 *The Wall Street Journal* cited that "the number of corporations collecting art has risen 50% in the past five years, to about 1,000."[11] By and

[9]Ibid.

[10]Calvin Tompkins, "Medicis, Inc.," *The New Yorker*, April 14, 1986, p. 87.

[11]Meg Cox, "Boom in Art Market Lifts Prices Sharply, Stirs Fears of a Bust," *The Wall Street Journal*, Nov. 24, 1986, p. 1.

large, these are contemporary collections since this art is more affordable and more plentiful; this demand alone has had an impact on sustaining a large number of artists and galleries. New branches of the art field have also sprung up to service these needs and interests: corporate curators, registrars, and art advisors. Calvin Tompkins conjectured that corporate collecting has bolstered more traditional styles of art as well, speculating that the increase in corporate buying may in fact be responsible for the return to favor of representational painting since the mid-1970s.[12] Conservatism in corporate collecting has also led to dubbing some art with the quasi-stylistic term "corporate art" (abstract prints or the mandatory steel sculpture sited in front of the corporate headquarters like a great logo).

IN THE 1970S THERE WAS INCREASED ATTENTION to art made outside of the center of New York, sometimes called regional art. Efforts were made, especially by new institutions like The New Museum of Contemporary Art, to give exposure to artists from other centers—Texas, California, Chicago, and elsewhere. In this atmosphere of opening up and enfranchising new groups into the art scene, places were being made (or at least talked about) for women artists, Blacks, Hispanics, and others.

In spite of the new awareness of the inequality of representation in the arts, and efforts to give recognition specifically to previously excluded groups in the arts, with the return to painting there was a reaffirmation of the leading, if not exclusive, role of men—that is white male artists from New York and Western Europe. With the return to art of "big bucks," there was a corresponding return to art by "big boys."

However, there was another history of the late 1970s and 1980s. Groups given some power and access earlier in the 1970s continued, although not in such a visible light. Important for the present exhibition were the sustained role and vitality of women artists. In fact, as Conceptual Art, photography, language art, and other related concerns seemed to fade from view in the late 1970s in the wake of bravado painting, it was the work of some of the most important contemporary women artists that kept the dialogue most alive. Barbara Kruger, Jenny Holzer, Sherrie Levine, Cindy Sherman, Sarah Charlesworth, Louise Lawler, Laurie Simmons, to name but a few included in this exhibition, all played a key role at the beginning of the period under discussion. And among the subjects that they dealt with in looking to the economics of the period was gender. Here feminist thought and Conceptualism found a sympathetic and fruitful union.

DURING THIS REAGAN ERA OF THE 1980S, not just the art world, but art itself has changed. The dynamics of the art world are more intertwined than ever, and it is no wonder that art—imitating life—is now imitating life in the art world. Not only have artists benefited from the decade's financial boom, but their art also reflects this new, closer relationship between art and commerce.

A new kind of art has arisen in the 1980s. The highest price-tagged items—Neo-Expressionism and Transavanguardia—and those artists whose subject

[12]Tompkins, "Medicis, Inc." (note 10), p. 90.

matter or style are reactionary or whose art stands outside the aesthetic issues of the moment are not the focus of the present exhibition. Rather, this exhibition focuses on those artists whose work has been directed and influenced by events of the art world in the last decade. Schooled in the Conceptualism of the 1970s (a movement whose link as antecedent is made clear in Anne Rorimer's essay that follows), these artists have redirected the strategies of Conceptual Art and of the business of art to the making of art. Theirs is a self-conscious art, which also finds precedence in the changing status of the artist during the twentieth century. The Dada readymade object gave the artist the right to bestow on anything the status of art; actual fabrication of the object was no longer necessary. Thus was dealt the first blow to the criteria of craftsmanship and originality that had previously defined a work of art. The success of the Pop artists, and most importantly Andy Warhol, not only added images from the mass media to this repertory of readymades, but also created the possibility for the artist to be a living star.

The relation of today's art to consumer society is perhaps even more complicated than that of the Pop artists. The subject now is not a product pulled from a grocery shelf, but art itself as a product for sale. Appropriating techniques of commerce and advertising for the content, mode of fabrication, and presentation of the work, artists are playing with the strategies of both the business and art worlds that have combined forces in so many ways over the past decade. As a result their work stands somewhere between criticality and complacency. To some it exposes and questions the more debased values of our times, whereas to others, such as Kay Larson, it is more accepting, as she wonders "How valid is any critique of capitalism that aims at total success within the system?"[13]

"A FOREST OF SIGNS" seeks not to present a final answer on this question. It attempts rather to be an exhibition about the 1980s turn-of-art-events and the recasting of how the artist approaches the making of art today. In accepting the challenge to do a truly contemporary exhibition, about ideas of the moment, we chose not to invent final answers nor close the book on a chapter in art history still in the making. More questions than answers are presented by these new artistic tendencies still in formation; this is a period-in-progress. The twelve years covered in this exhibition do not mark a period to presented like a string of influences that reflect a standard art historical sense of continuity. Twelve years is a very short time, and even though we have come to measure art history in years or months rather than decades, this exhibition looks upon this period in its totality. Artists are not represented by their first work nor locked into any sequential order of masters and followers, but instead are seen as a steady, even rapidly burgeoning group that has expanded ideas within today's critical dialogue. This exhibition certainly does not aim to present the guaranteed new art stars of the future. Rather these artists were selected because their work was particularly articulate and allowed for some understanding of today's aesthetics and its relation to the dynamics of the present art world. The diversity of approaches represented quickly shows there is not one style or solution in this new art. It is hoped that the forum for debate that this exhibition provides will enable us, as viewers, and even the artists, to have a better grasp of the issues of our time.

[13]Kay Larson, "Masters of Hype," *New York*, Nov. 10, 1986, p. 102.

BAIM−WILLIAMS

By Ann Goldstein

RICHARD BAIM's art is aligned with his occupation as a producer of corporate audio-visual events that communicate, seduce, and sell, facilely blurring the distinctions between entertainment and "corporate message." His art draws upon these same strategies in the production of elaborate slide shows of photographic images presented like cinema in a theater, and environmental multimedia installations or displays. Baim's intention is to examine critically such spectacularizing vehicles of presentation as the world's fair exposition, convention trade show, and the amusement park—which he sees as effectively "reestablishing consumption as the essential element in the perpetuation of the capitalist system."[1]

In *Rise and Fall* (1986), Baim has used this vehicle of display, "the exhibition," to explore the representation of male power. The work is a three-part "epic" slide show consisting of photographic images (taken by the artist) of fascist architecture, war monuments, bullfights, and businessmen, accompanied by a dramatic Wagnerian sound track. In *World/Fair* (1988), projected images of crowds in shopping malls and the industrial landscape are accentuated by a projected image of the utopian "cash register" pavilion from the 1939 New York World's Fair. Accompanied by a large floor tablet bearing song lyrics from a Radio City Music Hall production celebrating the World's Fair ("We're the rising tide come from far and wide/marching side by side on our way/for a brave new world/tomorrow's world/that we shall build today"), this installation takes on the didactic character of a world's fair "display" but with images that portray a future different from the utopia envisioned fifty years earlier.

The world's fair is of particular interest to Baim for what it represents as propaganda, commerce, and societal ideals for the future. Baim's extensive collection of 1939 World's Fair memorabilia, personal papers, and photograph albums of strangers that he has picked up in thrift stores,[2] as well as a multitude of photographs that Baim has taken himself, together comprise a massive archive of global history and memory. This collection marks pivotal moments in cultural history as experienced by Baim and others, and is the material source for his works. In turn, his art reflects this multiplicity of viewpoints.

Baim sees *Turn of the Century* (1988) (SEE CAT. NO. 1; SEE ILLS. PP. 66-67) as, in a sense, a sequel to *World/Fair*. This elaborate two-room display of slide projections and photographs emulates a world's fair type of exhibition. Whereas *World/Fair* talks about the "future" and the transition of the nineteenth to the twentieth century, *Turn of the Century* is about the transition from the twentieth to the twenty-first century—the future that *World/Fair* imagined. It addresses the obsolescence of the advances made or anticipated since the nineteenth century, where "obsolescence might be a term applied to culture or society instead of technology...."[3] Images of the industrial landscape of the Eastern and Western United States are incorporated into a series of framed black-and-white and color photographs and slide projections. Again, the use of visual "activators" (like the cash register image in *World/Fair*) sets a tone for the overall reading of the work. Images of lifeboats, gas tanks, machinery, power lines, etc., "aestheticized" by their blurred presentation, convey the transition of the nineteenth- to the twentieth-century cultural landscapes, and like memories or thoughts, blur the distinctions between past and present.

Richard Baim
WORLD/FAIR, *1988 (detail)*
Mixed-media installation with slide projections and floor tablet
Overall dimensions variable; detail: 12 x 25 ft.
Courtesy the artist

[1]Richard Baim, unpublished exhibition proposal, 1987.
[2]For example, the "cash register" image in *World/Fair* was found among a family's papers; Baim's research suggests that it was taken by a Nazi relative visiting at the time.
[3]Letter from the artist to the author, Aug. 11, 1988.

22

Since the late 1970s, JUDITH BARRY has considered "how space is ideological,"[4] critically examining the ascribed function of architectural spaces in relation to the individual's experience of them. Her work has encompassed video, film, slide presentations, installations, performances, critical texts, exhibition design, and fiction. Barry studied architecture and also worked early on as a space planner for a major hotel chain, an important influence on her interest in the symbolic dynamics of corporate architecture. Barry has written about her interest in architecture, likening the individual's experience of a public space to that of the cinema:

> For me, architecture as the bearer of the inscribed social relations
> structuring the world has been subsumed by media to such an extent
> that it no longer exists in the "platonic" way that architecture used to
> be thought about—the ideal, expressed in built form, to stand for-
> ever. Instead I see this architecture as most like the montage theo-
> ries of the cinema, particular images with symbolic importance
> which take on meaning as we move through the environments that
> shape our existence. For me, architecture has become transparent, a
> giant screen into which social life dissolves.[5]

Barry equates the experience of corporate architecture to the way one experiences cinema—passively, as a spectator. For example, in her soap opera-like videotape *Casual Shopper* (1980-81), a couple strolls somnolently through a shopping mall, passive shoppers whose identities become indistinguishable from the fashion models in the magazines they look through and the commodities they desire. As perpetual shoppers, the characters move within a timeless world without history.

Like these characters, Barry suggests that individuals in the real world are similarly destined to be perpetual consumers whose identities are formed in the reflections of the mass-media culture that surrounds them. She locates the myth of the vampire as an analogy for the spectator:

> He lives outside of time and, as such, has no history, no memory, nor
> is he bound by the conventions of daily life. He must live at that time
> when all else is dead, at night. He lives in a dreaded state of antici-
> pation and anxiety which carries with it a profound emptiness and
> loneliness not remedial even by death for he cannot easily die. He
> must spend his time watching the lives of others who are uncon-
> scious of his very existence. He cannot stand his reflection because
> it reminds him of his situation. He cannot constitute himself as an
> "other" through the mirror phase. He is doomed to be what he is, he
> cannot change the fact that he does not exist. The mirror does not lie
> here, does not allow him that feeling of mastery and control essential
> even to adult survival. It insists on showing him precisely the state
> that he is in.[6]

The vampiric reflection as symbolic of unrequited desire is examined in Barry's slide/film/sound installations *In the Shadow of the City... vamp r y* (1986) and *Echo* (1986) (CAT. NO. 2; ILLS. PP. 68-69). The latter refers to the myth of Echo who, in her unrequited love for Narcissus, pined away until only her voice remained,

[4]Judith Barry, "Pleasure/Leisure and the Ideology of Corporate Convention Space," in Lorn Falk and Barbara Fisher, eds., *The Event Ho-
rizon* (Banff, Canada: Banff Centre and The Walter Phillips Gallery,
and Toronto: Coach House Press, 1987), pp. 253-64.

[5]Judith Barry, quoted in Elke Town, *Dark/Light* (Toronto: Mercer
Union, 1986), p. 7.

[6]Judith Barry, "Willful Amnesia," in *Video by Artists 2* (Toronto: Art
Metropole, 1986), p. 46. For a critical discussion of Barry's notion of
the vampire, see Jean Fisher, "The Vampire of the Text," *Parkett* 14
(Fall 1987): 93-95.

Judith Barry
Maelstrom, *1988 (foreground)*
Film and slide projections, text,
and painted walls
Overall dimensions variable
Installation at the Whitney Museum
of American Art at Equitable Center,
New York, 1988

whereafter Narcissus was condemned to fall in love with his own image. Slow dissolves of slides projecting images of the AT & T building's lobby, the atrium of the IBM tower, and the "Globe" at the 1965 World's Fair in New York are inset with Super-8 video film loops of a businessman in various corporate settings—riding an escalator, exiting a building carrying a briefcase, and, like Narcissus, gazing at his own reflection in the pool of a company health club. The work addresses the contradictions of the corporate lobby or atrium, which attempt to blur the distinctions between inside and outside, public and private.

Barry's recent project *Maelstrom*, a video installation in progress since 1988, examines the impact of information technologies on the individual, thought processes, and communication. She questions the divisions between human being and machine in a deluge of video projections and texts painted on the walls, such as, "Are there still men or are there just computing, writing and thinking-machines?" Incorporating the architectural space, *Maelstrom* engulfs the viewers, intruding on their personal space, forcing them to confront their role as thinking individuals.

Since the late 1970s, Ericka Beckman has produced a cohesive and consistent body of work in Super-8 and 16mm film, and photographs. Beckman's films portray the complexities of the process of learning and socialization in child's play—how social and sexual roles are demonstrated, identified, and assumed, and how meaning is applied and developed. Her use of repetitive, childlike chants, sound effects, and musical scores, along with toylike props in primary colors and adults as childlike characters set in a disorienting black field, projects a dreamlike state of suspended fragments. Deceptively simple, Beckman's early Super-8 films, including *We Imitate; We Break Up* (1978), *The Broken Rule* (1979), and *Out of Hand* (1981) (CAT. NO. 3), represent the complex and ambiguous signals of how the world is represented in children's songs, nursery rhymes, and fairy tales, and in turn, reflect upon how that impact is manifest. Writing about Beckman's films, Sally Banes observed:

> The films are much more complicated than they might seem at first glance, because below their bright, light, charming surfaces and the apparently disconnected streams of imaginative icons one finds the most profound issues: questions of ethics, identity, gender, sexuality, acculturation, destiny, power, knowledge.[7]

This observation applies to Beckman's later films. The 16mm film *Cinderella* (1986) (CAT. NO. 3) is a feminist critique of the childhood tale. The story is transformed into a pinball-like game in which Cinderella is made aware of the social role and personal goals that she must learn and embrace, symbolically set forth as the successful outcome of the game: to get the dress, leave the shoe, and be home at midnight with the prince. In Beckman's film, Cinderella struggles to

[7]Sally Banes, "Imagination and Play: The Films of Ericka Beckman,"
Millenium Film Journal 13 (Fall / Winter 1983-84): 99.

Ericka Beckman
CINDERELLA, *1986*
Still from 16mm film, 27 min.
Courtesy the artist

master "how to play the game," failing on her first attempt; when she finally succeeds, she rejects the system.

Beckman has also shown Cibachrome photographs from her films, as well as installations that incorporate sculptural props. Recently, she has begun to "animate" the photographs with synchronized lighting and sound tracks. These installations of "Nanotech Players" (SEE CAT. NO. 4; SEE ILLS. PP. 70-71) refer to nanotechnology, a futuristic mixture of computer technology and biology in an industrial process of building materials from living cells—a process whereby computers run the life cycle. Beckman's "Nanotech Players" activate a space for the duration of a program, bringing the viewer into the work and giving the spectator a sense of the activities in her films, further illuminating through "play" the childlike experiences of socialization and symbolic learning depicted in her films.

In her work since the early 1980s, GRETCHEN BENDER has critically engaged the proliferation of mass media. Images of corporate logos, footage from broadcast news, reproductions of artworks, and advertising imagery are appropriated and re-presented (straight or modified through computer generation) in a changing repertory of forms including photographic constructions, installations, video, and video and film "performances." Bender catches the images in motion, diverting the flow for a momentary scrutiny, so that the systems and strategies that underlie these signs can be critically examined: "I quickly got caught up in the way in which TV moves, the current. The movement, not even the sequence, but the movement that flattened content. From that equivalent flow I tried to force some kind of consciousness of underlying patterns of social control."[8]

Bender identified the controlled obsolescence, equivalence of images, and seductive "defamiliarizing" tactics of the mass media: "I think of the media as a cannibalistic river. A flow or current that absorbs everything. It's not 'about.' There is no consciousness or mind. It's about absorbing and converting."[9] She has described how her strategy is to mimic the media in order to affect critically through provocation.[10]

Multichannel, multiscreen video/sound/film installations such as *Dumping Core* (1986) or *Total Recall* (1987) assume the form of a media spectacle

[8]Gretchen Bender, interview with Cindy Sherman, "Gretchen Bender," *Bomb* 18 (Winter 1987): 23.
[9]Ibid.
[10]Ibid.

with a profusion of images that bombard the viewer. Jonathan Crary wrote: "A single image can sustain an illusion of presence; but the proliferation of identical, dematerialized images that co-exist in time effaces the screen as object and the space it occupies. It is a vision of television as a black hole that absorbs energy and collapses in on itself."[11] The issue of production and consumption is also explored in works that incorporate film titles. *People in Pain* (1988) (CAT. NO. 5), is an expansive construction of heat-set sheets of vinyl illuminated from behind with white neon. Each sheet bears the title of a film scheduled for release in 1988. Bender chose the titles (approximately 120) from *The Film Journal*'s "Blue Sheets," a biannually published list of forthcoming feature films. Together, the entire work presents an expanse of melted "celluloid." It signals the transition of anticipation into the disappointment of arrival, and the cycle of this process, for as each film is released it renews anticipation for the next one. After all have been released, Bender's object remains as a massive archival record of a period of cinematic production; its bulk signifies the refuse of that process.

Since 1985 Bender has appropriated broadcast television into works that are comprised of television sets tuned to local channels with short phrases or words printed on the screens (SEE CAT. NO. 6). The television images are filtered through such texts as "Relax," "I'm going to die," "People with AIDS." Disengaged from their audio component, the images of the game shows, soap operas, broadcast news, etc. flow unemphasized by sound in a constant stream, their original meaning changed by their redirection through the textual overlays. As Gary Indiana wrote about *People with AIDS*: "Bender projects *the virus* into the electronic bloodstream, reconstitutes TV figures as physical bodies, infects inanity with anxiety and reveals a certain kind of *manufactured anxiety* as a hysterical spectacle."[12]

Gretchen Bender
UNTITLED *(People with AIDS), 1986*
Television, text on acetate, and steel
15 x 20 x 15 in.
Courtesy Metro Pictures, New York

[11]Jonathan Crary, "Gretchen Bender: Total Recall," in exh. brochure (Houston: Contemporary Arts Museum, 1988), unpag.
[12]Gary Indiana, "Clownphobia Today," *Village Voice* 32, 25 (June 23, 1987): 92.

Working exclusively since 1978 in video, producing single-channel tapes and video/sound installations, DARA BIRNBAUM investigates mass media's impact on the construction of individual identity. Birnbaum's interest in reexamining mass-media representations has itself been a response to the changing nature of access to television imagery (before and after the availability of VCR's for private use) and advancements in video technology. As her work has developed, Birnbaum has redefined her role as an artist addressing the impact of the mass media on the individual.

> I consider it to be our responsibility to become increas-
> ingly aware of alternative perspectives which can be
> achievable through our use of media—and to consciously
> find the ability for expression of the "individual voice" —
> whether it be dissension, affirmation, or neutrality
> (rather than a deletion of the issues and numbness, due
> to the constant "bombardment" which this medium can
> all too easily maintain). [13]

In her early video work (1978-82)—including *Technology/ Transformation: Wonder Woman* (1978), *Kiss the Girls: Make Them Cry* (1979), and *PM Magazine* (1982)—she appropriated and re-constructed images from commercial television in order to assess, through displacement and montage, the cultural representations and social strategies at play within the medium. Specifically, Birnbaum looked at TV's representation of women. Her process included repeti-tive editing of selected cuts and dynamic sound tracks of short dura-tion, emulating the seductiveness of the medium while isolating seemingly simple sections that reveal subtle social messages.

It was a tactic that Birnbaum relinquished in a series of works that constitute *Damnation of Faust* (1983-87) (ILL. P. 75), in which she originated rather than appropriated video footage to con-tinue her examination of identity. Her thirty-second *Art Break* for MTV (1987) appropriated Max Fleischner's popular, animated "Out of the Ink Well" series of the 1920s (in which animator and character wrestle for control over the pen) but Birnbaum replaced the usual characters with popular representations of women as a critique of those in the music videos.

Dara Birnbaum
TECHNOLOGY/TRANSFORMATION:
WONDER WOMAN,
© *1978*
Stills from color videotape, 7 min.
Courtesy the artist

Birnbaum's current project for the "Rio" shopping mall development in Atlanta is comprised of a twenty-five-monitor video wall that presents a montage of images from three sources: footage of the original site before the mall was built, live broadcasts of Atlanta-based CNN news, and an interactive video set up for shoppers in the mall. It is a work that speaks specifically of its site— its cultural and historical context; as it assembles information, a viewer is able to read the past through the present, and vice versa.

Birnbaum's installations incorporate large black-and-white photo-graphic display panels inset with monitors and mounted on painted walls. *PM Magazine*, first created in 1982 and since reconstructed in different venues (CAT. NO. 7; ILL. PP. 74), is a multichannel installation (of varying versions from one to five channels) that uses footage exclusively from broadcast television. Three-minute loops assemble footage from the opening sequence of the TV show "P.M. Magazine," a Wang computer commercial, ice skaters, a little girl licking an ice cream cone, etc., set to a fragmented audio track that includes The Doors' "L.A.

[13]Dara Birnbaum, "Talking Back to the Media," in *Talking Back to the Media* (Amsterdam: Stedelijk Museum, 1985), pp. 48-49.

Woman" and the musical theme of the TV show, producing what Craig Owens has called "a phantasmagoria of the media."[14] The photographic panels are blowups of two stills from the video, one of the girl eating ice cream and one of a woman at a computer terminal. Birnbaum's work is experienced in a dialectical relationship to the paintings and sculptures adjacent to it, and aligns itself within the conventions of painting, sculpture, and architecture; her intention is not to sequester the installation work into a separate video area, but to display it as any other work of art. (Interestingly, *PM Magazine* was made at a time when large-scale epic painting was in the forefront of attention.) Its presentation addresses the notion of display in an institutional setting, as discussed by Benjamin H.D. Buchloh, where "the framework of the museum is bracketed with the commercial display, on the one hand, and the historic dimension of agitprop montage on the other."[15]

"For me the greatest pleasure consists in reading meanings in details...."[16] BARBARA BLOOM's obsession with detail stems from an interest in the implicit, in possible meanings—hers is "a detective gaze."[17] Her curiosity is piqued by incongruence and coincidence, the distraction of associations that a "precious fragment" can engender—satisfied with that moment which becomes its own entity. Bloom's work—in the form of photographs, texts, graphic design, publications, films, found and fabricated objects, and installations—is not easily characterized. In her earlier work, Bloom focused on the mass media, producing stage-set-like tableaux, book covers, posters, and a film trailer for a nonexistent film, *The Diamond Lane* (1981), that emulated conventional vehicles of communication or display.

The formation of meaning through the experience of details has continued in Bloom's recent work, as she moves away from a specific mass-media orientation to works that engage the viewer in the process of looking at the representation of cultural details, drawing into her reading the context of a particular exhibition setting, whether it be a museum or a commercial gallery. In *The Gaze* (1985), Bloom created an installation that addresses the act of looking. Using institutional railings that are used to keep spectators away from artwork, she installed the barriers so as to create a path around the perimeter of the room, preventing the viewer from walking outside of the prescribed path. Works on the wall were veiled by diaphanous curtains that invited the viewer to part them and view mostly photographic works—images of people in various settings taken from behind—placing the viewer in the position of voyeur. Bloom's notions of presentation and installation are inextricable from the objects she presents in her recent theatrical, still-life-like installations such as *Esprit de l'Escalier* (1988) or *The Seven Deadly Sins* (1988). Special display cases or pieces of furniture selected on the basis of their stylistic or historical references are used to exhibit her objects and contribute to their meaning.

The Reign of Narcissism (1989) (CAT. NO. 8), a parlorlike installation of objects and furniture, recalls the *vanitas* of sixteenth- and seventeenth-century Dutch and Flemish painting. Those still-life paintings portrayed objects symboliz-

[14]Craig Owens, "Phantasmagoria of the Media," *Art in America* 70, 5 (May 1982): 98.

[15]Benjamin H.D. Buchloh, "Allegorical Procedures: Appropriation and Montage in Contemporary Art," *Artforum* 21, 1 (Sept. 1982): 56.

[16]Barbara Bloom, "Het Genot Van Het Detail, Jan Simons. Barbara Bloom Ovef Haar Werk," in *Talking Back to the Media* (Amsterdam: Stedelijk Museum, 1985), p. 43.

[17]Conversation with the artist, Nov. 16, 1987.

ing the inexorability of time and death while expressing the emptiness of material possessions. Bloom's work examines narcissism and vanity, not only as a prevalent condition endemic to our society, but also as a personalized statement on artistic production. Encompassing a variety of elements, including mirrors, upholstered chairs, plaster and architectural moldings, columns, busts, and antique cases containing watermarked porcelain cups, cameos, stationery, chocolates, and books—all bearing images of the artist, her silhouette, and her signature, or images of women gazing at their own reflections—this work obsessively displays the artist's self-consciousness as a producer. It is a work about how art represents the artist, and the desire for recognition—obsessively elaborating on the production of likenesses so as to expose the intimate complexities of the personal self-exposure inherent in that process.

The process of looking and making meaning has been eloquently addressed by TROY BRAUNTUCH since the late 1970s in photographic works, works on paper, and paintings. Images of images, Brauntuch's works offer minimal information; they are just barely decipherable from their background field—the images are distinguishable, but their specific subjects are unrecognizable. This loss of identity is of particular importance because Brauntuch's photographic sources include photographs of the Third Reich, among them personal drawings, sketches, and architectural renderings by Adolf Hitler and Albert Speer. The severe breakdown of these loaded images renders them mysterious, paradoxically "beautiful"; the visual and spatial ambiguity of these works is seductive because of their delicate execution. As the images rest at the threshold of decipherability, they are also at the threshold of meaning. Brauntuch's images are at the brink of collapsing into meaninglessness.

The obdurate reticence of the early photographs and works on paper (1979-81) (SEE CAT. NOS. 9-12) based on Third Reich imagery is a result of photographic mediation of visual and historical fragments—a very different treatment of cultural history than the bold Neo-Expressionist paintings of similar themes that were predominant in the late 1970s and early 1980s. Framed under glass, these works reflect the viewer in the process of looking, making the assessment of meaning even more problematic. "His work establishes an interplay between the forces of enticement and exclusion, creating an ambiguous space of fascinated entrapment for the gaze."[18]

Even the expanded scale of Brauntuch's large-scale paintings, the images derived from documentary or cinematic sources, does not offer the comfort of resolution. The recent works on paper (SEE ILLS. PP. 78-79) reduce the images—ranging from simple architectural forms, to a street person, to Third Reich imagery—to diagrammatic, sketchlike drawings on the verge of abstraction. Some, rendered as just a few charcoal lines on a white sheet of paper, are reminiscent of the early work—though their sources are no longer specific. Seemingly spectacular, Brauntuch's fragments are visual remains rendered ambiguous and equivocal in their mystery.

Troy Brauntuch
UNTITLED, *1978 (detail)*
Type-C prints
Three panels: 48 x 96 in.;
48 x 48 in.; and 48 x 48 in.
Lannan Foundation

[18]Rosetta Brooks, "Troy Brauntuch: Life After Dark," *Parkett* 11 (Dec. 1986): 7.

The conditions of photographic reality and the process of extracting meaning have engaged SARAH CHARLESWORTH since the late 1970s. Several comprehensive bodies of work, commencing with the prodigious "Modern History" (1977-79) and continuing with "Stills" (1979-80), "Tabula Rasa" (1980-81), "In-Photography" (1981-82), "Plaids" (1983), "Objects of Desire" (1983-87), and "Academy of Secrets" (1988-present), incorporate preexisting photographic images from newspapers, magazines, catalogues, etc.—familiar images that, according to Charlesworth, are "...part of our common dreamscape."[19] Charlesworth re-presents these images in a new context and form, thereby effecting new meaning in the viewer. "The work is not just a statement but a reordering, a re-seeing of something shared—a cultural experience."[20]

In her series of framed laminated Cibachrome photographs "Objects of Desire," Charlesworth used color reproductions for the first time. Images drawn from various cultural origins are rephotographed on color fields that provide new contexts for a symbolic reading. Charlesworth intends these iconic re-presentations to show "how desire is articulated in a public sphere."[21] The theme has evolved into a new series, "The Academy of Secrets," an articulation of a "cultural state of mind."[22]

Charlesworth has from the beginning considered the language of representation. In her voluminous "Modern History," she followed the international coverage of major current events in newspapers and applied a system for analyzing the representation of the events, such as the eclipse of the sun, the Pope's visit to Auschwitz, the assassination of ABC television newsman Bill Stewart, and the kidnapping and murder of Italian Prime Minister Aldo Moro. Front-page photographs are presented actual-size and, according to specifications set forth by the artist, all text has been deleted with the exception of some captions and the newspaper mastheads.

In *April 21, 1978* (1978) (CAT. NO. 13), Charlesworth followed the publication of a photograph of Aldo Moro released by his captors, the Brigate Rosse, following rumors that Moro had been killed. The image showed Moro with a newspaper in front of him bearing the headline "Moro Assassinato?," a device to prove that Moro was still alive (Moro was kidnapped on March 17, 1978, and his body recovered on May 10).

Approaching this information through systematic investigation, Charlesworth set up specifications for obtaining and processing information whereby the work would include "all countries, all available newspapers, all front pages, all photographs, all mastheads and dates" and would exclude "all other pages, all text." The resulting project (originally exhibited in Rome in 1978) is comprised of forty-five photographs and promotes scrutiny of the international coverage of this event. From one newspaper to the next, from one country to the next, a viewer can consider the size and cropping of the Moro photo and its placement on

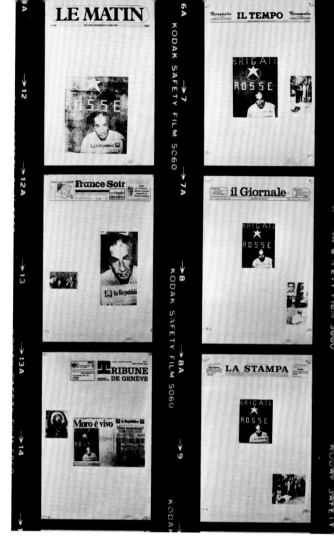

Sarah Charlesworth
APRIL 21, 1978 *from "Modern History,"*
1978 (detail)
Forty-five black-and-white photographs
Approx. 20 x 24 in. each
Collection of the artist
Courtesy Jay Gorney Modern Art, New
York, and Margo Leavin Gallery, Los Angeles

[19]Sarah Charlesworth, interview with Judy Glantzman, "Sarah Charlesworth," *Journal of Contemporary Art* 1, 1 (Spring 1988): 61.
[20]Ibid.
[21]Conversation with the artist, May 22, 1987.
[22]Ibid.

the page to assess its relative hierarchy to other events represented. Paradoxically, the photo of Moro with the newspaper was used as a device by his captors to prove that he was still alive. In highlighting specific information and deleting the rest, Charlesworth's investigation exposes gaps in the truth of newspaper reportage.

JACK GOLDSTEIN's work has been described as producing the quality of "imminence"[23] in a distanced view of experience. His work stems from a disbelief in the possibility of unmediated experience and a belief in the reality of representations:

> truth is always mediated. What can anyone be witness to in life? The films of Hitchcock, like Rear Window, answer that question. Anyway, is that which exists only in reproduction not truthful? Of course it is. The subject, the origin is always masked by language, by its own representation, condemned by it too, to be the object of its other. By "other" I mean its reproduction.[24]

Goldstein's work has encompassed film, performance, sound-recordings, records, aphorisms, and painting. Coming out of a background in Minimalist sculpture, Goldstein carried those concerns for the relationship between the viewer and the artwork into his early films, performances, and sound-recordings. He produced numerous 16mm films during the early to late 1970s (SEE CAT. NO. 14), and articulated concerns that have continued throughout his career: "There is always a distance—a space—between us and the world, that frustrates our attempt to get closer to that world. I can only understand the world through a distance, so I can never really understand the meaning of a thing except through its use."[25] Sound-recordings of special effects (from a tornado to a drowning man) gave Goldstein the opportunity to represent that which he could not do on film or that which was more effectively represented aurally rather than visually.

Goldstein's films such as *Shane* (1975) or *The Jump* (1978) create visual fragments by severely isolating and manipulating the image. For example, in *The Jump*, Goldstein applied an animation technique (rotoscoping) to transform footage of a diver so that the diving board and water are eliminated. Presented as a filmloop, this work repeatedly shows the diver jumping, diving, and disappearing into the blackness of the background. In a catalogue essay for a 1978 show of Goldstein's work, David Salle saw Goldstein's film images in terms of control: "one has to lie, in life and in art, in order to gain some measure of control over one's place in the environment which, even with the lie, is always slipping."[26]

Goldstein's activity as director has continued throughout his career. His films were shot by professionals and featured real actors; his paintings, which he began to produce in 1981, have always been produced by assistants. The notion of light is another constant in Goldstein's work, from the luminous images projected in his films to the light-filled paintings of spectacles of warfare, natural

[23] Jean Fisher, "Jack Goldstein: The Trace of Absence," *Artforum* 22, 3 (Nov. 1983): 63.

[24] Jack Goldstein, interview with Philip Pocock, "Jack Goldstein," *Journal of Contemporary Art* 1, 1 (Spring 1988): 40.

[25] Jack Goldstein, interview with Morgan Fisher, "Talking with Jack Goldstein," *Journal* 14 (Apr./May 1977): 42.

[26] David Salle, "Jack Goldstein; Distance Equals Control," in *Jack Goldstein* (Buffalo, N.Y.: Hallwalls, 1978), p. 3.

phenomena, or the recent paintings of computer-generated astronomical images (SEE ILL. P. 83). Goldstein describes his interest in white light:

> It is simultaneously presence and absence, everything and nothing, with no visible source or destination, the marking of an empty place....Too much light creates blindness or absence, and this property of light intrigues me. Light is pure information and communication; there are no longer any dark secrets. It removes the spectacle into the obscene.[27]

Goldstein's large black-and-white paintings of the early 1980s depict in a polished, airbrush technique almost photographic images of cityscapes with dramatic shows of light. Taken from photographs of cities under attack during World War II, the cinematic, seductive spectacle of the images overwhelms the viewer with their beauty.

The addition of color heightens the artificiality of the natural light phenomena in Goldstein's paintings of 1983-84 (SEE CAT. NOS. 15-17; SEE ILL. P. 82). The images of lightning, solar eclipses, and time-elapsed star tracks spectacularize the conditions of nature. Goldstein reflects on these works: "The heightened sense of reality in the phenomena painting is just about the sense of artificiality that undermines any sense of romantic transcendentalism. The pleasure of the beauty of the image is countered by the unpleasure of its elusiveness."[28]

Jack Goldstein
UNTITLED, *1981*
Acrylic on canvas
84 x 132 in.
Collection of Joan and Fred Nicholas,
Beverly Hills, California

[27]Goldstein / Pocock (note 24), p. 38.
[28]Ibid., p. 42.

While the notion of photographic "truth" has preoccupied many of the artists in this exhibition, verbal meaning has been challenged and obfuscated by JENNY HOLZER. Using written language exclusively since 1977, Holzer pushes language into a multitude of media: posters, bronze plaques, decals, LED electronic signboards, stone benches and sarcophagi, as well as public sites such as message boards in athletic stadiums, airport baggage counters, marquees, and recently, television spots. Her works engage the viewer by insinuation through the accessibility of language. They speak rhetorically the language of mass culture, but at the same time they "promiscuously"[29] confuse the authority of language as the validation of meaning.

In 1977 Holzer's first body of work, "Truisms," appeared anonymously (Holzer has stated: "Authorship blows your cover..."[30]) in the form of posters pasted on the exteriors of buildings in New York. Comprised of alphabetically ordered one-line statements, these logical, often disquieting, proclamations are presented in uppercase italics that project the authority of reason. The messages absorb and emulate a variety of viewpoints, both masculine and feminine, across the political spectrum. Emanating from a variety of voices, "the 'Truisms' emulate the force of the manifesto: each truism is a design for living, and collectively they are a manifesto saturated through the landscape."[31]

Following the "Truisms" (1977-79), Holzer produced series that engaged language using different themes, ranging from the assaultive "Inflammatory Essays" (1979-82), the neutral, conciliatory "Living" series (1980-82), the urgent messages of the "Survival" series (1983-85), and the lugubrious texts of "Under a Rock" (1986) and "Laments" (1989).

The "Inflammatory Essays" (SEE CAT. NO. 18; SEE ILLS. PP. 84-85) are a series of incendiary paragraphs—proclamations of righteousness, the tactics of terrorism, power of change, leadership, revolution, hatred, fear, freedom—that, unlike Holzer's other texts, have been produced only as posters or as texts in publi-

cations. The brightly colored square format employs an uppercase italic typeface. Addressing recognizable, common issues, their authoritative, aggressive, violent tone and poetry unnerve the viewer/reader.

Jenny Holzer
Beamed sign from "Survival Series,"
1985-86
Spectacolor board installation at
Times Square, New York, 1986
Courtesy Barbara Gladstone Gallery,
New York

[29]Hal Foster, "Subversive Signs," *Art in America* 70, 10 (Nov. 1982): 88. Hal Foster applied this term to the work of Holzer and Barbara Kruger: "...the work of both mixes promiscuously with signs of all sorts."

[30]Jenny Holzer, interview with Bruce Ferguson, "Wordsmith: An Interview with Jenny Holzer," in *Jenny Holzer: Signs* (Des Moines, Iowa: Des Moines Art Center, 1987), p. 71.

[31]Rex Reason, "Democratism or, I went to see 'Chelsea Girls' and ended up thinking about Jenny Holzer," *Real Life Magazine* 8 (Spring/Summer 1982): 11.

ON ONE OCCASION WHEN I WAS WALKING SUNSET BOULEVARD, AN ABSOLUTELY BEAUTIFUL MUTED GREEN CAR PULLED UP BESIDE ME. I HAD NEVER SEEN ANYTHING LIKE IT BEFORE, BUT I LEARNED IT WAS A JAGUAR XKE, AND I RECOGNIZED THE YOUNG MAN WHO WAS DRIVING IT. FOR PURPOSES OF OUR STORY, WE WILL CALL HIM QUINT VANTAGE, SINCE HE IS A WELL-KNOWN AND HIGHLY SUCCESSFUL ACTOR WHOSE SUCCESS IS LARGELY DEPENDENT UPON HIS AIR OF MACHISMO. "HOW FAR YOU GOING?" HE CALLED OUT. I TOOK ONE LOOK AT HIM AND ANSWERED, "ALL THE WAY."

Larry Johnson
Untitled (I Had Never Seen Anything Like It), *1988*
Type-C print
45-1/2 x 90 in.
Collection of Richard Prince, New York
Courtesy 303 Gallery, New York

LARRY JOHNSON's photographs reflect upon personal identification as they portray through texts "real life" characters made familiar through the mass media. Johnson anticipates the curiosities piqued and the "knowledge" acquired about the lives of famous strangers. His photographic texts are portraits—textual likenesses—picturing the characters through their words or those of others. Equivocated through format and aesthetisizing graphic design, their presentation further distances the actual subject.

Johnson's earlier appropriations of *People* magazine texts or *TV Guide* blurbs on such celebrities as Nancy Sinatra, John Lennon, and the Kennedy family incisively identify famous figures who have had enormous media attention devoted to their personal lives. For example, an untitled diptych from 1985 is composed of two statements taken from the *TV Guide* synopsis of a Kennedy mini-series. The texts take the life of Robert F. Kennedy from the point of John F. Kennedy's death to his own and reduce it to a four-sentence "characterization."

Johnson's series of "movie stars" prints the names of film celebrities who died tragic deaths (i.e., Marilyn Monroe, James Dean, Natalie Wood, etc.) either in white on a rust-red background, or blue on a background of clouds. Like still photographs or film titles, these images picture the stars; when exhibited together they form a "cast" which alludes to their common films, lives, and deaths. In later works, such as a 1987 series of untitled ektacolor photographs, Johnson constructed an anthology of American culture, with black squares emblazoned with multicolor texts ranging from an ill-fated pilot's "black box" transcription, the lyric sheet from the album "Los Angeles" by the rock group X, to a monologue by Bill Murray's character in the film *The Razor's Edge*, which becomes an on-screen elegiac conversation with the late John Belushi.

Five recent large-scale photographic text works (SEE CAT. NOS. 19-23) address male homosexuality, and bear the artist's assessment of his own identity. The unidentified texts from various sources are set in a consistent format and color scheme which renders them difficult to read. They include an "Amway" testimonial about achieving success, an excerpt from *The Joy of Hustling*, a text written by the artist, a transcription of the artist's courtroom testimony during a trial over a jaywalking incident in a gay district of Los Angeles that makes his own homosexuality public record, and a text from the auction catalogue accompanying the Liberace estate sale.

The recent photographs and related cast plastic sculptures with autographs of the comedians Rip Taylor (SEE ILL. P. 87), Charles Nelson Reilly, and Alan Seus describe the construction of an identity wherein desires become indistinguishable from those promoted by the mass media, where personal issues are rendered public record or sublimated into burlesque humor, and where fictional lives become real and real lives become fiction.

RONALD JONES's work has developed from his interest in architectural and graphic designs that have been associated with heinous events of contemporary history—"sites of political and social oppression."[32] Floorplans, maps, and diagrams are extensively researched and selected to represent these events. The seductive materials used are selected for their symbolic references. Jones's works become ironic cultural symbols, making concrete—even precious—that which provided a structure for or bore witness to the activities within. Jones engenders a consideration of the relationship between the architectural or schematic plans and that which actually occurred. These representations also extend a critique of Modernist aesthetics by imbuing seemingly neutral, Minimalistic, referenceless forms with "content."

Jones's subjects have included Hitler's bedroom, represented as a floor piece in carved black granite (that Jones noted was a favorite material of Hitler's); North Carolina's death chamber, represented as a series of etched "designs" in a sheet of frosted glass; German architect Eric Mendelsohn's "Columbushaus" (1933), a modern office building that the German SS used for a central prison, in effect the first German concentration camp during World War II (represented as a series of wooden floorplans); and the diagram for the "Mylai Massacre" during the Vietnam War (etched in a sheet of pink frosted glass—the code name for Mylai was "Pinkville"). The table used in the Vietnam War Paris Peace Talks is represented by small models of the proposed designs (six submitted by South Vietnam and the United States, and one submitted by North Vietnam and the National Liberation Front of South Vietnam).

Jones's research into the plans for the internment camps for Japanese-Americans during World War II has led to a site-specific work for MOCA (CAT. NO. 24; ILLS. PP. 88-89). He has designed stone inlays to be set directly into the floor of the Temporary Contemporary and into the sidewalk outside of the nearby, adjacent site for the planned Japanese American National Museum, formerly a Buddhist temple in which Japanese-Americans assembled for relocation during World War II. The work is a response to the manner in which these two cultural institutions are situated in the "Little Tokyo" section of downtown Los Angeles. As Jones researched the plans for the relocation centers, he noted that almost immediately following their arrival, the internees designated sites within the camps for cultural activities: art, literature, music. The Poston, Arizona, Relocation Project was the site for all three activities and Jones sought to commemorate it in three stone-and-marble inlaid floorpieces in the Temporary Contemporary. The designs portray the basic military block plan, encompassing barracks, mess hall, toilets,

[32]Conversation with the artist, Nov. 21, 1988.

and a cultural building. Each inlay represents the block plan that incorporated one of the three cultural activities. The selection of materials consists of black granite for the background, greenish slate for the barracks, and white Carrara marble for the enclosing road.[33] A stone inlay in the sidewalk at the entrance to the Japanese American National Museum represents another landmark; the design diagrams the corner of First Street and Central Avenue (the site of the inlay and the debarkation location) in 1942, the year that Poston started receiving internees. The sidewalk inlay also has particular meaning in Los Angeles, recalling the Hollywood ''Walk of Fame'' which commemorates celebrities of the entertainment industry.

Ronald Jones
UNTITLED (PEACE CONFERENCE TABLES DESIGN BY THE UNITED STATES AND SOUTH VIETNAM, *1969), 1987 (foreground)*
UNTITLED (PEACE CONFERENCE TABLES DESIGN BY NORTH VIETNAM AND THE NATIONAL LIBERATION FRONT OF SOUTH VIETNAM, 1969), *1987 (rear table)*
Lacquered oak and aluminum
28 x 48 in. each
Installation at Metro Pictures,
New York, 1987
Courtesy Metro Pictures, New York

MIKE KELLEY grapples with mass culture's representations, subjecting them to associations that turn them inside-out. He undermines the foundations of high culture's sacrosanct subjects (history, art, philosophy, religion, science, etc.) and their practitioners with popular culture's leveling—in effect, debasing—inscriptions. His strategy is to identify associations through implication, bringing forth that which exists in society but has been suppressed, is unexpected, or is socially incorrect. Howard Singerman has likened Kelley's attitude to that of the adolescent: ''While the self-conscious sexual energy of adolescence translates the lessons of history and geography into a metaphor for that energy, they also deconstruct the various categories of adult reality.''[34]

Kelley's practice stems from a background in performance in the late 1970s and has grown to encompass drawings, paintings, sculpture, photography, and numerous texts, often together comprising specific bodies of work. Such bodies of work have included *Monkey Island* (1982-83), a sexually charged adolescent cosmology, as represented by insects and monkeys; *The Sublime* (1984), an investigation of that concept; and *Plato's Cave, Rothko's Chapel, Lincoln's Profile* (1985-86), a cross-referencing demystification of the three figures of philosophy, art, and history. *Half a Man* (1987-88) presents a representative analysis of sexual difference through the accouterments of childhood and adolescence.

The position of the artist in society and the notion of artistic genius

[33]It was brought to Jones's attention by Katsumi Kunitsugu, of the Japanese American Cultural and Community Center in Los Angeles, that the Japanese-American 442nd Regimental Combat Team of the U.S. Army liberated Carrara, Italy.

[34]Howard Singerman, "The Artist as Adolescent," *Real Life Magazine* 6 (Summer 1981): 19.

Mike Kelley
BOOTH'S PUDDLE *from* PLATO'S CAVE,
ROTHKO'S CHAPEL, LINCOLN'S PROFILE,
1985
Acrylic on paper, tacked on stretched canvas
Two parts: 22 x 60 in. and 60 x 71 in.;
82 x 71 in. overall
Courtesy Rosamund Felsen Gallery,
Los Angeles

as the license to disavow the law or moral codes has been critically explored by Kelley in *Pay For Your Pleasure* (1988) (CAT. NO. 25; ILLS. PP. 90-91), an installation of forty-two banners bearing quotations which has included an artwork by convicted murderer John Wayne Gacy, as well as by the Los Angeles freeway killer, William Bonin.[35] Each banner, painted by a sign painter in a single color (as part of a repeated spectrum) is a portrait of a venerated figure including poets, philosophers, writers, painters, and even a Pope (all men)—accompanied by a statement by that man. Kelley debunks the words of such sacrosanct figures as Artaud, Baudelaire, Degas, Keats, Mondrian, Sartre, Veronese, and Yeats, with quotations claiming, for example, that artists, in the words of Pope Paul III on one banner, "ought not to be bound by law"; or as Baudelaire stated: "If rape or arson, poison or the knife, has wove not pleasing patterns in the stuff of this drab canvas we accept as life—it is because we are not so bold enough." Commemoration gives way to condemnation when this hall of great men is considered in the paradoxical context of an artwork by a man whose life is marked by heinous achievement, and whose art is a product of rehabilitative therapy. As Singerman noted in an essay on this work when it was shown with Gacy's self-portrait:

> Gacy is the man of action, the artist whose passions could not be restrained. But if Gacy is the true artist, it is, in Kelley's scenario, precisely not for his painting. For the forces that line the wall, that object is not the object of art but the image of restraint of socialization, of sublimation.[36]

Kelley has chosen consistently to place into the "high" art arena that which is outside of it. As a microcosm of society, the art world has difficulty absorbing that which coexists outside of the mainstream. The artworks by Gacy and Bonin emphasize this point, for these "artists" are not only outsiders to society but outsiders to the art world. Their art would not hang on MOCA's wall if it had not been incorporated into Kelley's work. Kelley, in setting up this dynamic, opens up to question the function of moral judgment as it relates to both artist and artwork.

[35] For the first presentation of the installation at The Renaissance Society at The University of Chicago in 1988, Kelley selected a painting, a small self-portrait as Pogo the Clown by John Wayne Gacy, the murderer of thirty-three adolescent boys in Illinois. For MOCA's presentation of the work, Kelley has chosen to be site-specific, substituting the Gacy painting with a drawing by William Bonin.

[36] Howard Singerman, "Mike Kelley's Line," in *Mike Kelley* (Chicago: The Renaissance Society at The University of Chicago, 1988), pp. 9-10.

"My work is very involved with the tragedy of unachievable states of being."[37] JEFF KOONS looks at the object as a sign capable of expressing and reflecting issues of personal and social identification. His work is about the contingency of meaning[38] as expressed through the legacy of the decontextualized Duchampian readymade. His bodies of work, comprised of manufactured objects (fabricated or purchased), are inspired by the artist's view of the function of the object as an indication of class status in capitalistic society. As Koons has stated:

> In the system I was brought up in—the Western, capitalistic system— one receives objects as rewards for labour and achievement. Everything one has sacrificed in life—personal goals or fantasies, for instance—in the effort to obtain these objects, has been sacrificed to a given labour situation. And once these objects have been accumulated, they work as support mechanisms for the individual: to define the personality of the self, to fulfill desires and express them....[39]

Koons produces works to function as symbolic objects for those who own and view them. His complicity with the capitalist system, and specifically the art market, is a practical program—to exploit the market, to elevate the status of his position among other artists, and to achieve notoriety in the public eye. His controversial interviews and glossy publicity portraits and ad campaigns package his persona and celebrate his desire for fame. His bodies of work have addressed a variety of personal and social issues that affect the desires of an individual.

Jeff Koons
STRING OF PUPPIES, *1988*
Polychromed wood
42 x 62 x 37 in.
Collection of Phoebe Chason, Harrison, New York

Koons's notion of "unachievable states of being" was first expressed in the Plexiglas-encased vacuum cleaners and rug shampooers of "The New" (1981–88). Their anthropormorphic quality as containers with "breathing" functions unsettles the viewer with the "newness" that only such unused machines can display. These works also display their obsolescence as they enter the sphere of cultural artifacts—as artifacts of both high art culture and mass culture.

Koons's "Equilibrium" series (1985), consisting of aquarium tanks filled with water displaying basketballs and soccer balls suspended midway or half-immersed, bronze castings of life-preserving objects (snorkel, aqualung, life boat), and framed Nike advertising posters (featuring mainly black basketball stars), also addresses unachievable states. The posters advertise class mobility and stardom through sports; the balls are suspended, fetuslike, in their "equilibrium" tanks; and the objects of survival, cast in bronze, have been rendered useless.

In "Luxury and Degradation" (1986), Koons looked at the accouterments of alcohol, objects indicating different class statuses (Jim Beam specialedition decanters, a Baccarat crystal set, pail, traveling bar) meticulously cast in the "proletarian luxury"[40] of stainless steel, as well as a series of paintings of liquor advertisements. The "Statuary" series (1987) also is comprised of castings of period objects specifically selected for their original function and signification

[37]Jeff Koons, interview with Giancarlo Politi, "Luxury and Desire: An Interview with Jeff Koons," *Flash Art* 132 (Feb./Mar. 1987): 75.
[38]Jeff Koons, in panel moderated by Peter Nagy, "From Criticism to Complicity," *Flash Art* 129 (Summer 1986): 48.
[39]Koons/Politi (note 37), p. 71.
[40]Ibid., p. 72.

as objects of social hierarchy—whether for the eighteenth-century French aristocracy or the twentieth-century American working class.

Koons's recent work (SEE CAT. NOS. 26-30) focuses on the "moral crisis of the bourgeois,"[41] presenting "dislocated imagery" of banality. These works push the object of desire into the realm of kitsch, engendering reactions that hover between fascination and repulsion. Porcelain and polychromed wood sculptures (presented life-size or larger) are fabricated by artisans in Italy and described by their titles: *Bear and Policeman*, *Michael Jackson and Bubbles*, *St. John*, *Woman in Tub*, *String of Puppies*, *Ushering in Banality*, etc. They are comprised of familiar images derived from mass culture, "democratizing"[42] their symbolic materials as they vulgarize their subjects. These works service and exploit desires for fame, wealth, sex, status, and religious affirmation, and indulge the collector with monumental, precious, symbolic objects.

Barbara Kruger
UNTITLED, *1988*
Billboard installation on 39th Street,
North of Queens Boulevard, in Queens,
New York, 1988-89
(part of a Public Art Fund Inc. program)
Courtesy the artist and Mary Boone Gallery,
New York

[41]Conversation with the artist, Dec. 9, 1988.
[42]Ibid.

Barbara Kruger has worked in a number of disciplines, including the production of photographic work, teaching, writing criticism, public art projects, book publishing, curating, and serving on boards of art organizations. She considers all of these activities to be part of her work.[43] Since 1980 Kruger has engaged in a coherent series of photographic montages of phrases and appropriated images. The visual consistency of her works (primarily black-and-white photo/text montages with red frames) has imbued it with the recognizability that is crucial to her practice. Kruger has acknowledged that the years she "spent performing serialized exercises with pictures and words"[44] as a graphic designer and photo editor for Condé Nast publications influenced her art. In her photographic works, she has applied the visual and verbal facility gained from her experience with commercial publications toward "ruining certain representations"[45] that such publications promote. Her work incisively addresses mass culture's representations of social constriction, sexual difference, identity, and power, in which "she exposes, opposes, deposes stereotypes and clichés."[46] Images are selected from a variety of sources, all bearing a nostalgic, dated appearance that nurtures the social agenda Kruger attempts to dismantle. The superimposition of written or modified mottos or catchword phrases plays language against image, "exposing the 'Rhetoric of the Image.'"[47] Kruger has stated, "I work with pictures and words because they have the ability to determine who we are, what we want to be, and what we become."[48] Her use of the personal pronoun brings the viewer into this process of engendered deliberation as the subject and object of the visual and verbal statements: "You make history when you do business"; "I will not become what I mean to you"; "We won't play nature to your culture"; "Give me all you've got."

This art unnerves by assertively exposing the powerful subtleties of socialization: "Kruger's work is not a confrontation between simplified notions of good and evil. Her images are powerful because they tap into the part of us that's been invaded and colonized—by the news media, an entertainment industry and political structure that promote tantalizing death, wondrous disaster and the unbridled abuse of power."[49] Her work has, through public artworks such as billboards, engaged a broad audience. Kruger's proposed site-specific project for "A Forest of Signs" (CAT. NO. 31), a monumental mural for the south wall of the Temporary Contemporary, takes the format of an American flag, incorporating MOCA's name and the "Pledge of Allegiance" as its stars and stripes. By inscribing MOCA into this work, Kruger has provided long-needed signage for the Temporary Contemporary. Presented the size of a building, the "Pledge of Allegiance," an institutionalized statement of personal patriotism, demands attention and scrutiny.

[43]Barbara Kruger, interview with Anders Stephanson, "Barbara Kruger," *Flash Art* 136 (Oct. 1987): 59.

[44]Barbara Kruger, interview with Jeanne Siegel, "Barbara Kruger: Pictures and Words," *Arts* 61, 10 (June/Summer 1987): 19.

[45]Barbara Kruger, interview with Jamey Gambrell, "What is Political Art…Now?," *Village Voice* 30, 42 (Oct. 15, 1985): 73.

[46]Craig Owens, "The Medusa Effect, or, The Specular Ruse," *Art in America* 72, 1 (Jan. 1984): 98.

[47]A reference to Roland Barthes's phrase made by both Owens, ibid., pp. 97-98, and Hal Foster, "Subversive Signs," *Art in America* (note 29), p. 90.

[48]Kruger/Siegel (note 44), p. 19.

[49]Carol Squiers, "Diversionary (Syn)tactics: Barbara Kruger Has Her Way with Words," *ArtNews* 86, 2 (Feb. 1987): 81.

LOUISE LAWLER'S work has consistently focused critically on the institutions of the art world, drawing attention to the conditions and conventions inherent in that system that affect the meaning of a work of art. She addresses the relationships that exist between the art object and the artist, the gallery, the critic, the collector, the historian, and the museum. Lawler's practice encompasses that which exists outside as well as within the "frame"; it is a critique of the conditions through which an artwork is read and how it is valued, identifying the contingency of its meaning (dependent upon the context of presentation and the ephemera and docu-

Louise Lawler
EXHIBITION 1987, *1987*
Two Cibachrome prints, thirty glasses,
ten brackets, wall paint, and text
90 x 260 in. overall
The Museum of Contemporary Art,
Los Angeles
Purchased with funds provided by
The Eli Broad Family Foundation

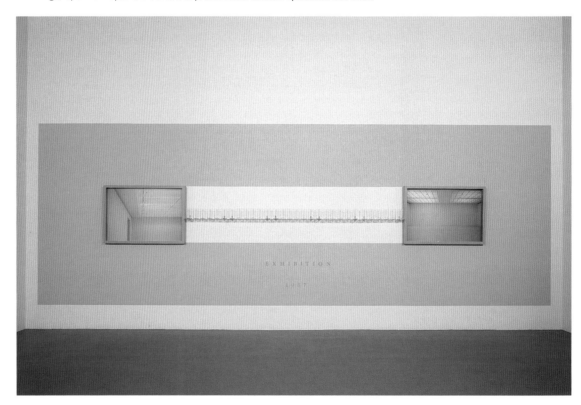

mentation that prove its existence). "Inescapably, Lawler's works demonstrate our investment in the very idea of a meaning—our desire to arrest the flux of significance, and to correlate the consequent stable to accredited value."[50] Her work addresses the "margins" of context, as Andrea Fraser has stated:

> Lawler transforms the seemingly irrelevant plethora of supple-
> ments—captions which name, proper names which identify, invita-
> tions which advertise (to a select community), installation photos
> which document, catalogues which historicize, "arrangements"
> which position, critical texts which function in most of these
> capacities—into the objects of an art practice.[51]

Lawler produces work that corresponds to the roles of the art world's participants—curator, artist, collector, archivist, registrar, etc. She does not seek to dismantle these roles but rather to make the viewer aware of those processes, of which she too, is a part. Like the museum registrar, Lawler examines and documents the conditions of a work's context, whether it is displayed or stored domesti-

[50]Kate Linker, "Rites of Exchange," *Artforum* 25, 3 (Nov. 1986): 100.
[51]Andrea Fraser, "In and Out of Place," *Art in America* 60, 1 (June 1985): 124.

cally in a private collection. But whereas the registrar may document, Lawler critiques presentation, noting how a work functions as decoration, personal embellishment, as a sign of status. For the archivist, she attends to the detail and production of "ephemera": invitations, announcements, matchbooks, that are often the only document of an exhibition or event. Like the curator, gallery, or collector, she "arranges" the objects according to a theme or underlying agenda and exhibits them as *her* work.

Lawler's production has included photographs, wall labels, matchbooks, gallery gift certificates, slide shows, drinking glasses, stationery, artist's books, photo editing, and "arrangements" of artworks by other artists. Her photographs are of artwork displayed and stored in collectors' homes, corporate settings, galleries, and museums. Her "arrangements" can be accompanied by new wall labels or by walls painted to refer to an issue outside of the works.[52] Lawler has also collaborated on projects with other artists, including Andrea Fraser, Sherrie Levine, and Allan McCollum.[53]

In 1986 Lawler visited MOCA's new California Plaza building before any art was installed. Lawler's work, *Exhibition 1987*, is the result of that visit (the work was subsequently purchased as a gift to MOCA's permanent collection). Two color photographs present a view of the north and south galleries. A red exit sign in the distance disrupts the pristine serenity of the cool blue-green space. These images, installed on a wall coordinated in color to that of the photographic images, are bridged by a glass shelf line with clear drinking glasses each printed with the message: "You could hear a rat piss on cotton." This line from jazz musician Charlie Parker disrupts the preciousness of the sanctified space of the museum and directly bridges art and commerce.

For this present exhibition, Lawler has again addressed MOCA, positioning photographs, labels, printed cards, and paperweights in "A Forest of Signs" and the concurrent exhibition at the Temporary Contemporary of works from MOCA's permanent collection. Her work, titled *"Standing Before You, Rather Behind You, To Tell You of Something I Know Nothing About"* (1989) (CAT. NO. 32), intervenes in MOCA's exhibitions, and addresses the experience of seeing images of well-known artworks reset in different contexts.

[52]For example, her contribution to the "Dissent" exhibition at The Institute of Contemporary Art, Boston, in 1986, presented three works from The Museum of Modern Art's permanent collection: two Warhol paintings from 1966 and a work by Henry Pearson also from 1966. The paintings were hung on a wall painted with a field of colors graphed to correspond to the percentages of the works acquired by MOMA through purchase, private gift, and corporate donation.
[53]A collaboration with McCollum appears in this catalogue: "Fixed Intervals"—objects that Lawler and McCollum have produced based on the "dingbats" that graphically denote the end of a passage, and have photographed for use throughout this text.

Thomas Lawson
HE DIED LIKE MANY OF HIS INNOCENT
VICTIMS, *1980*
Oil on canvas
51-1/2 x 41 in.
The Rivendell Collection

Our daily encounters with one another, and with nature, our ges-
tures, our speech are so thoroughly impregnated with a rhetoric
absorbed through the airwaves that we have no certain claim to the
originality of any of our actions. Every cigarette, every drink, every
love affair echoes down a never-ending passageway of references—to
advertisements, to television shows, to movies—to the point where
we no longer know if we mimic or are mimicked. We flicker around
the flame of our desire, loving the comfort of repeating a well-worn
language and its well-worn sentiments, fearful of losing all control to
that language and the society it represents.[54]

Since the late 1970s, THOMAS LAWSON has participated in the discourse of this
period through painting, critical writing, public art projects, and the editorship
(since 1979) of *Real Life Magazine*, a publication that focuses on art's relationship
to social and cultural issues. His practice has addressed critically the relationship
of art to its own history and conventions, directing it into a closer relationship to
mass culture, and in so doing, attempting to expose the factors that contribute to
the meaning of a work of art.

In the late 1970s, painting was an unlikely vehicle for radical critical
discourse; at the same time, painting saw a resurgence of critical and market interest. This "Postmodern," "New Image," "Neo-Expressionist" work drew upon past
styles and the visual and literary language of art history and literature. In his 1981
essay "Last Exit: Painting,"[55] Lawson criticized the work of artists associated with
Neo-Expressionism, writing that "the work of these artists must be considered part
of a last, decadent flowering of the modernist spirit....what they give us is a pas-
tiche of historical consciousness, an exercise in bad faith." "For by
decontextualizing their sources and refusing to provide a new, suitable critical
frame for them, they dismiss the particularities of history in favor of a generalizing
mythology and thus succumb to sentimentality."[56] Lawson concluded that the

[54]Thomas Lawson, "A Fatal Attraction," in *A Fatal Attraction* (Chicago:
The Renaissance Society at The University of Chicago, 1982), p. 3.
[55]Thomas Lawson, "Last Exit: Painting," *Artforum* 20, 2 (Oct. 1981):
40-47.
[56]Ibid., pp. 41-42.

most effective medium in which to maintain a critical stance and still be acknowledged and "radical" within the economic and institutional framework of the art world was "by resorting to subterfuge, using an unsuspecting vehicle as camouflage":[57] painting.

Working within the conventional medium of painting and its historical genre (portraiture, landscape), Lawson has engaged pictures taken from mass culture in his paintings. His earliest work depicts decontextualized, clichéd images of dogs, babies, and shoes isolated on a color field. In 1980 Lawson produced a series of paintings in which a small scene floats in the darkness of a black field. These images, lifted from a variety of sources—newspapers, detective magazines, pornography—depict anonymous victims of terrible acts of violence: rape, lynching, murder. The horrific imagery of these small paintings is barely decipherable, breaking down into brush strokes on closer inspection: "one sees them most clearly from a distance; from closer up the brushmarks assert primacy and the likenesses become ghostly."[58] A later series of paintings (1981), "portraits" of victimized children, was taken from snapshots or yearbook photographs in the *New York Post*, their titles the original newspaper headlines: *Shot for a Bike*, *Beaten to Death*, *Inches from Death*. Lawson described these paintings: "They are people of whom you have no expectations of seeing a portrait. Neither mass culture nor high culture, but absolutely anonymous strangers. Furthermore they are not my pictures. They are doubly anonymous—both photographed and photographer are anonymous."[59] Lawson's installation of these earlier paintings as well as a recent work on walls covered with blackboard paint and accompanied by a sound track from an audiowork, *45 Seconds of Billie Holiday*[60] (SEE CAT. NOS. 33-42), creates a somber atmosphere for the contemplation of the victims.

Lawson's later works depict images of architectural landmarks, statuaries, tourist attractions, and war memorials, rendered with distracting painted pattern overlays that make their reading problematic. His recent work has encompassed large-scale panoramas and site-specific public art projects (SEE ILLS. PP. 98-99) that draw upon and reread the conventions of public artworks, monuments, and displays, as well as the social and political context of their site.

SHERRIE LEVINE has consistently produced work that "celebrates doubt and uncertainty,"[61] unsettling the principles that have upheld the (male-dominated) conventions of mass culture's images or of Modernist representations. Levine's work in photography, painting, drawing, and printmaking has addressed issues of originality and authorship in an attempt to engage critically the history with which a woman artist is faced. Hers is a practice motivated by alienation—the alienation of lives from direct experience, the alienation of desires—the melancholic aftermath of unachievable pleasure. Levine wrote about this motivation:

> Certainly the best thing in life is ordinary sexual love. But we find unsanctioned sexual activity, like unsanctioned violence, frightening as well as exhilarating, because without manners or form, it yields no meaning or hope. It has no stake in the future.
>
> Reluctant moralists, we make art that suggests our simultaneous longing for anarchy and order—to have nothing and

[57]Ibid., p. 45.

[58]Jeanne Silverthorne, "Thomas Lawson, Metro Pictures," *Artforum* 23, 10 (Summer 1985): 111.

[59]Thomas Lawson, interview with D.A. Robbins, "An Interview with Thomas Lawson," *Arts* 58, 1 (Sept. 1983): 114.

[60]Originally created for "Untitled Sound Piece" on the record album *Just Another Asshole #5* (1982).

[61]Sherrie Levine, interview with C. Carr, "What is Political Art...Now?," *Village Voice* 30, 42 (Oct. 15, 1985): 81.

everything. An uneasy peace is made between the reassuring mythologies society and culture provide and our wish to see ourselves as free agents. The very best in art makes public our private anguish in the face of this ineluctable conflict.

We want images and stories which present us with ideals but at the same time are not innocent of the other side of the coin—our desire to have no ideals, no fetters whatsoever. We aspire to the best of both worlds.[62]

Early on Levine attempted to address this alienation by appropriating as her own rephotographed images of work by male artists into such series as "After Edward Weston" (1981), "After Walker Evans" (1981), "After Alexander Rodchenko" (1985-87). These images instill an uneasiness in the viewer through the artist's intervention of authorship: "it did seem embarrassing to be caught looking at these pictures too closely. You felt that the meaning of Levine's curiously covert art had to lie elsewhere, perhaps in the circumstances of its exhibition rather than in the images themselves."[63]

Other series of photographic "collages" followed, including "After Franz Marc" (1982), in which Levine collaged reproductions of Marc's paintings, and a large series of watercolors and drawings, "After Léger," "After Mondrian," "After Miró," "After Matisse," "After Paul Klee," which featured images the size of bookplates reproduced in catalogues. This work also signaled the reintroduction of the artist's own hand into the work, more densely knitting her own touch into these representations of the work of others.

Levine's paintings on panels, begun in 1984, signaled a new approach, appropriating the style or feeling of Minimalism or Surrealism in abstract paintings on mahogany, plywood, and lead. Levine subjected them to a repetition of format where the (commodified) variation on a theme is marked by the personal touch of the original.

A recent body of work based on George Herriman's comic strip, "Krazy Kat" (published 1913-44), features a narrative sequence involving two of the comic-strip characters: Krazy Kat and Ignatz Mouse. As the story goes, Krazy Kat (of ambiguous gender) is in love with Ignatz (a male). Krazy Kat's love is unrequited and a masochistic relationship ensues; Krazy Kat is repeatedly struck by a brick thrown by Ignatz, which he interprets as a sign of Ignatz's love. The relentless repetition of this sequence is the subject of two sets of untitled paintings by Levine of black casein on unpainted mahogany panels—one set of six, each depicting the same image of Ignatz as he is prepared to "Krease that Kat's bean with a brick," and six depicting the same image of Krazy Kat at the moment of being struck (SEE CAT. NOS. 43-54; SEE ILLS. PP. 100-101). Levine is among a number of artists, including Öyvind Fahlström, Willem de Kooning, Claes Oldenburg, and Philip Guston, who have been interested in the Krazy Kat comic strip. Her repetition of these images underscores the violence and tragedy in their humor.

Sherrie Levine
UNTITLED (After Alexander Rodchenko: 9), 1987
Black-and-white photograph
20 x 16 in.
Collection of Mera and Don Rubell, New York
Courtesy Mary Boone Gallery, New York

[62]Sherrie Levine, in Zeno Birolli, Horror Pleni: Pictures in New York Today (Milan: Padiglione d'Art Contemporanea, 1980), unpag.
[63]David Deitcher, "The Best of Both Worlds," in The Best of Both Worlds: Sherrie Levine's "After Walker Evans" (Evanston, Ill.: Mary and Leigh Block Gallery, Northwestern University, 1985), unpag.

In 1977 Robert Longo produced a work titled *The American Soldier and the Quiet Schoolboy*. This small, painted, cast-aluminum wall relief depicts a man in shirt, tie, and fedora, head thrown back, back arched, holding his left hand to his back. The image is that of a man at the moment of being shot in the back, taken from the 1970 R.W. Fassbinder film *Der amerikänïsche Soldat* (The American Soldier). Longo's treatment decontextualizes the image to the extent that a poetic ambiguity sets in. In selecting a still from a film sequence, Longo isolated a moment, freezing

Robert Longo
Untitled *from "Men in the Cities," 1987*
Charcoal, graphite, and ink on paper
96 x 60 in.
Collection of the artist
Courtesy Metro Pictures, New York

the image. The image, elegantly stylized in a "fluid grace,"[64] mitigates the original cinematic event, inviting questions as to what this man is doing. Douglas Crimp talked about this work, which was included in the 1977 "Pictures" exhibition at Artists Space in New York:

> In concretizing this climactic moment when the man is stopped by a bullet, Longo suspends the moment between life and death in the ambiguous stasis of a picture. And the odd result is that this picture/object has all the elegance of a dance.[65]

Longo has stated that his series "Men in the Cities" grew out of this work. Comprised of over sixty larger-than-life-size charcoal-and-graphite figures, "Men in the Cities" (SEE CAT. NOS. 55-61) was begun in 1975, but produced as a discrete series from 1977 to 1982, with additional works made since that time. The drawings were made from photographs Longo took of friends on his New York rooftop. Throwing tennis balls or corks at his models, Longo recorded their movements in response. Longo acknowledges the influence on this work of New Wave music (for example, The Talking Heads, Joy Division, and The Contortions); the choreography of his models approaches the moves of these musicians and performers.[66] The drawings made from the photographs isolate the figure on the paper, some floating on a blank field, others cropped by an imposing frame, pushing the ambiguity of meaning—are these people dancing or dying, and what is the effect on the viewer?

> Men in the Cities had such incredible hostility for the viewer, the act that was portrayed in the drawing occurs every time you look at the drawing. It's not a picture of someone being shot, the person's being shot every time you look at it.[67]

These huge drawings were also accompanied by lacquered cast-aluminum reliefs of New York buildings, including the Tombs and the New York Athletic Club. The highly truncated images complement the skewed viewpoint of many of the drawings. This concern with architecture has continued in Longo's work as an interest in the representation of power and grandeur often associated with the spectacular displays of fascism. Hal Foster wrote about this interest: "Longo traces not only our loss of the real but also our morbid attempt to compensate for this loss via the resurrection of archaic images and forms."[68]

Longo's work has encompassed performances, music, film, and video (including a number of music videos), as well as painting and sculpture. His early multimedia performances, such as "Sound Distance of a Good Man" (1978), "Surrender" (1979), and "Empire" (1981), employ the imminence of spectacular display with the ambiguity of vignettes that defy time and linear narrative. Cinema continues to be a constant reference in Longo's work and in his discussions of his work. For example, he has stated that he wants to "grow out of the living rooms of Aaron Spelling the way the thing pops of the guy's chest in *Alien*. You made me, now you have to deal with me."[69]

Longo's recent work continues to combine mass culture's images, significantly punctuated by his 1986 work *All You Zombies (Truth Before God)* (1986), which featured a bronze science-fiction monster as an apocalyptic specter. His work has also moved into new disciplines, directing rock music videos for such groups as New Order, R.E.M., and Megadeth, and in 1987 he completed *Arena Brains*, a thirty-minute film portraying a cynical view of the New York SoHo art scene.

[64]Robert Longo, interview with Richard Price, "Interview with Richard Price," in *Robert Longo, Men in the Cities* (New York: Harry N. Abrams, Inc., 1986), p. 88.

[65]Douglas Crimp, "Pictures," in *Pictures* (New York: Artists Space, 1977), p. 26.

[66]Longo/Price (note 64), p. 88.

[67]Ibid., p. 101.

[68]Hal Foster, "The Art of Spectacle," *Art in America* 71, 4 (Apr. 1983): 144-49, 195-98, esp. p. 145.

[69]Robert Longo, quoted in *The Art of Spectacle* (Los Angeles: LACE, UCLA, Some Serious Business, 1984), p. 26.

Allan McCollum
PLASTER SURROGATES, *1982-83*
Enamel on cast Hydrostone
Installation at Marian Goodman Gallery,
New York, 1983
Courtesy John Weber Gallery, New York

Art as a symbol of social and economic status and thus a means of exclusion has been the focus of ALLAN McCOLLUM's work since the late 1970s. The museum as well as the commercial gallery is implicated as a governing authority.[70] McCollum's work self-consciously addresses the production, distribution, acquisition, display, and reading of the artwork. He has done this through a limited production of "Surrogate Paintings" (1978-82), "Plaster Surrogates" (1982-present), "Perpetual Photos" (1981-present), "Perfect Vehicles" (1986-present), and "Individual Works" (1987-89), as well as works produced in collaboration with other artists (Louise Lawler, "Ideal Settings" [1983] and "Fixed Intervals" [1988]; and Laurie Simmons, "Actual Photos" [1985]). His "Surrogates," begun in wood in 1978 and in plasterlike Hydrostone in 1982, are painted castings, one-piece, self-framed and matted, imageless objects. Hung in salon-style arrangements, they function at once as signs for painting and as art objects. They can be assimilated into the art system and they infiltrate it, exposing the economic and social forces that produce desire for a specialized, symbolic object. The "Surrogates" function repetitively, drawing attention to the labor in the production of a work of art and the value of labor in mass production.[71] Each *Surrogate* is unique. Produced in quantity, they are reduced to "simple tokens of exchange,"[72] to symbolic commodities, as Craig Owens remarked:

> ...the potentially endless repetition of essentially identical objects prevents us from mistaking difference for uniqueness. For although it is possible to view each work as a mirror reflecting all the others, at the same time, it is impossible to forget that each is merely a reflection of all of the others.[73]

The "Perpetual Photos" are rephotographed details from photographs McCollum made of TV screens where "surrogate"-like images appeared in the background of various television programs. Blown-up, matted, and framed,

[70]Allan McCollum, interview with Daniela Salvioni, "Interview with McCollum and Koons," *Flash Art* 131 (Dec. 1986/Jan. 1987): 66-68.

[71]McCollum's parents were both assembly-line workers and this background continues to influence his work.

[72]Allan McCollum, interview with D.A. Robbins, "An Interview with Allan McCollum," *Arts* 60, 2 (Oct. 1985): 40-44, esp. p. 44.

[73]Craig Owens, "Repetition and Difference," in *Allan McCollum: Surrogates* (London: Lisson Gallery, 1985), p. 6.

these "Perpetual Photos" become indecipherable grainy forms, no longer resembling their unknown originals.

The "Perfect Vehicles," objects shaped like Ming ginger jars, are painted, solid castings of Hydrostone that "function" as art. McCollum has written about them: "In extinguishing absolutely the possibility of any recourse to utility, I mean to accelerate the symbolic potential of the *Vehicles* toward total meaning, total value. I aim to fashion the most perfect art object possible."[74] The recent giant "Vehicles" accentuate the body shape of urnlike objects that are larger than an average adult male.

The "Individual Works," small, approximately two-by-five-inch painted Hydrostone objects, have been produced in two sets, each numbering approximately 10,000. The first set (1988) (SEE ILLS. PP. 104-105) is aqua-blue, and the current set for MOCA (CAT. NO. 62) is salmon—each object cast from two molds comprising castings of household objects (cologne bottle tops, bottle caps, candy molds, etc.). These objects were assembled according to a mathematical structure that ordered their stacked compositions and ultimately ensured their "individuality." Their excessive production subsumes each piece into a sea of like objects divisible into wholesale "lots," their "individuality" mitigated by their quantity. Andrea Fraser considered the "Individual Works" in relation to McCollum's other production:

> If McCollum's Plaster Surrogates *are signs for painting, and his* Perfect Vehicles *signs for the antique or exotic objet d'art, his* Individual Works *are not signs for anything. They're simply bibelot; small, decorative, household objects. They are not now, symbolic objects, but, rather, they are made to become symbolic objects, in use, as souvenirs, keepsakes, tokens of affection; little mnemonic traces.*[75]

In a seminal 1980 essay on the work of MATT MULLICAN, Allan McCollum discussed the identification of reality as a socially constructed system of material and symbolic relationships drawn between an individual and the world.

> Through his work, we watch a drama unfold—one which we all experience in our day-to-day lives, but unconsciously —as he represents the way he constructs, assimilates, disintegrates, modifies, reconstructs, and generally works to maintain his personal sense of reality.[76]

Mullican's work since the mid-1970s has developed as a "model of a cosmology," "a social order of signs"[77] that represents an individual's relationship to the world. His works are models for understanding the universe as depicted through the symbolic system of art, comprised of an encyclopedic compendium of pictographic signs assigned to represent the broad ranges of empirical knowledge, subjective experience, artistic creativity, and philosophical thought. Mullican's work has consistently followed this path and has encompassed a multitude of media: performance, drawings, posterlike paintings, sculpture, banners, even stained glass, carved granite floorpieces, and bulletin boards of assembled objects.

[74]Allan McCollum, "Perfect Vehicles," in *Damaged Goods: Desire and the Economy of the Object* (New York: The New Museum of Contemporary Art, 1986), p. 11.

[75]Andrea Fraser, *Allan McCollum: Individual Works* (New York: John Weber Gallery, 1988), unpag.

[76]Allan McCollum, "Matt Mullican's World," *Real Life Magazine* 5 (Winter 1980): 5.

[77]Matt Mullican, interview with Dan Cameron, "Worlds within Worlds: A Conversation with Matt Mullican," in *Mullican* (Bath, England: Artsite Gallery, 1988), p. 8.

Mullican has systematically ordered subjective experience into his cosmological categories: the "World Framed," "World Unframed," "Subjective," "Elemental," "Signs," "Arts," "History," "Evolution," and such spiritual concepts as "Life," "Death," "Before Birth," "God," "Heaven," "Hell," "Fate." He has undergone hypnosis to achieve these various subjective states.

The signs that Mullican has developed resemble the language of international symbols, visually identifying gender, facilities, and directions. As McCollum noted, our understanding of these symbols is predicated on self-awareness and personal identification with a "class of like objects" (for example, men or women, in the case of public restrooms).[78]

Matt Mullican
Untitled (bulletin board), 1982
Mixed media on board
97 x 49 in.
Courtesy the artist and Michael Klein, Inc.,
New York

In a series of bulletin boards begun in 1979 (SEE CAT. NOS. 63-68), assembling photographs, drawings, and objects (generators, minerals, a skeleton) displayed on pedestals, Mullican categorized different visual and material artifacts into representations of subjective experience that constitute a retrospective of his work. As Germano Celant commented:

These function not only as literal, matter-of-fact anchors for the work but also as "absolute" signs connoting sacred mysteries, images transcending the precarious human condition. They serve to remind us of how the sensory refers to the extrasensory, of how signs circulate in both the physical and the metaphysical realms, on real and abstract levels, as both corporeal and psychic manifestations. The objects form part of the uncontained matter of Earth; organized into art, they become the cardinal points for an interpretation of the world through the collective consciousness.[79]

One example of this activity can be traced back to a 1975 performance in which Mullican photographed a cadaver and documented himself "experiencing in entirely as an object,"[80] photographing the cadaver's ear and the dissected sections of the abdomen, putting his hand in the cadaver's mouth, and being unable to distinguish between thinking of the cadaver as "him/person" and "it/body."[81] One photo of the cadaver is shown next to a photo of a decayed doll's head, the doll projecting more "life" than the dead man. McCollum raised questions in this comparison of these images: "Is a dead body more dead than 'dead' matter? Or less dead? Is a living fictional person more alive than a real dead one?"[82]

[78]Fraser (note 75), unpag.
[79]Germano Celant, "Between Atlas and Sisyphus," *Artforum* 24, 3 (Nov. 1985): 78.
[80]Mullican/Cameron (note 77), p. 6.
[81]Ibid.
[82]Fraser (note 75), unpag.

An individual's engagement of the world through the intervention of signs produced by mass culture has been critically addressed by PETER NAGY since the early 1980s.[83] He montages or juxtaposes images lifted from commercial sources: product design, illustrations, logos, art reproductions, and architectural images, presenting them as photocopies or enlarged onto black-and-white paintings, and metal engravings and reliefs.

This strategy has operated from his early photocopy works, which he presented mounted on cardboard or Masonite boxes, laminated in plastic, or as labels on a box. In *The 8-Hour Day* (1983), for example, he replaced the numbers on a watchface with reproductions of artworks, while in *International Survey Condominiums* (1985) he overlaid corporate logos and condominium floorplans over the gallery plans for The Museum of Modern Art in New York. The interest in juxtaposition and overlay continued with the series of "Cancer" paintings (1985-86), the "Industrial Culture" (1987) series of metal reliefs, and the recent paintings incorporating amalgams of photocopied architectural images.

Peter Nagy
BELIEF IN STYLE, *1988*
Acrylic on canvas
72 x 72 in.
Collection of John L. Stewart, New York

Interest in theorist Jean Baudrillard's discussion of cancer as a model for the capitalistic social structure, as well as personal experience with the disease (his father and grandmother died from cancer in the same year), Peter Nagy's "Cancer" paintings incorporate the "pathology of cancer applied to the production of signs."[84] In such works as *America Invented Everything*, *Leger*, and *Mondo Cane* (CAT. NOS. 72-74), images are comprised of layered amalgams of photocopied logos and clip-art (readymade illustrations) in a composition modeled on the cellular structure of cancer. The visual structure of these varyingly recognizable images emulates the process of cancer, presenting the analogy of a metastatic production of signs, whereby "New logos are created by the juxtaposition of old ones."[85]

The recent paintings (1988) (SEE CAT. NOS. 75-77) continue this interest in the collaged imagery and structural strategy of the "Cancer" series. Architectural images from different historical periods and genres (secular and religious), particularly representations of seventeenth- and eighteenth-century Baroque and Rococo art, form the theme. For example, *L'Age d'Or* shows a Rococo church altar in Munich inset with a French clock from the J. Paul Getty Museum, Los Angeles, and *Belief in Style* includes imagery of the Bernini altar in Rome's St. Peter's, seamlessly assembled. The work focuses on European images of opulence for American audiences, and vice versa when they are presented in Europe, in order to emphasize the distance of these fragments. The photocopy process equivocates the imagery, flattening and distorting it in a conflation of styles and sources.

[83]From 1982 to 1988 Nagy ran Nature Morte Gallery (cofounded with artist Alan Belcher) in New York's East Village. There he showed the work of many of the artists in this present exhibition.
[84]Conversation with the artist, Nov. 22, 1988.
[85]Martin Guttmann, "On Peter Nagy's Cancer Paintings," *Flash Art* 134 (May 1987): 43.

Stephen Prina
A STRUCTURAL ANALYSIS AND RECONSTRUC-
TION OF MS7098 AS DETERMINED BY THE
DIFFERENCE BETWEEN THE MEASUREMENTS
OF DURATION AND DISPLACEMENT, *1980-84*
(detail)
*12 in. phonographic record, poster,
merchandising display, and publicity
photograph*
*Installation at Music Man, Ghent, Belgium,
1980*

Applying logical systems of analytic discourse that undermine the conventional readings of cultural representations, STEPHEN PRINA's work touches on the functions of the artist, authorship, systems of production, display, distribution, and historicism. His work systematically addresses the theoretical, critical, historical, and philosophical systems of representing and interpreting cultural production.

Prina addresses specific hallowed historical works or masterpieces. "As vested cultural structures, they are severed from their rhetorical moorings, restructured and re-presented, or hoisted into bondage on a critical telemetry of the artist's devising."[86] Prina's bodies of works are composed of fragments that represent a whole; his intervention opens up through extended examination or elaboration that which is considered complete.

For example, in an audio work, an LP produced in 1980 titled *A Structural Analysis and Reconstruction of MS7098 As Determined by the Difference Between the Measurements of Duration and Displacement*, Prina "reconstructed" Glen Gould's original recording of *Arnold Schoenberg: The Complete Music for Solo Piano* according to an algebraic equation analyzing the duration of the recording versus area traversed by the phonographic needle. Prina's intervention consists of the addition of new bands of silence (the original bands remain as they were) and the ultimate erasure of twenty-one seconds from the recording. His subtle intervention disrupts the completeness of the works, breaking them into fragments that cannot be reconstituted—it brings forth questions not only concerning the threshold of authorship, but about the threshold of a work's toleration of analysis (structural or interpretive) before it unravels. Prina has likened his bands of silence to historical disruptions: "Schoenberg meets Cage once again."[87]

Untitled, Version I (1987) and *Untitled, Version II* (1987-88) are each comprised of twenty-four computer-generated drawings on vellum, each a

[86]Timothy Martin, "In the Years Preceding *Olympia*: Notes on the Systems Activity of Steve Prina," *Visions* 3, 1 (Winter 1988): 6.
[87]Conversation with the artist, Oct. 26, 1988.

fragment of the statement "It's in Our Own Best Interests." This work also encompasses the computer diskettes used to produce the drawings. Composed in a block format and gridded into twenty-four squares, the fragmentation of this directive statement (a reference to the work of Holzer and Kruger[88]) through the strategy of the Modernist grid, "a device for dividing and conquering," and displayed in a continuous line that links one-half of one version to one-half of the other, renders the original statement unreadable. The drawings, conventionally treated (matted, framed, and signed by the artist), look very similar or, in some cases, even the same. The selection of a single drawing presents a problem for the collector/connoisseur who desires to choose the "best."

Prina's *Exquisite Corpse: The Collected Works of Manet*, is an ongoing project begun on January 1, 1988. Sepia wash drawings without images each refer in size and by title (on the accompanying label card) to a work by Manet. Each drawing is accompanied by an offset lithographic print that in 1:72 scale reproduces Prina's entire enterprise (556 works), providing a catalogue or legend of Prina's, and Manet's, work. Prina has produced and exhibited the drawings in the same order in which they were produced by Manet. His process of reconstructing an existing but dispersed body of work is itself being dispersed through sales—making the eventual exhibition of the completed work problematic.

Upon the Occasion of Receivership (CAT. NO. 78; ILLS. PP. 110-111) uses as its material a 1969 work by artist Lawrence Weiner, A TRANSLATION FROM ONE LANGUAGE TO ANOTHER (SEE RORIMER, P. 138). The title of Prina's work is an excerpt from Weiner's statement that applies to all of his work: "1. THE ARTIST MAY CONSTRUCT THE WORK 2. THE WORK MAY BE FABRICATED 3. THE WORK NEED NOT BE BUILT EACH BEING EQUAL AND CONSISTENT WITH THE INTENT OF THE ARTIST THE DECISION AS TO CONDITION RESTS WITH THE RECEIVER UPON THE OCCASION OF RECEIVERSHIP." As a "receiver," Prina has taken literally Weiner's statement and has produced sixty-one works on paper, each of which presents the statement translated into a different language. The translations, performed by the Berlitz translation house in Woodland Hills, California, representing the full range of their expertise, are presented laserprinted on the company letterhead.[89] Seeing Weiner's work as "tautological,"[90] Prina too is creating a tautology and addressing the question, "Is a tautology of a tautology a tautology?" "Collapsing spectatorship and production," he addresses the role of the viewer as participant/author: "I am on the receiving end and this is what I do with it."

[88]Conversation with the artist, Nov. 7, 1988.
[89]Prina has organized the translation into four language type categories (see Catalogue of the Exhibition), a now obsolete system used by Berlitz for pricing translations. For MOCA's presentation of this work, Prina has chosen to omit three works: *English* (Language Type A), *Spanish* (Language Type A), and *Japanese* (Language Type C), a reference to MOCA's inaugural exhibition in 1983, "The First Show," wherein each work was accompanied by a label in English, Spanish, and Japanese.
[90]Conversation with the artist, Nov. 7, 1988.

Recognition of and belief in the blurred distinctions between fiction and reality have characterized Richard Prince's practice, which since the late 1970s has encompassed photographs, written texts, and paintings. Writing about his early photographic work, Kate Linker observed: "By functioning as a simulator, by remaking and thereby intensifying signs that are already fabricated from existing materials and techniques, he acts to expose (literally, 'set forth') the extent to which our reality has been invaded by fiction."[91]

In 1976 Prince published in *Tracks Magazine, Eleven Conversations*—texts lifted from the verso of Elvis Presley bubble-gum cards. The next year he produced a series of three photographs of living rooms lifted from *The New York Times*. These unaltered images, straight "unaesthetisized" photographs of photographs, heightened their "normal" look, while their comparison pushed them into equivalence and emphasized their visual likeness. This process of "re-photography" that continues in his photographic practice was described by Prince:

> Re-photographing someone else's photograph, making a new picture effortlessly. Making the exposure, looking through the lens and clicking, felt like an unwelling…a whole new history without the old one. It absolutely destroyed any associations I had experienced with putting things together.[92]

Richard Prince
Untitled, *1980-84*
Ektacolor print
20 x 24 in.
Courtesy Barbara Gladstone Gallery,
New York

Following the living rooms, Prince re-photographed advertising pictures of luxury items (watches, jewelry, lighters, perfume bottles, etc.), in series of different images that look similar (people looking in similar directions, hands holding cigarettes). These images selected and cropped by the artist were re-photographed in color whether or not the original image was in color, because "color film would give them a more even quality. It would create an equivalence which made them look even more real."[93] In later series Prince manipulated the images, as in "Sunsets" (1981), in which the travel-and-leisure images are cut from their original backgrounds and re-photographed in a severely grainy black and white against a superreal "sunset" backdrop.

Begun in 1980 and continuing into the present, Prince's series of "Cowboys" have excised the models in the Marlboro cigarette advertisements. The continuity of the project (both the ad campaign and concomitantly Prince's project) indicates the effectiveness of the imagery, whereby the Marlboro campaign itself "is parasitic to and overshadowed by the cowboy imagery."[94]

In 1984 Prince initiated his series of "Gangs" (continuing to the present). Literally taken from the economical printing process of "ganging up" images on a page, Prince's "Gangs" assemble images from American genre magazines (biker, surfing, hot rod, etc.), as well as recycling images he has used in previous series.

The "Jokes" began in 1986, initially in "Gangs" assembled out of *New Yorker* cartoons, and later, handwritten on sheets of paper, pencil on canvas, and recently silkscreen on canvas (SEE CAT. NOS. 79-87; SEE ILLS. PP. 112-113). Prince's jokes chronicle America's sexual fantasies and frustrated desires: one-liners, standup comedy, burlesquelike jokes.

Prince's work has also encompassed his own texts that continue to

[91]Kate Linker, "On Richard Prince's Photographs," in *Richard Prince: Pamphlet* (Lyon, France: Le Nouveau Musée, 1983), p. 4.
[92]Richard Prince, interview with Barbara Kruger, "All Tomorrow's Parties," *Bomb* 3 (1982): 42.
[93]Richard Prince, interview with David Robbins, "Richard Prince," *Aperture* 100 (Fall 1985): 13.
[94]Daniela Salvioni, "On Richard Prince," *Flash Art* 142 (Oct. 1988): 88.

reference and describe the familiar vernacular of mass culture from the perspective of the mass media's "characters." Written in the first or third person, the texts no longer distinguish between fiction and nonfiction or autobiography. Regarding Prince's literary and photographic projects, Brian Wallis has written:

> ...Prince's writing centers on the validity of the photographic image: the characters in his stories are an attempt to make true the fiction of the advertising photograph by supplying a narrative and a coherence to the images of the models.[95]

As Wallis elaborated, Prince's interest in history, in "the fictiveness of history" (also described by the artist as "wild history"), has not only led Prince to identify the truth in fiction, but to identify *with* it: "I'd like to be remembered in a movie. I know that sounds preposterous. But having someone else play me is pretty much what I think I'm already doing."[96]

CINDY SHERMAN has focused on the construction of an engendered identity that reflects representations from the mass media. She has designed and directed her own photographs, until recently using herself exclusively as model—posing as different characters, particularly women. Her work addresses the narcissism of the spectator, whose self-awareness in response to society's prescribed roles and appearances is enhanced by her images. Sherman looked into a mirror to set her pose, but referred to the reflected image in the third person:

> It's not like I'm method acting or anything. I don't feel that I am that person. I may be thinking a certain story or situation, but I don't become her. There's this distance. The image in the mirror becomes her—the image the camera gets on the film. And the one thing I've always known is that the camera lies.[97]

Sherman's earliest work, a voluminous series of "Untitled Film Stills" (1977-80), black-and-white photographs that emulate actual or general stereotypical female roles styled after movies of the late 1950s and early 1960s, originally appeared poster-sized (thirty-by-forty-inch format) (SEE CAT. NOS. 88-97), and subsequently as eight-by-ten-inch stills. The believability of these cinematic images stems from the familiarity of their style and genre. And like film stills, they catch Sherman at a particular moment—her facial expressions as well as the particular location and camera angle implying a narrative or situation.

Following the "Untitled Film Stills," Sherman produced work in color, including images using rear-screen projected backdrops like those used in nonlocation films. In 1981 she was commissioned to do a work for *Artforum*. She chose the centerfold format, translating that into a series of images that continue the cinematic reference with strong, screenlike horizontals, which she also incorporated formally into the images—all horizontal poses strictly contained by the edges of the photographic frame.

Later series such as large-scale photographs of Sherman "modeling" designer fashions (1983)—a commission by the store Dianne B.—were followed by more androgynous images (1984) and later by more fantastic ones, as Sherman posed as nonspecific fairy-tale or mythological characters (1985-86), in which props and dramatic makeup obfuscate her face and body. The removal of the artist

Cindy Sherman
UNTITLED FILM STILL *(#14), 1978*
Black-and-white photograph
10 x 8 in.
Collection of the artist
Courtesy Metro Pictures, New York

[95]Brian Wallis, "Mindless Pleasure: Richard Prince's Fictions," *Parkett* 6 (Sept. 1985): 61.
[96]Prince/Robbins (note 93), p. 13.
[97]Cindy Sherman, quoted in Gerald Marzorati, "Imitation of Life," *ArtNews* 82, 7 (Sept. 1983): 81.

herself from the images was all but complete in a series of large-scale horrific images (1987) (ILLS. PP. 114-115) elaborately orchestrated with fake blood, worms, vomit, bugs, and fake body parts. This series unsettles the viewer with its unnerving representations of the pathologies of narcissism—binge-purge, pornographic shots, personal hygiene, disease, and cosmetic concerns—an apocalyptic aftermath of obsessive self-consciousness.

Laurie Simmons
WOMAN OPENING REFRIGERATOR, 1979
Color photograph
6 1/8 x 9 1/4 in.
Courtesy Metro Pictures, New York

"I realized early on that artifice attracted me to an image more than any other quality."[98] This is artifice "in the sense of staging, heightened color and exaggerated lighting, not a surreal or fictive moment." Throughout LAURIE SIMMONS's career, extending back to the late 1970s, she has engaged this interest exclusively in photographic works of varying scales, whether by staging "artificial" elements: miniature sets composed with dolls and props, or dolls or live models posed in front of projected backdrops of landmarks. This melding of real and artificial elements exposes the stereotypical "identities" that animate the dolls or transform the live models into mannequins. Until recently focusing almost exclusively on women, Simmons's photographs do not portray individuals, but rely on engendered types, "surrogates, stand-ins for women oppressed (and mass-produced) by their environment."[99]

Simmons's work has a specific chronology to its production, each series she produces "contingent on what happened before."[100] The "Color Coordinated Interiors" (1983) and "Tourism" (1984) series consist of color-coordinated, blown-up images and monochrome plastic dolls with rear-projected images; in her "Fake Fashions" (1984), the dolls have become live models stiffly posed like mannequins, again color-coordinated to the projected backdrop. A collaboration with artist Allan McCollum led to "Actual Photos" (1985), fifty-one photographic "portraits" of the faces of microscopically enlarged tiny cast plastic figurines, their minute forms differentiated and disturbingly readable despite their minute size.

Simmons's recent series, "Ventriloquism" (1986-present) (SEE ILL. P. 117), includes photographs, taken at the Venthaven Museum of Ventriloquism in

[98]Laurie Simmons, interview with Cindy Sherman, "The Lady Vanishes," in Laurie Simmons (Tokyo: Parco Co., Ltd., 1987), p. 11.
[99]Roberta Smith, "Allan McCollum and Laurie Simmons at Nature Morte," Art in America 74, 1 (Jan. 1986): 139.
[100]Conversation with the artist, May 19, 1987.

Kentucky, of ventriloquist's dummies (sometimes with the ventriloquist) and "talking objects"—actual objects like a purse or ukulele anthropormorphized into puppets. It also includes a series of large-scale, black-and-white photographs of "walking objects" that are animated by a real person (SEE CAT. NOS. 98-103; SEE ILL. P. 116). These works portray and dramatize these objects (a camera, a purse, a cake, etc.) as representations of people, especially types, and the particular dynamics of the ventriloquist/dummy, puppetmaster/puppet relationship in which "the ventriloquist is a rather kindly character and the dummy his hostile alter-ego."[101] Her interest also extends that relationship to the viewer: "We're willing to accept the dummy's words as his own rather than admit to hearing one man with two voices."[102]

HAIM STEINBACH's work since the late 1970s has focused on found objects of various cultural origins, presenting them unmodified on the privileging space of the shelf. Steinbach has described his practice as having "a stronger sense of being complicit with the production of desire, what we traditionally call beautiful seductive objects, than being positioned somewhere outside of it."[103] His practice has been viewed as "essentially a curatorial endeavor...with objects selected for what they said about their real or imagined owners, about their context, about each other and about the curator himself."[104] The recontextualized objects become "cultural artifacts....Removed as they are from their other lives, the lives for which they were

Haim Steinbach
UNTITLED (WAKAMBA GOURDS), *1989*
Formica-laminate shelf with gourds
49 x 80 x 22 in.
Courtesy Jay Gorney Modern Art, New York, Margo Leavin Gallery, Los Angeles, and Sonnabend Gallery, New York

[101] Simmons/Sherman (note 98), p. 13.
[102] Ibid.
[103] Haim Steinbach, "From Criticism to Complicity," *Flash Art* (note 38), p. 46.
[104] Holland Cotter, "Haim Steinbach: Shelf Life," *Art in America* 76, 5 (May 1988): 159.

made, the objects are now engaged in a process of initiation and mythicization through their location in another life, in art."[105]

In 1979 Steinbach made *Display no. 7*, an installation at Artists Space in New York, comprised of a variety of objects—ranging from a high-tech tea kettle to a wooden vase filled with feathers—arranged on shelves made of simple boards on brackets installed on walls painted or covered with strips of wallpaper. In the early 1980s, Steinbach isolated objects on handmade shelves, setting up a contrast between a single object and its support. Around 1984 he developed a particular type of shelf, a Formica-laminated wooden wedge structure (recalling Donald Judd's wall-reliefs and Richard Artschwager's Formica objects) as the support for an arrangement of multiple objects.[106] In *supremely black* (1985), Steinbach assembled mass-produced American cultural objects—two black ceramic water jugs and three "Bold" detergent boxes, while *Untitled (jugs, mugs) #1* (1987) displays hierarchically on two tiers two types of crockery: an assembly of Israeli pottery on the top shelf and a variety of mass-produced "kitsch" coffee mugs on the lower shelf.

Steinbach's practice is highly conscious of the systems of display, exploring different permutations of the shelf as a conventional support for the institutional and domestic display of symbolic objects. It draws upon the various roles that are ascribed to the cultural object, namely, as previously noted, the curatorial role, but also that of the consumer who purchases objects and makes aesthetic, functional, and socio-economic choices, and the private collector who accommodates these works into the home, and to whom Steinbach entrusts these objects to be maintained as "art."

Recent installations have encompassed a broader repertory of objects that consider the polarities of cultural dynamics and hierarchies. A recent installation at Lia Rumma Gallery in Naples thus included "cheap" regional handicrafts, African marble perfume urns, and cast-iron pots, all purchased locally. Steinbach also attended to the walls, painting them the color of Pompeiian pottery or covering them with moiré fabric.

Steinbach's installation for "A Forest of Signs" incorporates a shelf work, *Untitled (Wakamba gourds)* (1989), into an installation that includes two "funhouse"-type mirrors and a phrase painted on a wall (CAT. NO. 104). The shelf piece presents four Kenyan gourds used for storing beer on "teak" and "mahogany" laminated shelves. Together with the mirrors which distort the viewer's reflection, and the phrase, "Side order of facts,"[107] a fragment from an electronics advertisement, the work addresses issues of difference and otherness (the four gourds of the same family each grow into a different form), distortion (the distorted shapes of the gourds and their placement in an art context, the distortion of the viewer in the mirrors), and the idea of fact (as emphasized by the phrase and the reflections in the mirrors).

[105]Germano Celant, "Haim Steinbach's Wild, Wild, Wild West," *Artforum* 26, 4 (Dec. 1987): 75.

[106]The supports are unique, built specifically for the objects. The relationship of the objects to the shelves extends to the purchase price of the work; the price of the shelves is figured separately from that of the objects.

[107]See also ills. pp. 118-119 for a similar work using the phrase and an advertisement image of truffles.

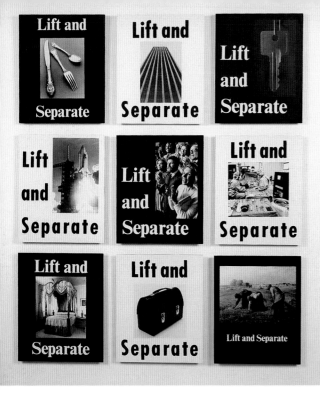

Mitchell Syrop
LIFT AND SEPARATE, *1984*
Black-and-white photographs
mounted on board
Nine panels: 24 x 20 in. each
Collection of Gregory Linn, Los Angeles

In rereading the texts and images of advertising, MITCHELL SYROP has, since the late 1970s, produced works that recall the look of corporate advertising. It has been Syrop's program as an artist to identify with the strategies of the advertising agencies—their command over the production of desire in the consumer through the production of symbolic visual and textual representations and powerful implicit messages in the mass media. Recently in an article on Jay Chiat, chairman of the Los Angeles-based advertising agency Chiat/Day, Sean Mitchell described the style of the agency:

The award-winning creative agency specializes in the "big hit," or what chairman Chiat likes to describe as "crashing through the rubble," a reference to the 20,000 advertising messages that he estimates the average American is subjected to every week. [108]

Syrop's works address this practice, bringing it into the discourse and conventions of art, just as the advertisers have aestheticized representations of their clients' products or functions in their ads. [109] Syrop combines common catchword phrases or colloquialisms with images lifted from a variety of sources, assuming in their juxtapositions the power over these elements to offer new meanings or insight into hidden meanings:

> *This willingness to allow meanings to proliferate anarchically while at the same time implying an underlying order marked a new direction.
> ...he has focused on the difference between meanings deliberately hidden in images and phrases, and meanings spontaneously produced by them.* [110]

It is the viewer who interprets the combinations suggested by the artist. For example, in his work starting in the early 1980s, Syrop combined text with predominantly black-and-white photographs. Such works as *Stoop to Conquer, Lift and Separate,* or *Sit in Judgement* (CAT. NOS. 117, 112-113, 108) bear the visual and textual authority of advertisements. Their meaning is the result of a complete interdependency of text and image—Syrop promotes the reading of text into image and vice-versa. In later works, phrases are combined with black-and-white photographs that have been hand-colored (by the photo lab). The application of color to these black-and-white images can be likened to the colorization process applied to vintage films—it is an assignment of color laid over black and white used for nostalgic seductive enhancement under the guise of realism.

In addition to the photographic works, Syrop has produced a number of "products" (soaps, sponges, decals, rubber stamps, balloons) bearing the same slogans but functioning as art commodities that insinuate the messages into less specialized or privileged "art" contexts.

Since 1987 Syrop's work has moved from rephotographing images with texts to using ready-made posters and large-scale photographic wallpaper murals as the material and source for his recent works (SEE ILL. PP. 120-121). The images he has selected—scenes of deserted tropical beaches at sunset, fields of tulips, New England autumns, crashing waves or cascading waterfalls—all project visions of paradise, Eden, heaven. These hyperreal travel images promote desire; they offer decoration and distraction in domestic or office situations. Symbols of

[108]Sean Mitchell, "Off the Wall on Madison Avenue," *Los Angeles Times Magazine* 4, 37 (Sept. 18, 1988): 10-12.
[109]See Syrop's discussion of the aestheticization of gender and biological functions in "Demenstruation," *Journal* 5, 41 (Spring 1985): 57-63.
[110]Lane Relyea, "Mitchell Syrop at Kuhlenschmidt/Simon," *Art in America* 75, 3 (Mar. 1987): 147.

freedom and leisure, these familiar images instill the desire to escape, to travel— the viewer becomes a tourist. Instead of overlaying his texts, Syrop rips them out of the posters. Phrases such as "You Are Beautiful/I Love You," "Blind Spot," "Academic Freedom," or "Live Nude," are divided in half; the resulting works reunite the phrases with one-half of the poster with letters dropped out and the other with ripped out letters on a blank background. A visual equivalence is set up through implied but not actual replacement of the letters between the two halves and the literal unification as text and image are inextricably read together—though the images cannot be reconciled. The act of ripping and the resulting torn edges lend a particular anxiousness, if not a pathology, to these images of idealized paradise.

JAMES WELLING's interest in issues of representation has, since the late 1970s, remained essentially a photographic practice. His interest in appropriation has been directed not to mass media's imagery, but rather to "a classic photographic style and the institutional presentation that goes along with 'straight' photography."[111] The style of representation in Welling's work invites a certain readability, a specific accessibility to meaning. A tension arises from the illusive nature of the imagery, the concomitant multitude of associations it engenders, and its adherence to traditional genre that make the images more difficult to identify— photographs of old diary pages that are not readable, "landscape" photographs that are not landscapes, or photographs of modern buildings composed in the styles of a different time.

Welling's work traverses a variety of subjects that can be located within the traditional pictorial genre of landscape and still life. Its continuity lies in its incomplete closure of meaning. In a 1980 conversation with David Salle, Welling remarked that the intention in his work was "To get at meaninglessness through representation."[112] Welling's early series of small black-and-white photographs of diary pages and romanticized landscapes (1977-80) (SEE CAT. NOS. 119-130) are not easily interpreted chronologically. The diary pages can be located in a different point of time as indicated by the style of the handwriting and the occasional date, but the content is illegible. The landscapes appear "antique" as well because they become associated with the diary pages and the genre of vintage nineteenth-century photographs. The images printed in black and white on a cold-toned paper belie the "antiqueness" of their subject matter.

James Welling
UNTITLED, *1977-80*
Silver print
4-5/8 x 3-3/4 in.
Courtesy the artist and Jay Gorney Modern Art, New York

[111] James Welling, interview with Trevor Fairbrother, in David A. Ross and Jürgen Harten, *The BiNATIONAL: American Art of the 80s* (Boston: The Institute of Contemporary Art and Museum of Fine Arts, and Cologne: Du Mont Buchverlag, 1988), p. 219.

[112] James Welling, in "Images That Understand Us: A Conversation with David Salle and James Welling," *Journal* 27 (June-July 1980): 43.

A later series of photographs of crumpled aluminum foil (1980-81) invites interpretation and can be read as landscapes: "What interests me is this primitive desire to look at shiny, glittering objects of incoherent beauty. I'm trying to locate a place outside of the dominating power of language where these sensual landscapes can exist."[113] The later series of images composed of photographs of gelatin, tiles, filo-dough flakes on folds of drapery, and the recent black-and-white and color Polaroids of drapery—all "straight" photos—hover ambiguously between abstraction and representation. A series begun in 1985 of farm images relates to early Romantic landscapes. Accompanying a selection of the early diary/landscape photographs in this exhibition is a selection of Welling's recent photographs of H. H. Richardson architecture (SEE CAT. NOS. 131-139; SEE ILLS. PP. 122-123). This late nineteenth-century American architect's revivalist designs of Romanesque and Gothic architecture struck Welling as a form of appropriation. Looking at Welling's austere images, the viewer looks into the past to see a utopian future.[114] He noted: "The nineteenth century represents our origin and utopia in terms of technological and cultural values. It's an almost unimaginable world which created and then was obliterated by modernism."[115]

CHRISTOPHER WILLIAMS's work since the early 1980s has dialectically addressed the interpretation of photographic imagery, fragmenting meaning in a multiplicity of references (historical, cultural, aesthetic, political, etc.). His resources are institutional repositories of categorized information: photographic archives, commercial stock photo companies, publications, libraries, and museums, and his work has looked at these repositories in relationship to notions of power. His images fall within the conventions of pictorial genre (portraiture, landscape, still life), within the conventions of photographic history (photojournalism, documentation, publicity, and art), and within the convention of photographic presentation—production of the image (production of a negative, cropping, production of a positive) and display (matting and framing, contextualization, identification through label cards and captions), publicity (announcement cards), and reproduction.

The range of Williams's practice can be examined through three works. In 1981 Williams produced *Source, The Photographic Archive, John F. Kennedy Library....* The title is a text, which is presented separately from the rest of the work, and a descriptive disclosure of its production.[116] This work is comprised of

[113]Welling/Fairbrother (note 111), p. 220.
[114]Conversation with the artist, May 13, 1988.
[115]Welling/Fairbrother (note 111), p. 221.
[116]The full title of this work which has appeared on the announcement cards for its exhibition is: *SOURCE: The Photographic Archive, John F. Kennedy Library, Columbia Point on Dorchester Bay, Boston, Massachusetts, 02125, U.S.A.; CONDITIONS FOR SELECTION: There are two conditions: the photograph or photographs must be dated May 10, 1963, and the subject, John F. Kennedy, must have his back turned toward the camera. All photographs on file fulfilling these requirements are used. TECHNICAL TREATMENT: The photographs are subjected to the following operations: rephotography (4 x 5" copy negative), enlargement (from 8 x 10" to 11 x 14" by use of the copy negative), and cropping (¹/₁₆" is removed from all sides of the rephotographed, enlarged image). The final component of the title, PRESENTATION, is a variable as it cites the name, title, and date of the exhibition, and name and address of the venue, followed by the name of the artist.*

Christopher Williams
SOURCE, THE PHOTOGRAPHIC ARCHIVE,
JOHN F. KENNEDY LIBRARY..., 1981
Gelatin silver print
9-1/2 x 13-12/16 in.
Collection of Coosje van Bruggen
and Claes Oldenburg, New York

four photographs (three black and white and one color) of John F. Kennedy on May 10, 1963 (a day selected by Williams to have no other historical or cultural references) that were re-photographed from those on file at the John F. Kennedy Library. These photographs can be classified as portraiture, while also addressing journalistic notions of the "photo-opportunity" (and a president who invited the press into his daily life); the subject of these images, John F. Kennedy (who in that year was assassinated by a "shot" from the rear); and standard photographic practices. As Anne Rorimer wrote, "The work's meaning incorporates the entire system that governs the dispensation and manipulation of photographic information."[117]

In his series of photographic works (begun 1984) *On Amsterdam*, *On Ghent*, *On Paris*, *On New York* (I & II) (ILL. P. 124), and *On Naples* (each comprised of three photographs), Williams utilized images from two photographic sources: a Pulitzer Prize winning photograph of a 1971 execution in Bangladesh (a "photo-opportunity") distributed by AP/Wide World Photos, and a stock photo "tourist" or "postcard" image selected to represent each city in which the work is presented. These photographic representations speak of issues of context (relationships between picture and place, site-specificity of an artwork, and the politicizing of imagery with references at once to tourism and travel, journalistic photo opportunities, and the itinerary of the exhibition of the work itself. Abigail Solomon-Godeau wrote about this work:

> In juxtaposing the spectacle of the execution with the very different
> kind of spectacle afforded by the glossy tourism photo of the city, and
> inscribing both within a kind of epistemological grid that charts the
> norms and forms of what could be termed exhibitionality, Williams
> performs a multivalent critique that embraces systems of photo-
> graphic representation and dissemination even as it calls attention
> to the most disturbing aspects of photographic substance.[118]

[117]Anne Rorimer, "Introduction," in *74th American Exhibition* (Chicago: The Art Institute of Chicago, 1982), p. 9.
[118]Abigail Solomon-Godeau, "Photography at the Dock," in *The Art of Memory / Loss of History* (New York: The New Museum of Contemporary Art, 1986), p. 51.

Williams's recent photographic project, *Angola to Vietnam**[119] (CAT. NO. 140; SEE ILL. P. 125), is a portfolio of twenty-seven black-and-white photographs of glass botanical models produced by Leopold and Rudolf Blaschka during 1887-1936 in Dresden, housed in the Botanical Museum at Harvard University. Checking a list of thirty-six countries identified in a report on terrorism as countries where disappearance is practiced against the labels for 847 glass models in the Botanical Museum, Williams found twenty-seven of these countries represented in the museum. The glass models are photographed from different angles, some clinically documenting the repaired cracks, the wire supports, the catalogue number, others looking quite "real." In addition, one image is repeated twice (a flower that represents both Angola and Togo), while in the case of Namibia and South Africa, Williams produced two different photographs from one negative to represent the individual countries. These still-life photographs engage the genre of flower photography and nineteenth-century vintage images (with references extending back to August Sanders's typological investigation, *Citizens of the Twentieth Century: Portrait Photos 1892-1952*, the films of Carl-Theodore Dryer, and the botanical photographs in Karl Blossfeldt's *Üformen der Kunst*). Yet their titles (the names of the countries—notably Third World countries) and the additional information about the glass models on the accompanying label cards beget a wholly different set of readings pertaining to terrorism, colonialism, and propaganda, that resonate with Williams's earlier travel work. His use of the museum as repository for these representations, "in perpetual bloom,"[120] speaks of the collection's original function as specimens—the models were made because real flowers die.

[119]The asterisk refers to the following text which appears on the verso of the title page for a book by Williams of the same title published by Imschoot, Uitgevers Voor IC, Ghent, Belgium, 1989: "*Angola to Vietnam**, an abbreviation of the list of twenty-seven countries, is the result of filtering the list: *Angola, Argentina, Bolivia, Brazil, Central African Republic, Chile, Colombia, Cyprus, Dominican Republic, El Salvador, Ethiopia, Guatemala,* Guinea, *Haiti, Honduras, Indonesia,* Iran, Iraq, *Lebanon, Mexico,* Morocco, *Namibia,* Nepal, *Nicaragua, Paraguay, Peru, Philippines,* Seychelles, *South Africa, Sri Lanka,* Syria, *Togo, Uganda, Uruguay, Vietnam,* and Zaire—thirty-six countries where disappearances are known to have occurred during 1985 as noted on page twenty-nine of *Disappeared!, Technique of Terror*, a report for the Commission on International Humanitarian Issues, 1986, Zed Books, Ltd., London and New Jersey—through the 847 life-size models representing some 780 species and varieties of plants in 164 families from the Ware Collection of Blaschka Glass Models, the Botanical Museum, Harvard University, Cambridge, Massachusetts." The italicized country names refer to those represented in the Ware Collection.

[120]David Deitcher, "Angola to Vietnam: Unnatural Selection," *Visions* 3, 1 (Winter 1988): 24.

RICHARD BAIM

TURN OF THE CENTURY

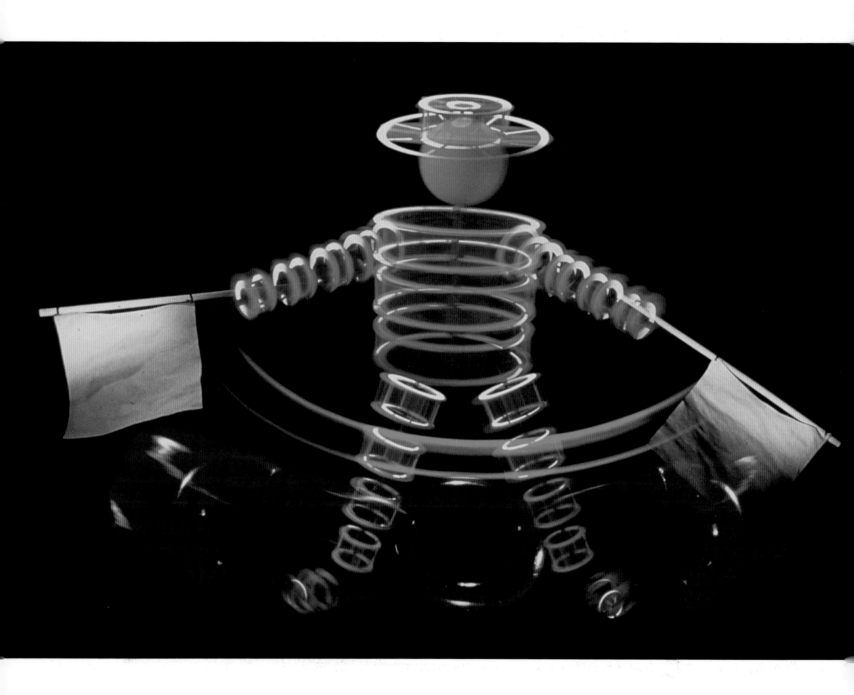

ERICKA BECKMAN

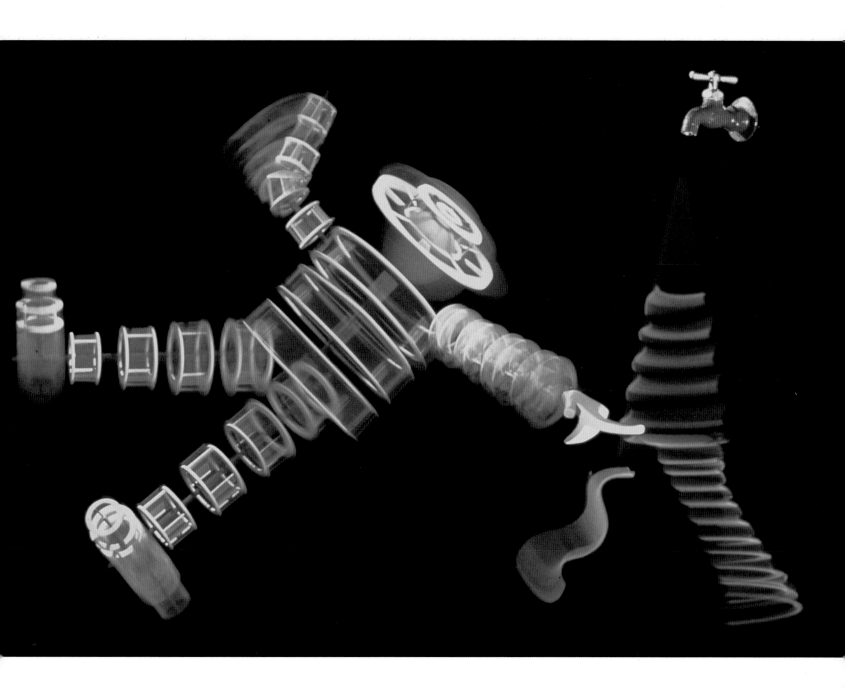

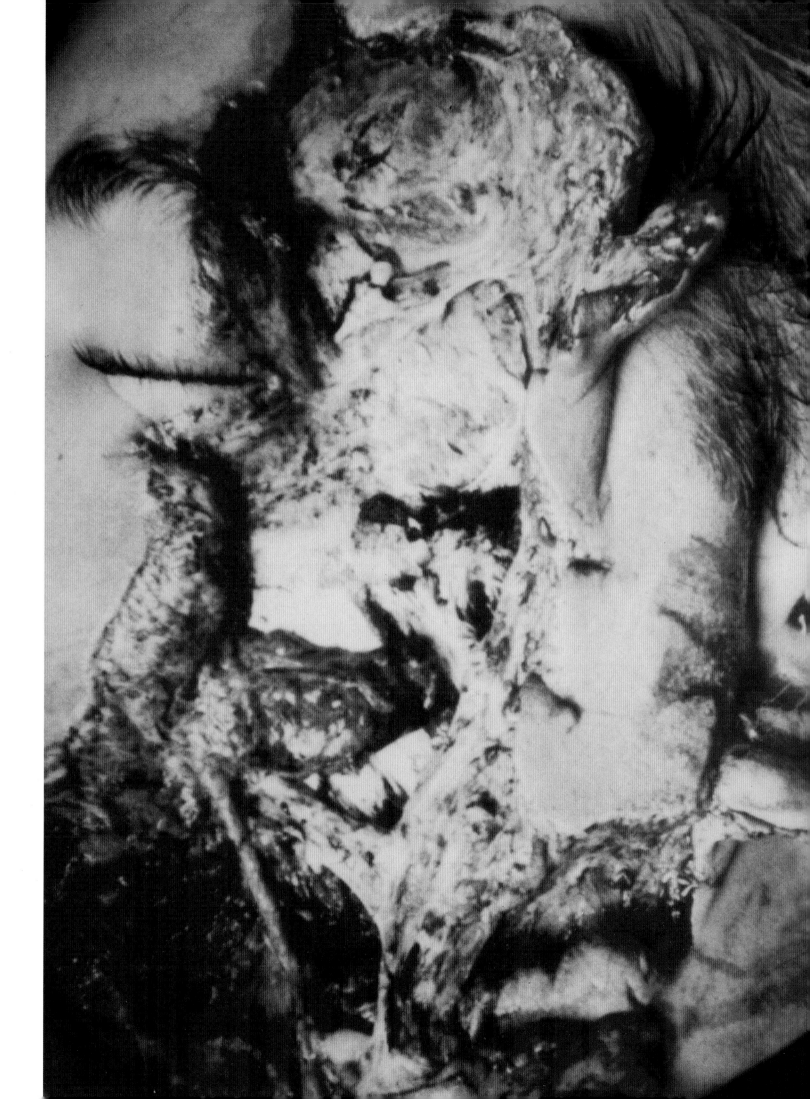

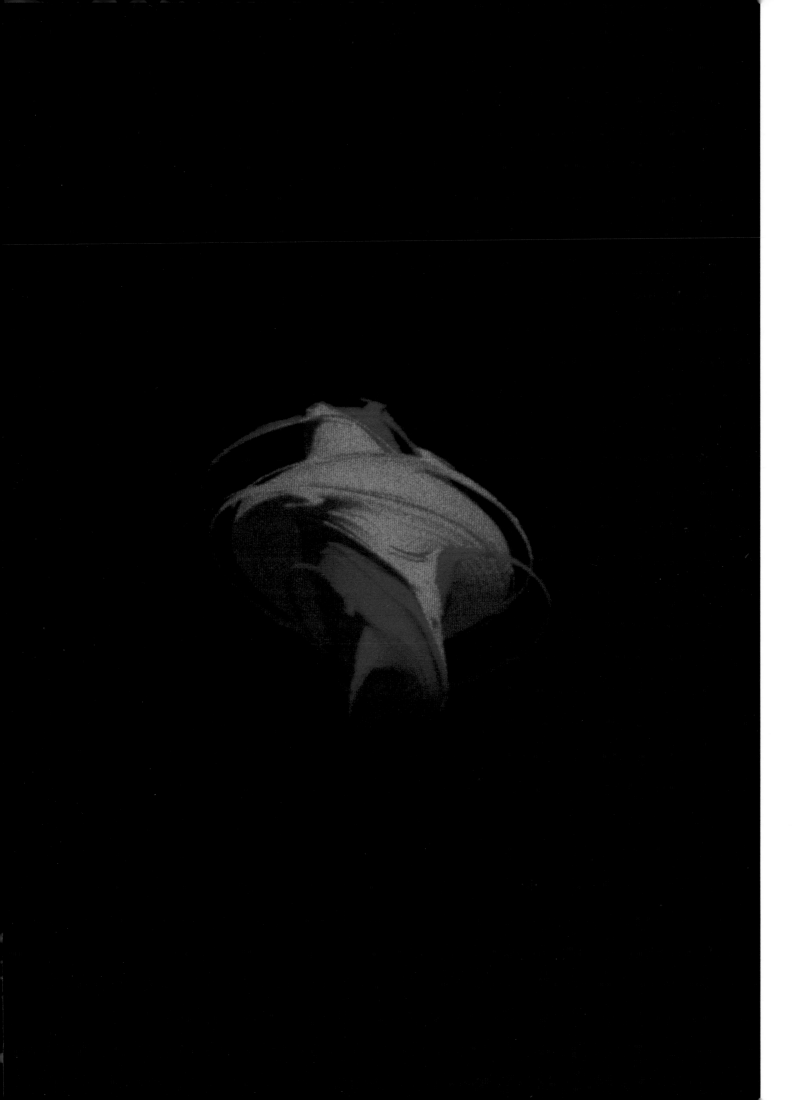

DARA BIRNBAUM

PM MAGAZINE © 1982

PM Magazine / Acid Rock: (L.A. Woman)

L.A. (Los Angeles)
I see
I see your hair is burning
Hills are filled with fire
If they say I never loved you
You know they are a liar

Cops in cars
Topless bars
Never saw a woman
So all alone
So all alone
alone, alone, alone

(I) took a look around
To see which way the wind blows

Still from videotape installed for *Documenta 7*, Kassel, Germany, 1982

Partial installation view at The Institute of Contemporary Art, Boston, 1984

…the works completed from 1978–87 are "altered states," with earlier works, such as PM Magazine, *composed of TV-fragments and structured on the reconstructed conventions of television: new "readymades" for the late twentieth century. It was my desire for the viewer to be caught in a limbo of alteration where she / he would be able to plunge head-long into the very experience of TV. I wanted to establish, and set as a representative model, the ability to explore the possibilities of a two-way system of communication—a "talking back" to the media.*

Detail of installation at The Institute of Contemporary Art, Boston, 1984

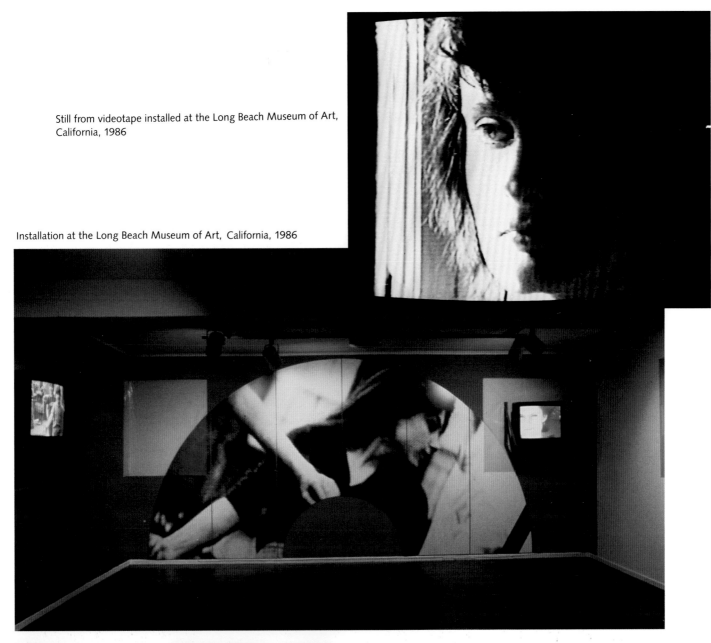

Still from videotape installed at the Long Beach Museum of Art, California, 1986

Installation at the Long Beach Museum of Art, California, 1986

Endemic in "characters" such as the animated figures in PM Magazine *or the teenager on the streets of NYC in* Damnation of Faust, *are the forms of restraint and near suffocation imposed through our current technological society; pressures which force a person to find the means of openly declaring, through communicated gestures, their own identity.*

Still from videotape installed at the Long Beach Museum of Art, California, 1986

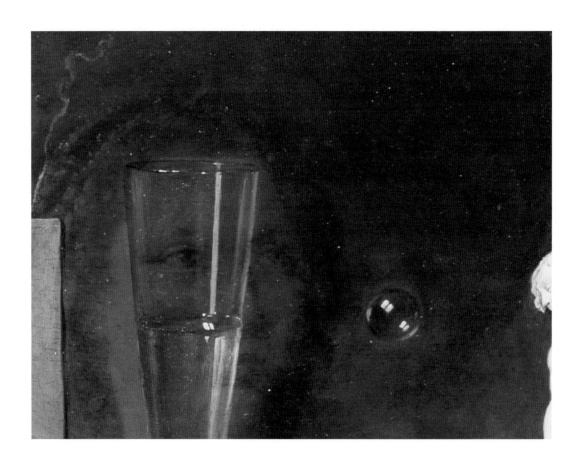

BARBARA BLOOM

TROY BRAUNTUCH   *Untitled*, 1988

Untitled, 1988

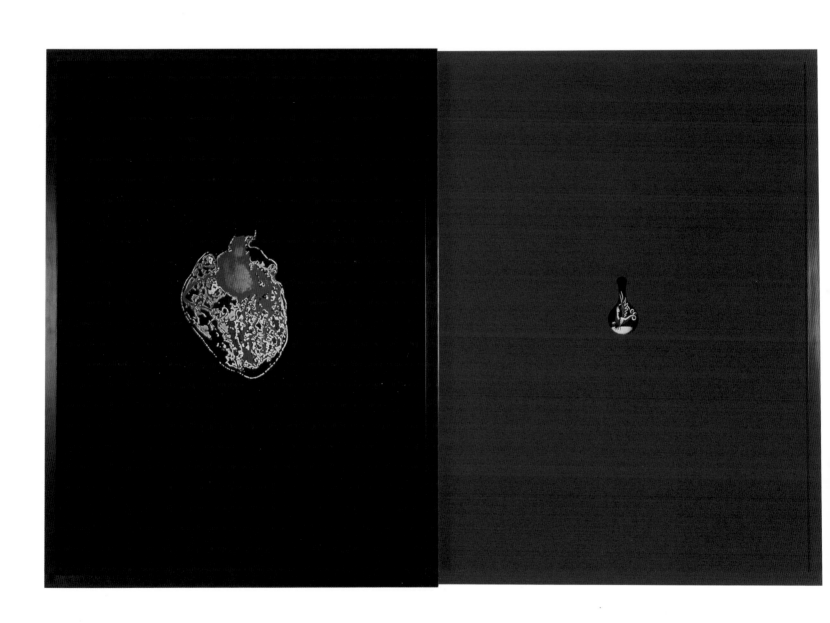

SARAH CHARLESWORTH

Heart's Retort, 1988

Work, 1988

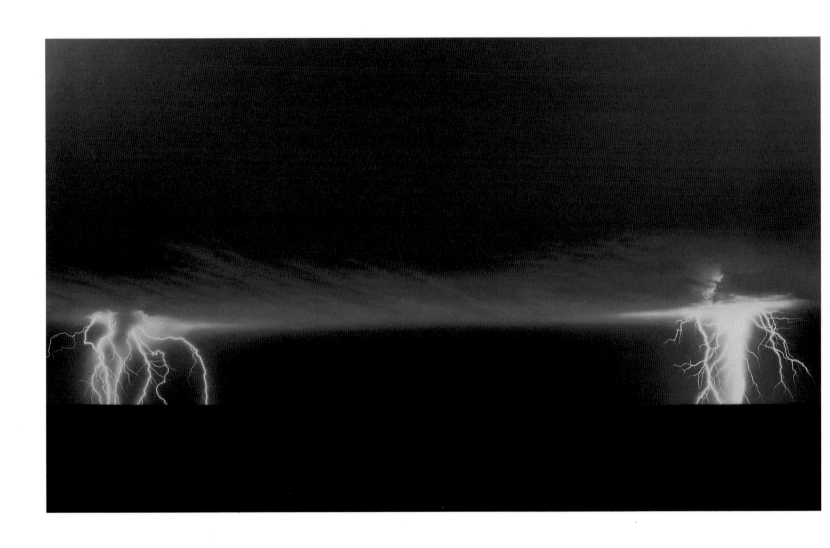

JACK GOLDSTEIN   *Untitled*, 1983

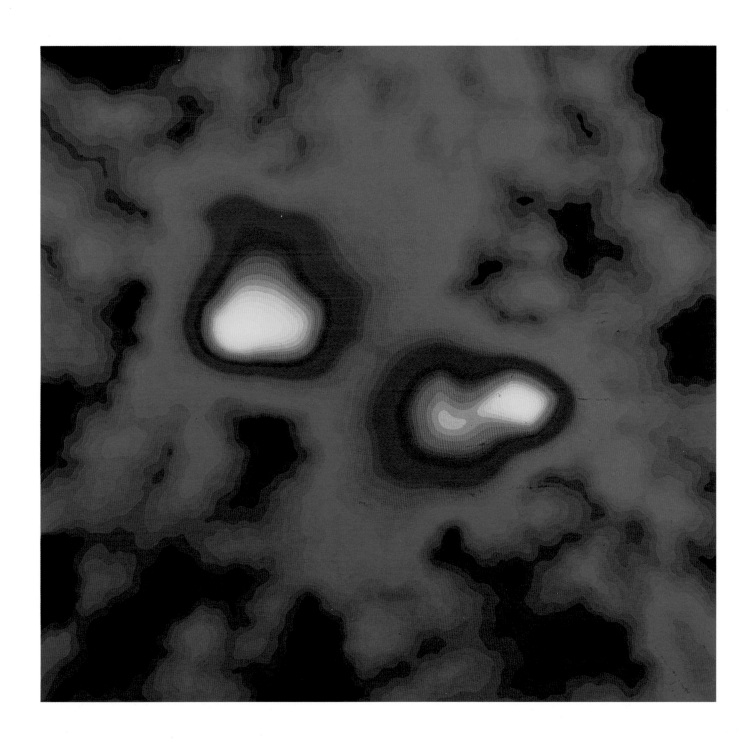

Untitled, 1987

SHRIEK WHEN THE PAIN HITS DURING INTERROGATION. REACH INTO THE DARK AGES TO FIND A SOUND THAT IS LIQUID HORROR, A SOUND OF THE BRINK WHERE MAN STOPS AND THE BEAST AND NAMELESS CRUEL FORCES BEGIN. SCREAM WHEN YOUR LIFE IS THREATENED. FORM A NOISE SO TRUE THAT YOUR TORMENTOR RECOGNIZES IT AS A VOICE THAT LIVES IN HIS OWN THROAT. THE TRUE SOUND TELLS HIM THAT HE CUTS HIS FLESH WHEN HE CUTS YOURS, THAT HE CANNOT THRIVE AFTER HE TORTURES YOU. SCREAM THAT HE DESTROYS ALL KINDNESS IN YOU AND BLACKENS EVERY VISION YOU COULD HAVE SHOWN HIM.

DON'T TALK DOWN TO ME. DON'T BE POLITE TO ME. DON'T TRY TO MAKE ME FEEL NICE. DON'T RELAX. I'LL CUT THE SMILE OFF YOUR FACE. YOU THINK I DON'T KNOW WHAT'S GOING ON. YOU THINK I'M AFRAID TO REACT. THE JOKE'S ON YOU. I'M BIDING MY TIME, LOOKING FOR THE SPOT. YOU THINK NO ONE CAN REACH YOU, NO ONE CAN HAVE WHAT YOU HAVE. I'VE BEEN PLANNING WHILE YOU'RE PLAYING. I'VE BEEN SAVING WHILE YOU'RE SPENDING. THE GAME IS ALMOST OVER SO IT'S TIME YOU ACKNOWLEDGE ME. DO YOU WANT TO FALL NOT EVER KNOWING WHO TOOK YOU?

LARRY JOHNSON   *Untitled (MOOCA), 1988*

To
M.O.C.A
Jalways use it
m Place of MOOCA
Thank you
to Including
new my wig
thanks
Rip Taylor

無題（日系人が戦時強制収容所へ向うための集合場、
セントラル街と1街、ロスアンジェルス市、カリフォ
ルニア州、1942年、）、1988年。

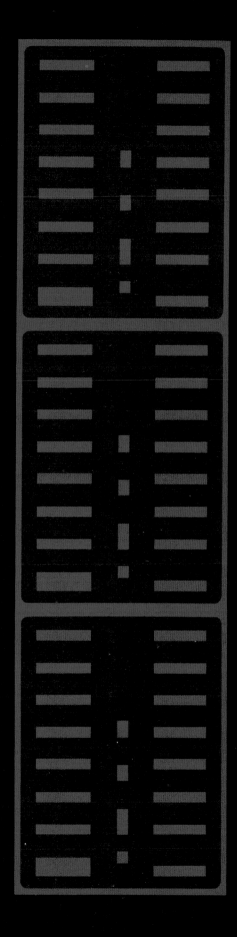

無題（版画部、建物15番、60町目、G街とH街間のH街、
ボストン第1区、ボストン戦時収容所、ボストン、ア
リゾナ州、戦時移転プロジェクト、コロラド川戦時移
転プロジェクト、1942年。）、1988年。

無題（日本詩の部、建物13番、310町目、C街とD街間の
2街、ボストン第3区、ボストン戦時収容所、ボストン、
アリゾナ州、戦時移転プロジェクト、コロラド川戦時移
転プロジェクト、1942年。）、1988年。

無題（音楽部、建物15番、44町目、G街とH街間の8街、
ボストン第1区、ボストン戦時収容所、ボストン、ア
リゾナ州、戦時移転プロジェクト、コロラド川戦時移
転プロジェクト、1942年。）、1988年。

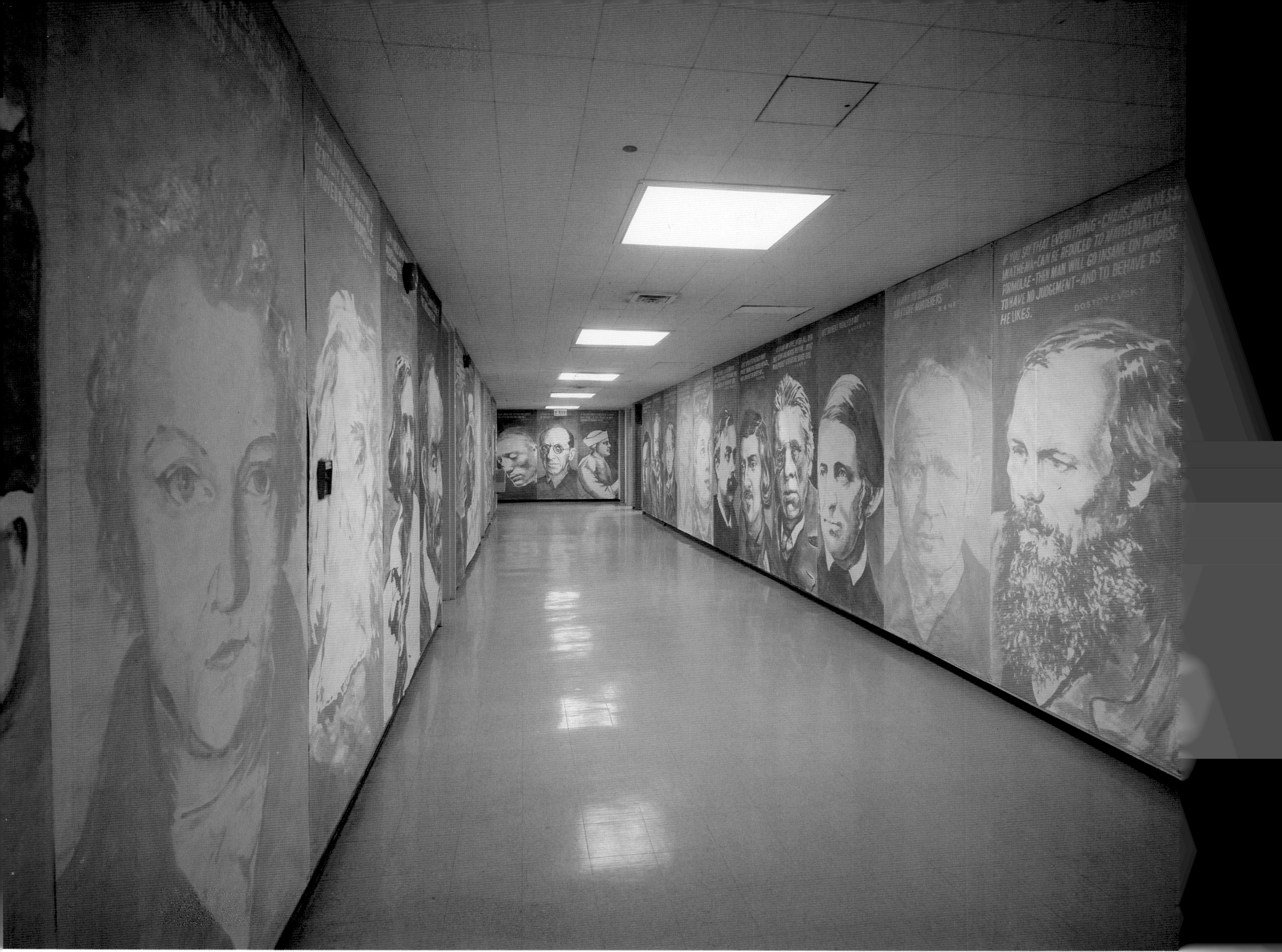

MIKE KELLEY

Pay For Your Pleasure, 1988

You can't see the forest for the trees

DOES ANDY WARHOL MAKE YOU CRY?

LOUISE LAWLER

DOES MARILYN MONROE MAKE YOU CRY?

TOLERANCES (EXCEPT AS NOTED)	MANHATTAN MUNICIPAL BUILDING SCAFFOLDING PROJECT			
DECIMAL ±	Scaffold bridges in entrance courtyard	SCALE 1"= 24"	DRAWN BY Thomas Lawson	
			APPROVED BY Art Commission, NY	
FRACTIONAL ±	TITLE Portrait of New York			
ANGULAR ±	DATE Aug 88	DRAWING NUMBER Central archway facing West		

MADE IN U.S.A.

SHERRIE LEVINE   *Untitled (Krazy Kat: 2)*, 1988

Untitled (Ignatz: 1), 1988   101

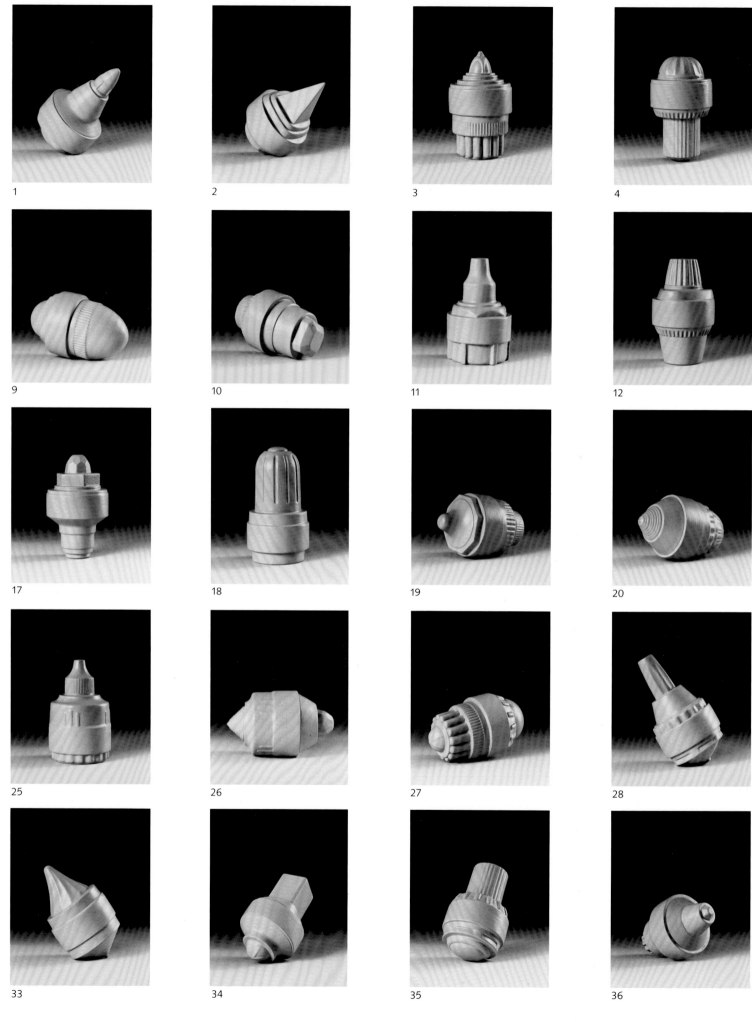

1

2

3

4

9

10

11

12

17

18

19

20

25

26

27

28

33

34

35

36

ALLAN McCOLLUM   *Individual Works, 1988*

5

6

7

8

13

14

15

16

21

22

23

24

29

30

31

32

37

38

39

40

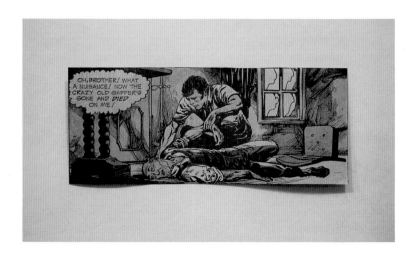

MATT MULLICAN

Untitled (Working Model for a City), 1988

8 Dead Cartoon Characters, 1973

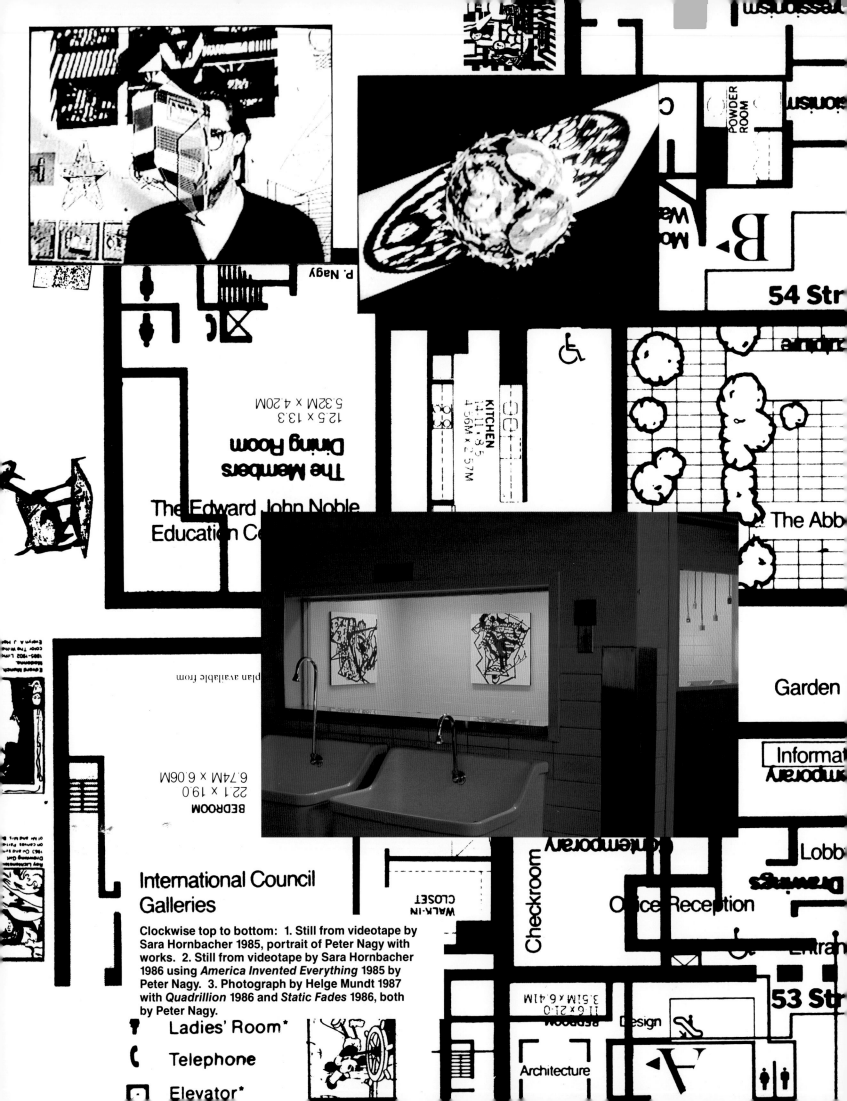

International Council
Galleries

Clockwise top to bottom: 1. Still from videotape by
Sara Hornbacher 1985, portrait of Peter Nagy with
works. **2.** Still from videotape by Sara Hornbacher
1986 using *America Invented Everything* 1985 by
Peter Nagy. **3.** Photograph by Helge Mundt 1987
with *Quadrillion* 1986 and *Static Fades* 1986, both
by Peter Nagy.

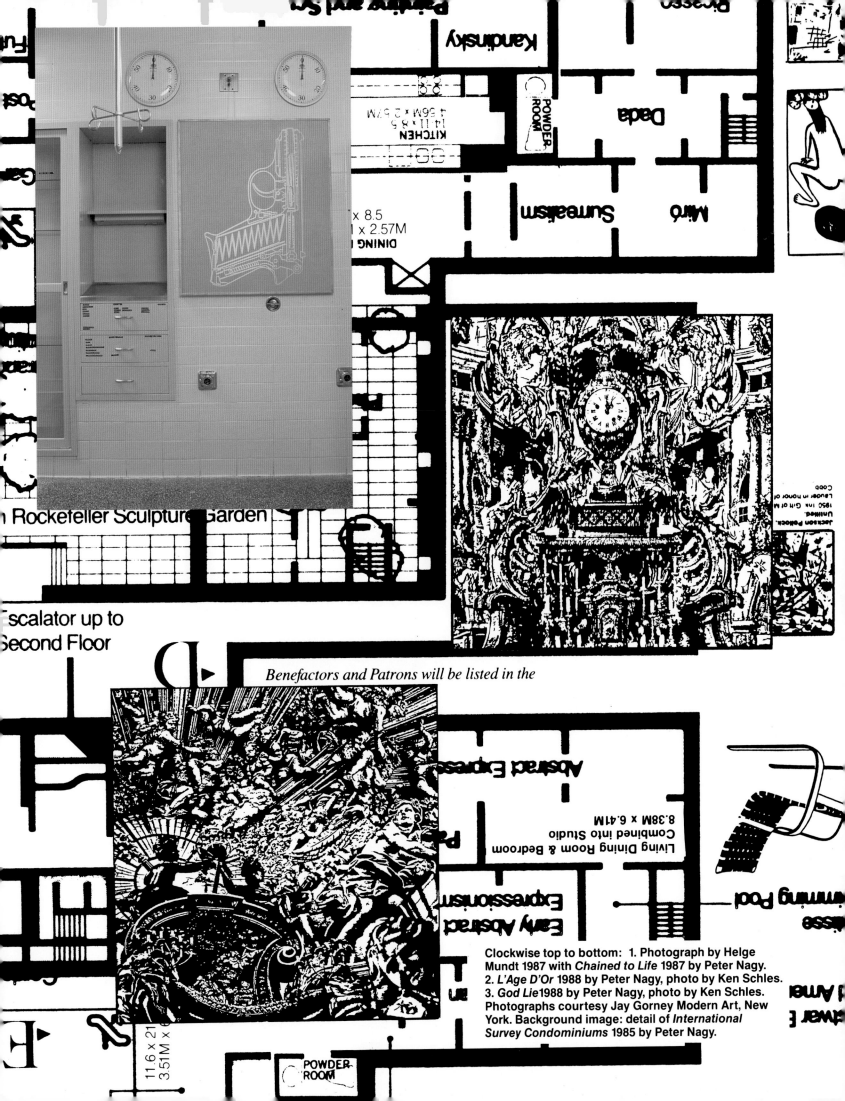

KITCHEN 14'11 x 8.5
4.56M x 2.57M

POWDER ROOM

DINING x 8.5
x 2.57M

Dada

Kandinsky

Miró

Surrealism

Picasso

Jackson Pollock.
Untitled,
1950. Ink Gift of M
Lauder in honor of
Cobb

Rockefeller Sculpture Garden

Escalator up to
Second Floor

Benefactors and Patrons will be listed in the

Abstract Express

Living Dining Room & Bedroom
Combined into Studio
8.38M x 6.41M

Early Abstract Expressionism

Swimming Pool

Matisse

POWDER ROOM

11.6 x 21
3.51M x 6

Clockwise top to bottom: 1. Photograph by Helge
Mundt 1987 with *Chained to Life* 1987 by Peter Nagy.
2. *L'Age D'Or* 1988 by Peter Nagy, photo by Ken Schles.
3. *God Lie* 1988 by Peter Nagy, photo by Ken Schles.
Photographs courtesy Jay Gorney Modern Art, New
York. Background image: detail of *International
Survey Condominiums* 1985 by Peter Nagy.

*Stephen Prina

UPON THE OCCASION OF RECEIVERSHIP: Language Type C, Indonesian, 29 of 61, 1989

Lawrence Weiner, **A TRANSLATION FROM ONE LANGUAGE TO ANOTHER,** Amsterdam, 1969;
laserprinting on letterhead stationery. 18-5/16 x 15-5/8″

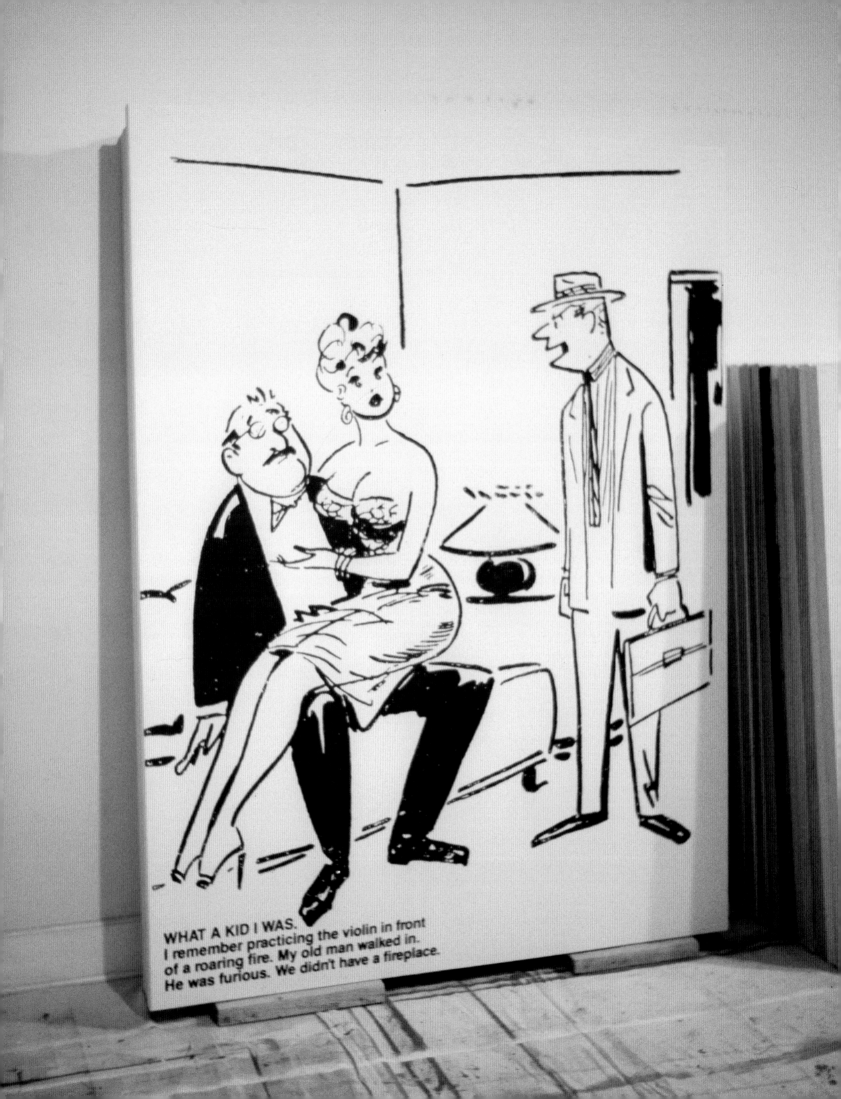

The old man stood at the gates of the cemetery and wept. A passer-by stopped to comfort him. "Why are you crying?" the latter asked softly. "My daughter is laying in there," explained the weeping one. "Sometimes I wish she was dead."

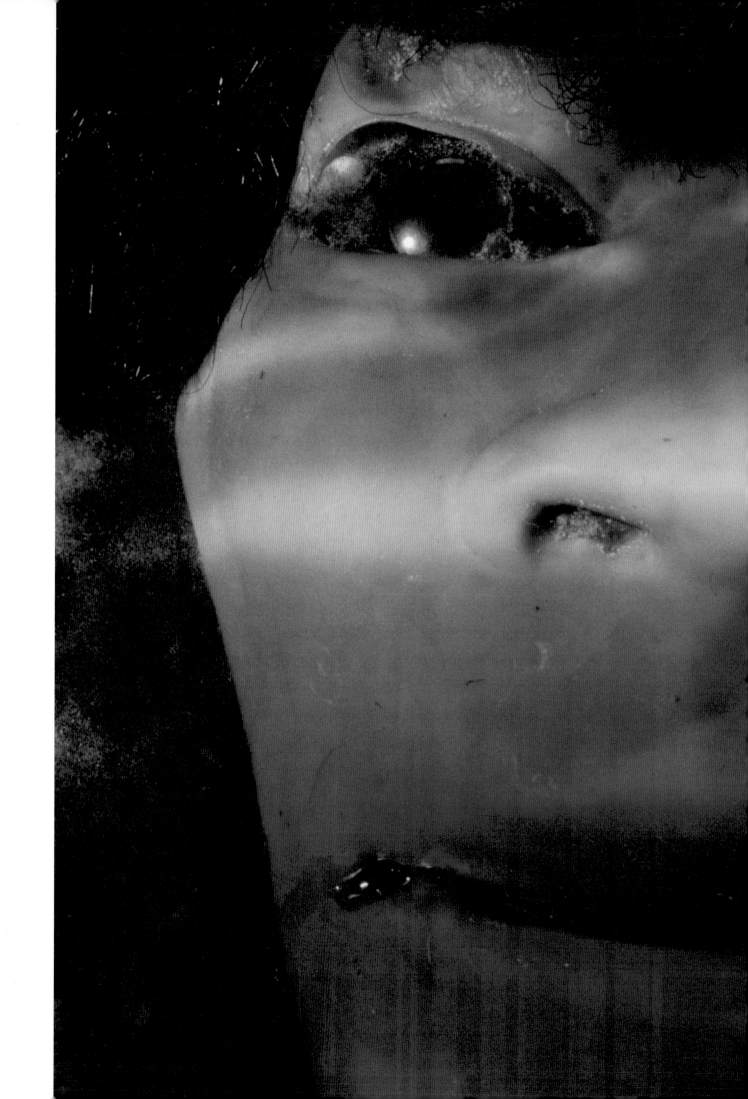

LAURIE SIMMONS

Side order of facts.

JAMES WELLING   *Stack Wing, Ames Free Library, North Easton, MA; 1877–79, 1988*

Winn Memorial Public Library, Woburn, MA; 1876–79, 1988

On New York (detail), 1985
Cibachrom, Ilford Cibachrome II Paper CRC .44M
10 x 14 in. [25 x 35.5 cm.]
The Image Bank–Peter M. Miller
Courtesy of the artist

CHRISTOPHER WILLIAMS

Angola, 1989
Blaschka Model 439, 1894
Genus no. 5091
Family, Sterculiaceae
Cola acuminata (Beauv.) Schott and Endl.
Cola Nut, Goora Nut
Gelatin silver print, Ed. 1/5
14 x 11 in. [35.5 x 28 cm.]
Courtesy of Galerie Crousel-Robelin, Bama, Paris

ILLUSTRATIONS

The following is a list of works reproduced in the preceding Portfolio of Artists' Projects.

RICHARD BAIM 66 - 67

TELEPHONE POLE, 1988
   Silver print
   8 x 10 in.
   Courtesy of the artist
LIFEBOATS, 1988
   Silver print
   8 x 10 in.
   Courtesy of the artist

JUDITH BARRY 68 - 69

ECHO, 1986
   Installation of slides, video transferred to Super-8 film,
   and audiotape at The Museum of Modern Art, New York,
   "Projects," 1986
   Collection of the artist

ERICKA BECKMAN 70 - 71

FLAG BEARER and COOL DOWN/WIND DOWN from "Nanotech
   Players," 1988
   Type-C prints
   44 x 64 in.
   Courtesy Bess Cutler, New York

GRETCHEN BENDER 72 - 73

DAYDREAM NATION: NARCOTICS OF REALISM, 1989
   Type-C prints
   Quaternion fractel image courtesy Alan Norton,
   IBM Research
   Courtesy Metro Pictures, New York

DARA BIRNBAUM 74 - 75

PM MAGAZINE, © 1982
   Five-channel color video with six-channel sound, two
   black-and-white photographic enlargements, and
   painted walls
   Dimensions variable
   Courtesy the artist, Josh Baer Gallery, New York, and
   Rhona Hoffman Gallery, Chicago
DAMNATION OF FAUST, © 1984
   Two-channel color video with quadriphonic sound, black-
   and-white photographic enlargement, and painted walls
   Dimensions variable
   Courtesy the artist, Josh Baer Gallery, New York, and
   Rhona Hoffman Gallery, Chicago

BARBARA BLOOM 76 - 77

THE AGE OF NARCISSISM, 1989
   David Bailly, STILL LIFE c. 1651, oil on canvas, 89.5 x 122
   cm., Stedelijk Museum "de Lakenhal," Leiden,
   The Netherlands

TROY BRAUNTUCH 78 - 79

UNTITLED, 1988
   Charcoal on handmade paper
   11-1/8 x 8 in.
   Courtesy Kent Fine Art, New York
UNTITLED, 1988
   Handstamps, ink, and shellac on handmade paper
   14-1/2 x 11-1/4 in.
   Courtesy Kent Fine Art, New York

SARAH CHARLESWORTH 80 - 81

HEART'S RETORT, 1988
   Laminated Cibachrome print with lacquer frame, ed. 1/4
   40 x 60 in.
   Courtesy Jay Gorney Modern Art, New York, and
   Margo Leavin Gallery, Los Angeles
WORK, 1988
   Laminated Cibachrome print with lacquer frame, ed. 1/4
   40 x 60 in.
   Courtesy Jay Gorney Modern Art, New York, and
   Margo Leavin Gallery, Los Angeles

JACK GOLDSTEIN 82 - 83

UNTITLED, 1987
   Acrylic on canvas
   84 x 96 in.
   Speyer Family Collection
UNTITLED, 1983
   Acrylic on canvas
   84 x 132 in.
   Collection of B.Z. and Michael Schwartz, New York

JENNY HOLZER 84 - 85

Two offset paper posters from "Inflammatory Essays,"
   1979-82
   17 x 17 in. each
   Courtesy Barbara Gladstone Gallery, New York

LARRY JOHNSON 86 - 87

UNTITLED (MOOCA), 1988

RONALD JONES 88 - 89

UNTITLED (SITE FOR THE DEBARKATION OF JAPANESE AMERICANS TO
   RELOCATION CENTERS, CENTRAL AVENUE AT 1ST STREET, LOS
   ANGELES, CALIFORNIA, 1942.), 1988
UNTITLED (DEPARTMENT OF BLOCKPRINTING, BUILDING 15, BLOCK
   60, 11TH STREET BETWEEN G AND H STREETS, POSTON-UNIT I
   AREA, POSTON RELOCATION CENTER, POSTON, ARIZONA, WAR
   RELOCATION PROJECT, COLORADO RIVER RELOCATION PROJECT,
   1942.), 1988
UNTITLED (JAPANESE POETRY DEPARTMENT, BUILDING 13, BLOCK
   310, 2ND STREET BETWEEN C AND D STREETS, POSTON-UNIT III
   AREA, POSTON RELOCATION CENTER, POSTON, ARIZONA, WAR
   RELOCATION PROJECT, COLORADO RIVER RELOCATION PROJECT,
   1942.), 1988
UNTITLED (MUSIC DEPARTMENT, BUILDING 15, BLOCK 44, 8TH
   STREET BETWEEN G AND H STREETS, POSTON-UNIT AREA I,
   POSTON RELOCATION CENTER, POSTON, ARIZONA, WAR
   RELOCATION PROJECT, COLORADO RIVER RELOCATION PROJECT,
   1942.), 1988
   Design and plans for mixed-media installation with
   marble, granite, and slate floor inlays commissioned for
   the exhibition

MIKE KELLEY 90 - 91

PAY FOR YOUR PLEASURE, 1988
  Oil on canvasboard by John Wayne Gacy and forty-two
  painted Tyvek banners
  Canvasboard: 20 x 16 in.; banners:
  approx. 96 x 48 in. each
  Installation at The Renaissance Society at The University
  of Chicago, 1988
  Collection of Timothy and Suzette Flood, Chicago
  Promised gift to The Museum of Contemporary Art,
  Los Angeles

JEFF KOONS 92 - 93

PAPARAZZI SHOT (JEFF, BUBBLES, & KATIE), 1989
  Black-and-white photograph
  Courtesy Sonnabend Gallery, New York

BARBARA KRUGER 94 - 95

UNTITLED, 1989
  Courtesy the artist and Mary Boone Gallery, New York

LOUISE LAWLER 96 - 97

DOES ANDY WARHOL MAKE YOU CRY?, 1988
  Cibachrome print
  26 x 40 in.
  Collection of Gabriella de Ferrari, New York
DOES MARILYN MONROE MAKE YOU CRY?, 1988
  Cibachrome print
  26 x 40 in.
  Collection of Raymond J. Learsy, Sharon, Connecticut

THOMAS LAWSON 98 - 99

PORTRAIT OF NEW YORK, MANHATTAN MUNICIPAL BUILDING
  SCAFFOLDING PROJECT, 1988
  Proposal for municipal building project
  Courtesy the artist and Metro Pictures, New York

SHERRIE LEVINE 100 - 101

UNTITLED (KRAZY KAT: 2), 1988
  Casein on wood
  18 x 15-1/2 in.
  Courtesy Donald Young Gallery, Chicago
UNTITLED (IGNATZ: 1), 1988
  Casein on wood
  24 x 20 in.
  Courtesy Mary Boone Gallery, New York

ROBERT LONGO 102 - 103

THE FIRE NEXT TIME, 1988 (detail)
  Plexiglas, graphite, and cast aluminum bonding
  72 x 222 in.
  The Rivendell Collection
NOSTROMO, 1988
  Copper, wood, wax, pigment, felt, steel, lead, and brick
  120 x 156 in.
  Collection of Fredrik Roos, Zug, Switzerland
  Courtesy Metro Pictures, New York

ALLAN McCOLLUM 104 - 105

"Individual Works," 1988 (Nos. 1-40)
  Enamel on Hydrocal
  Approx. 2 x 3 in. each
  Courtesy John Weber Gallery, New York

MATT MULLICAN 106 - 107

8 DEAD CARTOON CHARACTERS, 1973
  Newspaper print
  Courtesy Michael Klein, Inc., New York
UNTITLED (WORKING MODEL FOR A CITY), 1988
  Mixed media
  4-1/4 x 41-3/4 x 90 in.
  Courtesy Michael Klein, Inc., New York

PETER NAGY 108 - 109

ON THE TELEVISION, IN THE HOSPITAL, AT THE CHURCH, AROUND THE
  MUSEUM, 1988

STEPHEN PRINA 110 - 111

UPON THE OCCASION OF RECEIVERSHIP, 1989
  Lawrence Weiner, A TRANSLATION FROM ONE
  LANGUAGE TO ANOTHER, Amsterdam, 1969
  Laserprinting on letterhead stationery
  Sixty-one units: 18-5/16 x 15-5/8 in. each (framed)
  Courtesy the artist and Luhring Augustine Gallery,
  New York
UPON THE OCCASION OF RECEIVERSHIP: LANGUAGE TYPE C,
  INDONESIAN, 1989
  Unit twenty-nine of sixty-one

RICHARD PRINCE 112 - 113

WHAT A KID I WAS, 1988
  Acrylic and silkscreen on canvas
  58 x 75 in.
  Courtesy Barbara Gladstone Gallery, New York
WHY ARE YOU CRYING?, 1987
  Acrylic and silkscreen on canvas
  56 x 48 in.
  Courtesy Barbara Gladstone Gallery, New York

CINDY SHERMAN 114 - 115

UNTITLED, 1987
  Two color photographs
  96 x 120 in.
  Courtesy Metro Pictures, New York

LAURIE SIMMONS 116 - 117

WALKING OBJECT #1, and FEMALE VENT, 1989

HAIM STEINBACH 118 - 119

SIDE ORDER OF FACTS, 1989

MITCHELL SYROP 120 - 121

SKID ROW/RODEO DRIVE, 1988
  Offset lithograph poster mounted on board
  Two panels: 55-1/3 x 40 in. each
  Courtesy the artist and Richard Kuhlenschmidt Gallery,
  Santa Monica, California

JAMES WELLING 122 - 123

STACK WING, AMES FREE LIBRARY, NORTH EASTON, MA; 1877-79,
    1988
    Silver print
    18 x 22 in.
    Collection of Alain Clairet, New York
    Courtesy Thea Westreich Associates, New York
WINN MEMORIAL PUBLIC LIBRARY, WOBURN, MA; 1876-79, 1988
    Silver print
    18 x 22 in.
    Collection of Alain Clairet, New York
    Courtesy Thea Westreich Associates, New York

CHRISTOPHER WILLIAMS 124 - 125

ON NEW YORK, 1985 (detail)
    Cibachrome, Ilford Cibachrome II Paper CRC .44M
    10 x 14 in.
    The Image Bank—Peter M. Miller
    Courtesy the artist
ANGOLA, 1989
    Blaschka Model 439, 1894
    Genus no. 5091
    Family, Sterculiaceae
    COLA ACUMINATA (Beauv.) Schott and Endl.
    Cola Nut, Goora Nut
    Gelatin silver print, ed. 1/5
    14 x 11 in. [35.5 x 28 cm.]
    Courtesy Galerie Crousel-Robelin, Bama, Paris

PHOTOGRAPHY–LANGUAGE–CONTEXT: Prelude to the **1980s**

By Anne Rorimer

THE THIRTY ARTISTS IN THIS EXHIBITION, whose careers were formed by the end of the 1970s or beginning of the 1980s, share significant attitudes and methods of working, and address important issues in common. Thematically revolving around the nature of representation as it has been defined in the last ten years, the exhibition includes works in photographic and temporal media, works using language, and works made up of preexisting, commercial objects. The confrontation with this wide range of visual expression by artists of the same generation prompts one to ask how the goals of these artists differ from those of the immediately preceding generation.

Jackson Pollock
NUMBER 1, *1949*
Enamel and aluminum paint on canvas
63 x 102-1/2 in.
Private Collection

In a recent essay in which she reflected on the transformations that took place in art during the late 1960s, the art critic Barbara Rose concluded that, after the transitional year of 1967, "things would never be again as they once were."[1] Having written about Minimal and Pop Art as these movements were developing,[2] Rose contemplated in retrospect the winds of change that were ushering in yet other approaches to artistic production now broadly labeled Conceptual Art. In this regard she succinctly stated:

> If I could sum up the shift that occurred in art and criticism in 1967, it would be the widespread assault on the dogma of modernism as an exclusively optical, art-for-art's sake, socially detached, formalist phenomenon that inevitably tended toward abstraction....[3]

This widely acknowledged shift characterizing the art of the 1970s prepared the ground for the art ascribed to the 1980s. A consideration of the specific purposes of a

number of artists who first began working over twenty years ago—with no attempt at historical all-inclusiveness—brings the artistic issues of the 1970s (initially defined in the late 1960s) into relief in relation to developments in the 1980s (commencing in the late 1970s). It also presents the opportunity to reflect on particular manifestations of, in Rose's words, the "assault on the dogma of modernism" or, in less combative terms, the gradual erosion of Modernist doctrine.

"Modernism," in its more recent and limited usage, has been predominantly associated with the views of the eminent art critic Clement Greenberg.[4] Regarded as the father of American art criticism,[5] Greenberg is renowned for his writings since the late 1930s and for his early support in the 1940s and 1950s of Abstract Expressionist artists such as Willem de Kooning, Franz Kline, Barnett Newman, Jackson Pollock, and Mark Rothko, as well as the slightly later Color Field painters such as Morris Louis and Kenneth Noland, whose work, he found, fulfilled the Modernist tendency of art to progress toward being a reflection of itself as opposed to a representation of external reality. "The essence of Modernism lies, as I see it," Greenberg summarized in 1965, "in the use of the characteristic methods of a discipline to criticize the discipline itself—not in order to subvert it, but to entrench it more firmly in its area of competence."[6]

For Greenberg, the work of art, as an idealist construct, explores its formal potential within the prescribed limits of painting or sculpture without interference from the economic, social, or political realities that exist outside of its borders. In order to defend the highest cultural values "against the prevailing standards of society," the artist, "retiring from public altogether," and "in search of the absolute ... tries in effect to imitate God by creating something valid solely on its own terms. ... Content is to be dissolved so completely into form that the work of art or literature cannot be reduced in whole or in part to anything not itself."[7] To accomplish successfully its "task of self-criticism"—in order to "find the guarantee of its standards of quality as well as of its independence"[8]—the work of art should not transgress the specifically defined boundaries of its discipline, whether painting or sculpture. That is, quoting Greenberg once again, "a modernist work of art must try, in principle, to avoid dependence upon any order of experience not given in the most essentially construed nature of its medium."[9]

[1]Barbara Rose, "Remembering 1967," in Janet Kardon, ed., *1967: At the Crossroads* (Philadelphia: Institute of Contemporary Art, University of Pennsylvania, 1987), p. 39.
[2]The artists whose work is linked with these movements had begun their careers by the second half of the 1950s or early 1960s.
[3]Rose (note 1), p. 34.

[4]For discussions of Modernism in relation to Postmodernism, see Brian Wallis, ed., *Art After Modernism: Rethinking Representation* (New York: The New Museum of Contemporary Art, 1984). See also Hal Foster, ed., *The Anti-Aesthetic: Essays of Postmodern Culture* (Port Townsend, Wash.: Bay Press, 1983).
[5]Donald B. Kuspit, *Clement Greenberg, Art Critic* (Madison: The University of Wisconsin Press, 1979), p. 19.
[6]Clement Greenberg, "Modernist Painting," in Gregory Battcock, ed., *The New Art: A Critical Anthology* (New York: E.P. Dutton & Co., 1966), p. 101.
[7]Clement Greenberg, "Avant-Garde and Kitsch," in *Art and Culture* (Boston: Beacon Press, 1961), pp. 5-6.
[8]Greenberg, "Modernist Painting" (note 6), p. 102.
[9]Greenberg, "The New Sculpture," in *Art and Culture* (note 7), p. 139.

A work of art, according to Greenberg, is meant to transcend the chaos of modern life and the contradictions of society.[10] Seeking to attain its own reality within the dictates of its particular medium, it is an autonomous, self-sufficient object that contends with either its two-dimensional or three-dimensional nature as painting or sculpture. Within this scheme, the representation of recognizable subject matter in painting gives way to the "abstract"[11] so as to ensure to the extent possible the actual two-dimensionality and "flatness"[12] of the canvas against the slightest allusion to figuration since even "the fragmentary silhouette of a human figure, or of a teacup"[13] leads to associations with false, illusionistic, three-dimensional space. Insofar as sculpture is concerned, being three-dimensional, it "exists for and by itself literally as well as conceptually."[14]

Modernist theory in some respects applies more stringently to the work of Minimal and Pop artists than to that of the Abstract Expressionists, although Greenberg himself did not endorse these ensuing movements.[15] The frequently quoted remark by Frank Stella about his painting, that there is nothing there "besides the paint on the canvas" and that "only what can be seen there *is* there,"[16] cogently characterizes the paintings and sculptures that, responding to and reacting against Abstract Expressionist works, further clarified the objective nature of their formal content. During the 1960s, for example, Donald Judd, Carl Andre, and Sol LeWitt succeeded in bringing sculpture to its "purist"[17] state as a nonreferential object that essentially is about the fact of being sculpture. With the intent of eradicating all figurative reference and hierarchically arranged compositional elements in order to move "away from illusionism, allusion and metaphor,"[18] as their contemporary Robert Morris has articulated, these artists have stressed the material presence of sculpture for its own sake.

Paradoxically, the reintroduction of imagery into painting by Jasper Johns in his *Flag* (1954), and thereafter by Roy Lichtenstein with his enlarged depictions of existing comic-book scenes, or by Andy Warhol with his use of existing commercial illustration, confirmed rather than abrogated the flatness of the picture plane so crucial to Greenberg's thinking. Representation of recognizable subject matter, in the form of already flat imagery, reemerges as a

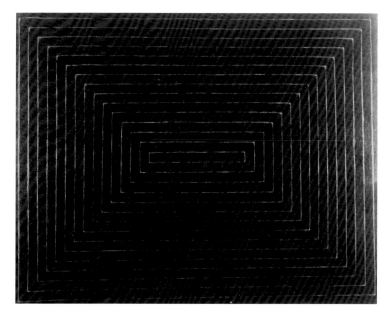

significant factor in painting, but coincides with and indicates its two-dimensionality instead of, as Greenberg feared, obscuring its literal flatness. In this regard, Lichtenstein has claimed that his work "doesn't look like a painting *of* something; it looks like the thing itself."[19] It might further be noted that the insertion of real objects by Robert Rauschenberg into his early paintings—whether the artist's bedding, tipped up and used for *Bed* (1955), or the full-scale stuffed goat standing in *Monogram* (1955-59)—confirmed the pure materiality of paint as paint while also denying illusionism. No longer tied to associative or representational purpose, paint portrays its own reality in Rauschenberg's "Combine Paintings" at the same time as items from the "real" world are absorbed into the framework of art without falsifying the two-dimensionality of the canvas surface. Self-referential and nonillusionistic, works of the late 1950s and 1960s may thus be said to have remained within the Modernist idiom.[20] However, having imported materials that do not conform to "the most essentially construed nature" of the mediums of painting and sculpture as traditionally conceived, they signaled the need for the expansion or reappraisal of Greenberg's criteria.

Attentive to preceding achievements, artists in the late 1960s who followed in the wake of Minimal and Pop Art, on the one hand, continued the self-reflexive critique of painting and sculpture. On the other hand, however, they reinterpreted what its "characteristic methods" might encom-

Frank Stella
TOMLINSON COURT PARK, *1959-60*
Enamel on canvas
84 x 108 in.
Collection of Robert A. Rowan

[10]Kuspit (note 5), p. 41.
[11]Greenberg, "Avant-Garde and Kitsch," in *Art and Culture* (note 7), pp. 5-6.
[12]Greenberg, "Modernist Painting" (note 6), passim.
[13]Ibid., p. 104.
[14]Greenberg, "The New Sculpture," in *Art and Culture* (note 9), p. 145.
[15]See Kuspit (note 5), pp. 114-116.
[16]Frank Stella, quoted in Bruce Glaser, "Questions to Stella and Judd," in Gregory Battcock, ed., *Minimal Art, A Critical Anthology* (New York: E.P. Dutton & Co., 1968), pp. 157-58.
[17]See Greenberg, "The New Sculpture," in *Art and Culture* (note 9), p. 139: "The arts are to achieve concreteness, 'purity,' by acting solely in terms of their separate and irreducible selves."
[18]Robert Morris, "Notes on Sculpture, Part IV: Beyond Objects," *Artforum* 7, 8 (Apr. 1969): 54.

[19]Roy Lichtenstein, quoted in G.R. Swenson, "What is Pop Art?," in John Coplands, ed., *Roy Lichtenstein* (New York: Praeger Publishers, 1972), p. 55.
[20]For a more specific account of Pop Art in relation to Modernism, see Carol Anne Mahsun, *Pop Art and the Critics* (Ann Arbor: UMI Research Press, 1987), pp. 23-40.

Edward Ruscha
ACTUAL SIZE, 1962
Oil on canvas
72 x 67 in.
The Los Angeles County Museum of Art
Anonymous gift through the Contemporary
Art Council

Robert Rauschenberg
BED, 1955
Combine painting
75-1/4 x 31-1/2 x 6-1/2 in.
Collection of Leo Castelli, New York

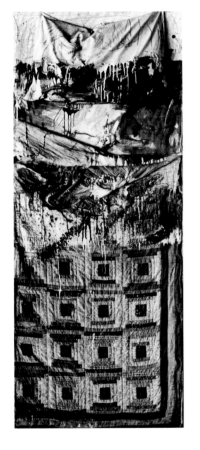

pass. Active experimentation at this time resulted in further reengagement with pictorial and sculptural representation, as well as in the so-called "dematerialization"[21] of the object, and undermined the assumptions of Greenberg's Modernism on two major accounts. Through the exclusive use of photography and/or language, a number of artists called into question the limitation to specific mediums imposed on painting and sculpture, while other artists negated the self-sufficient status of the physical object through the investigation of the contextual conditions of art.

Works of the 1970s break from subordination to an all-encompassing painted framework or sculptural format, while contending with the formal and material issues pertaining to the disciplines of painting and sculpture. Photography and language, employed separately or together, as of the late 1960s provided an avenue for the ongoing exploration of alternatives to previous pictorial and sculptural convention. With major consequence for the art of the 1980s, artists of the 1970s are responsible for having established

the independent use of photography and language as mediums for representation.

An important and immediate precedent for the application of photography and/or language to the purposes of painting or sculpture was set by Ed Ruscha in the early 1960s. As opposed to photographs or photographic imagery from the media introduced into painting by Rauschenberg or Warhol during the same period, photographs in Ruscha's work operate outside of the framework of traditional painting, contained instead within the format of a book. In 1963 Ruscha published *Twenty-six Gasoline Stations*, followed by other self-produced books of photographs that include *Some Los Angeles Apartments* (1965), *Every Building on the Sunset Strip* (1966), and *Thirty-four Parking Lots in Los Angeles* (1967). Noted for their direct approach to subject matter that is stripped of inessentials, as well as for their subject, these small publications single out vernacular structures of the Los Angeles landscape, relegating each example to a separate page. With the camera as witness, Ruscha highlighted the

[21]For a year by year account, see Lucy Lippard, *Six Years: The dematerialization of the art object from 1966 to 1972* (New York: Praeger Publishers, 1973).

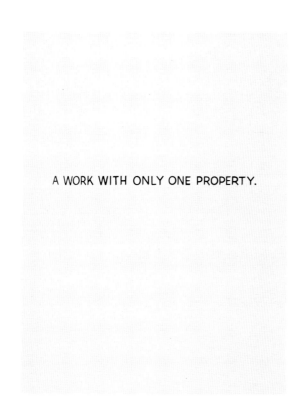

A WORK WITH ONLY ONE PROPERTY.

Joseph Kosuth
One and Three Chairs, 1965
Wooden folding chair, photograph,
and photographic text panel with dictionary
definition of chair
Chair: 32-3/8 x 14-7/8 in.;
photo: 36 x 24-1/8 in.;
text panel: 24-1/8 x 24-1/2in.
The Museum of Modern Art, New York
Larry Aldrich Foundation Fund

John Baldessari
A Work with Only One Property,
1966-68
Acrylic on canvas
59 x 45-1/4 in.
Collection of The Grinstein Family,
Los Angeles

features of the contemporary urban environment that typify the commercial aspect of the culture.

Just as the implementation of photography by Ruscha foreshadowed ensuing artistic developments, so did his incorporation of language into painting. As early as 1959, he had introduced a solitary word into a painting as a major part of its composition, juxtaposing "Sweetwater" (the name of a town) in the lower portion with painterly, abstract brushwork above. Since then single words or phrases have dominated much of his imagery. A work of 1962, *Actual Size*, allots nearly half of its six-foot area to the word "Spam," painted in large letters across the top of the canvas. An image of the product's label—scaled to "actual size"—floats in the canvas field below. From Ruscha's extensive body of work, one might further mention *Smash* (1964), with its large letters spanning the painting's entire width; *City* (1968), with this word floating in the sky like an image made of water; *Vanishing Cream* (1973), consisting of egg yolk on moiré rather than oil on canvas; or the pastel on paper *Those of Us Who Have Double Parked* (1976). Ruscha's words or statements in each case remain within the traditional confines of painting, although he has stretched painting to embrace a wealth of substances, from spinach on paper to blood on satin. Having been impressed with the work of Jasper Johns, particularly with his paintings of flags and targets as well as with his paintings with words,[22] Ruscha, along with others of his generation categorized as Pop Artists, has pursued a propensity for imagery culled from the culture at large, whether from its urban landscape, its products, or its phraseology. From within the traditional two-dimensional context of painting, he has rendered words or phrases as self-reliant images in a multiplicity of nonpainterly ways, representing them as objects. Using words as representational subject matter, Ruscha anticipated the work of artists who were to enlist not only photography but also language independently of a painted context.

Like harbingers of the decade of the 1970s, the early works of Joseph Kosuth, dated 1965, thematically announce the radical break from categorized adherence to traditional concepts of medium. His works of this date consist of three parts: a black-and-white photograph to scale of a utilitarian object—a broom, chair, hammer, lamp, or umbrella, for example; the object itself; and an enlarged photostat of a printed dictionary definition of the object shown. Like readymades—functional objects chosen by the artist in the tradition of Marcel Duchamp—Kosuth's objects stand on their own, materially untransformed. Not part of an overall painted or sculptural context, they are bracketed by their mechanically reproduced image and by their linguistic definition. Having been extracted from the "real" world of use and replaced to function within the work of art, the objects represent themselves. Believing that "art is the definition of art,"[23] and that it is not concerned "with questions of empirical fact,"[24] but "exists for its own sake,"[25] Kosuth has represented the idea of representation per se as it may be incurred by photographs or words. As the combination of three equal parts—photography, object, and text—these pieces are statements of fact, not simply about external reality, but about the means to register it.

The work of John Baldessari, Bernd and Hilla Becher, and Douglas Huebler, based on photography, and that of Robert Barry, Bruce Nauman, and Lawrence Weiner, relying on language, illustrate how these two systems of signification have lent themselves to the artistic purposes advanced in the 1970s. Photography—as an imprint of visible actuality—and language—a series of abstract lexical units that are contiguous with what they mean—affirm the reality of the work in terms of its formal/material self *and* in terms of its represented content. Because of their inherent representational nature, photography and language exempt the artist from the direct manipulation of materials or the determination of form so that the resulting work might be both what it *is* and what it is *of* simultaneously.

Early paintings by Baldessari done between 1966 and 1968 betoken his motivation for terminating an involvement with painting on canvas in the interest of photographic representation. By 1965 he "was weary of doing relational painting and began wondering if straight information would serve."[26] Desiring to expunge the accepted "art signals" from painting, he sent standard-size canvases primed by someone else to a sign painter who lettered them as simply as possible across the surface with the statements he provided. These lettered statements, taken from his notebooks, from art books, or from manuals, include such phrases as "A Work With Only One Property," or "Everything Is Purged From This Painting But Art; No Ideas Have Entered This Work." A text covering the entire canvas is, as its title heading states, "A Painting That Is Its Own Documentation." In a number of these early pieces, furthermore, photographs "taken to violate then current photographic norms" or "taken pointing out the window while driving," accompany pronouncements about "correct" photographic procedures.

[22] See "Chronology," in *The Works of Edward Ruscha* (New York: Hudson Hills Press in association with the San Francisco Museum of Modern Art, 1982), pp. 157, 159.

[23] Joseph Kosuth, "Art After Philosophy," in Gerd de Vries, ed., *On Art: Artists' Writings on the changed notion of art after 1965* (Cologne: M. Dumont Schauberg, 1974), p. 158.
[24] Ibid., p. 150.
[25] Ibid., p. 156.
[26] John Baldessari, in *John Baldessari* (Eindhoven: Municipal van Abbemuseum, and Essen: Museum Folkwang, 1981), p. 6.

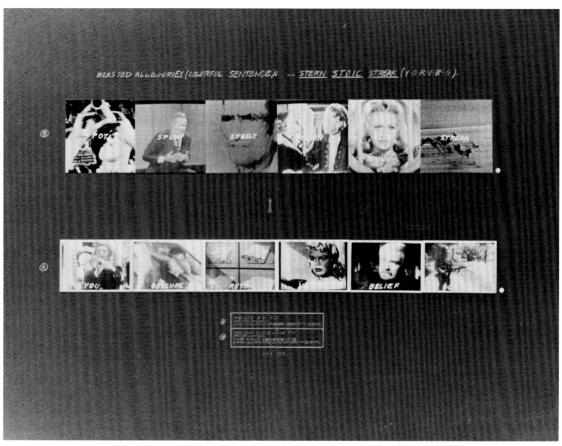

Works by Baldessari from this period derive their formal content from their linguistic content and from the application of measures that allowed him to abstain from direct intervention in the act of invention.

With its ability mechanically to reproduce reality, photography has enabled Baldessari to find and arrange existing imagery without having to create it himself. Works such as *Cigar Smoke to Match Clouds that Are Different (By Sight-Side View)* (1972-73) and *Throwing Balls in the Air to Get a Straight Line (Best of 36 Tries)* (1972-73) demonstrate the way in which the camera positions the artist in relation to his material, not so much as the traditional creator who inspires the work by "putting himself into it," as one might say, but more as an arbiter of situations set up in advance that seemingly permit the work to transpire of its own accord. In the former piece, Baldessari selected photographs in which his own cigar smoke most closely resembled clouds in the sky. In the latter, photographs document his attempt to a make a straight line with four balls tossed into the air. Works such as these are governed by the outcome of events that have been instigated by the artist to preclude his subjective input.

Subsequent works by Baldessari utilize photographic imagery from the media as well as photographs derived in response to whatever proviso he has devised. Newspapers, television, or film furnish him with given representation with which to question and redefine the traditional principles of pictorial composition. For a work of 1978 titled *Blasted Allegories*, images from the television screen "provided the raw material for by-passing aesthetic judgments."[27] Single, previously unrelated images from commercial television programs—combined by chance through a series of calculated maneuvers—paired with single, randomly obtained words, occasioned the formal structure of this work. A series of diverse scenes from the television screen were used "as a window into the world,"[28] each in conjunction with a superimposed, isolated, and disconnected word. Having destroyed

Bernd and Hilla Becher
BLAST FURNACE HEADS, *1988*
Nine black-and-white photographs
on board
20 x 16 in. each; 62-3/4 x 50-3/4 in. overall
Courtesy Sonnabend Gallery, New York

[27]John Baldessari, in a lecture to The Society for Contemporary Art, The Art Institute of Chicago, 1984.
[28]For further discussion of this work, see Baldessari, *John Baldessari* (note 26), p. 49.

a hierarchical or syntactical reading of the work, Baldessari has left narrative or allegorical interpretation open to speculation.

More recently, *Fitcher's Bird* (1982) exemplifies the way in which Baldessari has utilized the stills from a variety of different films to allude to a story from Grimm's Fairy Tales bearing the same title as the work. As a grid of twelve separate stills, the work offers only clues to the tale's plot. Because no single still takes narrative or formal precedence over another, the work may be viewed in any and all directions at once—vertically, horizontally, and diagonally. As all components are the same size and carry equal thematic weight, Baldessari has avoided the creation of a subjectively imposed hierarchy of compositional elements and forms while nonetheless succeeding in the creation of a cohesive representational work.

Like Baldessari, the Bechers have relied on photographic methods to engender pictorial form. Known since the 1960s for their portrayal of industrial architecture, by the late 1950s the Bechers had already found photography to be more suited than painting to their comprehensive study of these structures. For nearly three decades, they have traveled throughout the industrial regions of Europe and the United States documenting industrial buildings: water towers, cooling towers, winding towers, coal silos, lime kilns, blast furnaces, preparation plants, grain elevators, houses, etc. Individual works by the Bechers may be comprised of separate photographs showing different examples of one particular kind of structure all taken frontally, or may consist of a series of photographs of the same structure from different viewpoints. Images within each work are scaled to identical size and are aligned in equally proportioned rows.

Seeking "to provide...a grammar for people to understand and compare different structures,"[29] the Bechers have maintained for a long time that "what we would like is to produce a more or less perfect chain of different forms and shapes."[30] To this end, they render the building in question as objectively as possible, without the "artistic" effects of figures, trees, cloud formations, or surrounding vistas. Taking advantage of the camera as an instrument of exclusion as well as of inclusion, the Bechers systematically isolate and frame each piece of architecture, either from predetermined and straightforward angles or with regard to particular details. In this way they are able to predicate their work on the permutations of forms that, arising out of functional need, already exist in the industrial landscape and which, with the aid of the camera, they are able to single out, classify, and arrange according to the dictates of their formal enterprise.

Photography has presented artists such as Baldessari and the Bechers with the means of distancing themselves from the traditionally required procedures of constructing a work, while also affording the possibility of producing visual relationships, founded in reality, that would not otherwise be incurred. The work of Douglas Huebler makes this further evident. Having initially built sculptures with many sides in an attempt to convey all possible angles of an object, Huebler became dissatisfied with making sculpture that physically imposed on its environment. Concluding his construction of Formica-covered plywood objects in the late 1960s, he turned to systems of documentation—descriptive language and photographs as well as maps and drawings—as a more successful procedure for making a work "that has no privileged position in space."[31]

In a noted statement of 1969, now emblematic of the period, Huebler declared, "The world is full of objects, more or less interesting; I do not wish to add any more."[32] Ensuing photographic documentation, as it appears in Huebler's "Duration," "Location," or "Variable Pieces," results from verbal stipulations that give each work its temporal, spatial, and conditional parameters. For example, *Vari-*

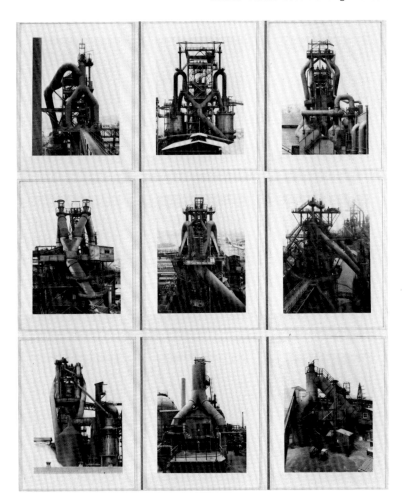

[29]Bernd and Hilla Becher, interview with Lynda Morris, in *Bernd & Hilla Becher* (London: The Arts Council of Great Britain, 1974), unpag.
[30]Bernd and Hilla Becher, "Anonyme Skulpturen," *Kunst-Zeitung Nr.2,* Jan. 1969, trans. Richard Bairstow, unpag.
[31]Douglas Huebler, in *Douglas Huebler* (Evanston, Ill.: Dittmar Memorial Gallery, Northwestern University, 1980), unpag. Originally quoted in the exhibition catalogue *Primary Structures* (New York: The Jewish Museum, 1966).
[32]Douglas Huebler, in *January 5 - 31, 1969* (New York: Seth Siegelaub, 1969), unpag.

Bruce Nauman
HUMAN NATURE/LIFE DEATH, *1983*
Neon tubing
74 x 72 x 4-1/2 in.
Permanent outdoor installation on State
Street in Chicago
Collection of the City of Chicago

136

able Piece No. 20, Bedford, Massachusetts, 1971, reads as follows:

> On January 23, 1971, for eleven minutes, the specific physical location of the artist was photographically documented at exact 30 second intervals as, at each of those instances, he relocated himself within an extremely fluid spatial environment.
>
> 23 photographs join with this statement to constitute the form of this piece.

The photographs accompanying this statement capture their subject *in media res* at various stages of unposed activity playing basketball in a gym. Individually, each represents just one of an infinite number of possible, incidental, and accidental moments that could be frozen in time. Together, in a series, they inform and structure the work. Unmomentous, haphazard details in themselves, which the camera—and only the camera—is able to single out from reality as a whole, they instate their specific photographic reality as such. By relying on the camera as an instrument that indiscriminately arrests motion and frames objects within its field of vision, Huebler uses it "as a duplicating device whose operator makes no 'aesthetic' decisions."[33] Instead of attempting to distill an essential, meaningful moment, he seeks to make visible otherwise undetected or uneventful moments or details of an open-ended, unstructured continuum. In works by Huebler of this kind, segments of time in conjunction with the camera's eye, replacing the artist's discriminating eye, dictate its visual components.

In the work of Baldessari, the Bechers, and Huebler, the camera, functioning in accordance with the *a priori* conditions or situations decided in advance by the artist, serves as a tool for focusing on external fact in order to circumvent internally generated fabrication. In the art of the 1970s, the photograph is subject to—as well as the subject of—the work as a total construct that comprises the sum of its systemically related, endemic parts, relationally extracted from reality. For these artists, the photograph, resulting from the treatment of the medium as a craft to be mastered, with emphasis on the tonal qualities of the print or in relation to the formal aspect or message of its image, is not a sought-after end.[34] By exempting the artist from subjective decisions regarding compositional content and arrangement, it acts instead to assure the work its own structured reality in direct alliance with forms acquired from reality at large.

As in the case of photographic images, the

Douglas Huebler
Variable Piece No. 20, *1971 (detail)*
Photographic documentation
Reproduced from the catalogue
Douglas Huebler,
Westfälischer Kunstverein,
Münster, West Germany, 1972

physical form of words and what they mean are contingent one upon the other. By using language, Bruce Nauman, Lawrence Weiner, and Robert Barry have made radical use of this relationship within their respective oeuvres. In the work of these artists, language does not encompass a literary aim—although it may possess "poetic" qualities—but is a vehicle for nonillusionistically fusing form and content.

The continuing search for methods to create meaningful form underlies the diversity of Nauman's work in general and reflects the desire to re-form traditional sculpture. In Nauman's production, words take part in the realization of three-dimensional objects. Two color photographs from a set of eleven, *Untitled* (1966-67), suggest the nature of Nauman's endeavor. In one, subtitled *Eating My Words*, the artist is shown as he sits at a kitchen table spreading jam on cut-out "words" made of bread, which he is about to eat. In the other, *Waxing Hot* (ill. p. 138), one sees the artist's hands in the process of applying wax to individual, standing wooden letters that spell "hot." Creating scenarios by acting out "plays" on words to the letter, so to speak, Nauman has represented words as material, three-dimensional objects, infusing them with physicality. With expressions providing imagery, words take shape.

From 1967 to the present, Nauman has intermittently used neon as a medium to translate verbal form and expression into sculpture. His neon pieces are based on the phonetic, phonemic, figurative, and referential properties of words. Minor changes in the positioning/repositioning, or the addition/subtraction, of single letters in works such as *Raw/War* (1970) or *Death/Eat* (1972) cause major changes in meaning. Illuminating each word in alternating succession, these works in neon often touch on the human and social condition. Sometimes treading the thin line between sense and non-sense, they explore elements that render verbal meaning. Resembling anonymous advertising signs that serve to draw attention,[35] they confer material form on signification and, in this way, alternatively bestow signification on material form.

Whereas language in Nauman's work plays a sculptural role in conjunction with other materials, in Weiner's work, language—because of its representational ability to stand *for* something—stands on its own as sculpture. Weiner came to the conclusion in 1967 that language by itself was sufficient for the production of visual form and meaning. Since then he has created a wide range of works within a broad thematic scope. These works may be either

[33]Douglas Huebler, in de Vries (note 23), p. 118.
[34]For an important consideration of relationships between photography and art, see Abigail Solomon-Godeau, "Photography After Art Photography," in Wallis (note 4), pp. 75-85.

[35]Brenda Richardson, *Bruce Nauman: Neons* (Baltimore: The Baltimore Museum of Art, 1982-83), p. 20.

mentally grasped by the viewer or actually physically constructed to yield any number of possible results. In every case, the precise, descriptive interpretation of the work is left open. The piece MANY COLORED OBJECTS PLACED SIDE BY SIDE TO FORM A ROW OF MANY COLORED OBJECTS (1979), for example, does not spell out how many objects might be involved, or of what these objects might consist, or where they should be placed. As the artist maintains in a statement that accompanies all of his work, "the decision as to condition rests with the receiver upon the occasion of receivership."

Using language as his material, Weiner deals with the three-dimensional concerns of sculpture by means of pure wording, that is, by what the piece describes. Lettering (or, in some cases, speech) gives the work its necessary presentational form. Usually shown as stenciled, Lettraset, outlined, or hand-drawn words on the walls of exhibition spaces, Weiner's works may also be printed in books or on posters or displayed in countless other ways. By employing language to create specific pieces with unspecified readings and the potential for ubiquitous placement, Weiner frees his work from sole reliance on a particular space or on the spaces designated for art. The shifting contexts in which his works appear alter the frames of reference through which they may be seen so that it is the viewers who, informed by the cultural context in general, ultimately bring their own frame of reference to bear.

Weiner treats language neutrally as a means to impart information about the verifiable, external world, and all of his works are grounded in the actuality of observable or possible qualities, processes, conditions, actions, substances, or things. His works vary semantically in the degree of their specificity from a piece like ONE QUART EXTERIOR GREEN INDUSTRIAL ENAMEL THROWN ON A BRICK WALL (1967) to ones such as TAKEN TO A POINT OF TOLERANCE (1973) and MADE QUIETLY (1972).

Referential and self-referential at the same time, works by Weiner *are* what they describe. A majority deal solely with their own physical nature, as does WITH A TOUCH OF PINK / WITH A BIT OF VIOLET / WITH A HINT OF GREEN (1977), while others may make an intangible occurrence concrete, as in the case of A TRANSLATION FROM ONE LANGUAGE TO ANOTHER (1969), through its materialization in language and "translation" into art. By adopting language as his exclusive representational medium and thereby deriving the substance of his work from the import of words, Weiner has succeeded in uniting the subject represented with the object of art. The reality

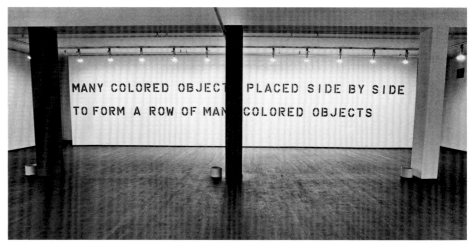

of the former and that of the latter are thus inseparably joined.

Since 1969 Barry has predicated his work on words as both linguistic content and formal configuration. Whereas his early word pieces present a series of short, highly generalized, and descriptive phrases such as "It is changing," typed on standard sheets of paper in single columns, later works consist of unrelated words or phrases variously and subtly disposed on paper, exhibition walls, outdoor architectural surfaces, or, more recently, on painted canvases. Spoken sound pieces or slide projects are similarly based on words or phrases. Whether printed, drawn, incised, or spoken, isolated words and truncated phrases perform, instead of abstract shape, line, brushwork, or figuration. Having extracted words (as, for example, those used in a specific plan for a wall piece of 1979) such as "Of course," "Change," "Deadly," "Too Much," "Apparent," "I will," "Nothing else," and "Disagree" from a grammatical whole, Barry reorders them within the spatial confines of the work, often arranging them to emphasize or delineate its physical perimeter.

Lawrence Weiner
MANY COLORED OBJECTS PLACED
SIDE BY SIDE TO FORM A ROW OF
MANY COLORED OBJECTS, *1979*
Installation at Leo Castelli Gallery,
New York, 1979
Collection of Annick and Anton Herbert,
Ghent, Belgium

Bruce Nauman
WAXING HOT, *1966*
Color photograph
20-1/6 x 20-1/4 in.
Whitney Museum of American Art,
New York

Words do not function sequentially or descriptively in Barry's work, as they do in Weiner's, but are evocative. As the artist has suggested, "they speak out to the viewer,"[36] who may posit the missing connections. As definitive signs that suggest the infinite possibilities of linguistic recontextualization, his words—simultaneously concrete and abstract entities—activate their surrounding space or surface by imbuing it with the potential for endless readings. By allowing for the viewer's insertion of other words in between the given words to fill the existing void, Barry represents the infinity of mentally conceived space in concert with its physically perceived limits.

Serving to eliminate the signs of execution involving brushwork or manual skill along with the signs of the mental decision-making process, photography and language remove evidence of the artist's participation in the formation of the artwork, so that the form of the work and its content might mutually express one another without subjective comment by the artist. Works of the 1970s employing photography or language further the objective aims of Minimal and Pop artists, who also abolish reference to internally expressive content. As the widely read French philosopher Michel Foucault (quoting Samuel Beckett) has asked, "What does it matter who is speaking?"[37] Moreover, his contemporary Roland Barthes, in a now well-known text, has asserted that, after all, "it is language which speaks, not the author."[38]

Concerned essentially with representation as a tool for social analysis, Victor Burgin and Hans Haacke turned to photography and language at the beginning of the 1970s as a means to bring aspects of the contemporary social situation into their representational purview. Burgin has maintained: "I wasn't concerned with objects as much as with events in the life of the observer."[39] In early pieces of 1969-70, he sought to implement language objectively in order to meet "the demands of a situation"[40] with relation to the viewer rather than to create a material object. His initial involvement with language as a link between viewer and environment instead of with physical objects led him to a consideration of how photographic representation, as a language of images, is manipulated in contemporary Western culture.

Robert Barry
Untitled, 1980
White ink on blue paper
5-7/8 x 5-3/4 in.
Courtesy Leo Castelli Gallery, New York

[36]Robert Barry, "Discussion: Robert Barry & Robert C. Morgan," in Erich Franz, ed., *Robert Barry* (Bielefeld: Karl Kerber Verlag, 1986), p. 75.

[37]Michel Foucault, "What Is an Author," in Josué V. Harari, ed., *Textual Strategies: Perspectives in Post-Structuralist Criticism* (Ithaca, N.Y.: Cornell University Press, 1979), p. 141.

[38]Roland Barthes, "The Death of the Author," in *Image-Music-Text* (New York: Hill and Wang, 1977), p. 143. For a discussion of the relevance of Foucault's and Barthes's definitions of authorship to recent art, see Craig Owens, "From Work to Frame, or, Is There Life after 'Death of the Author?,' " in *Implosion: a postmodern perspective* (Stockholm: Moderna Museet, 1988), pp. 207-213.

[39]Victor Burgin, in catalogue entry on *Room* (1970), in *The Tate Gallery 1972-74: Biennial Report and Illustrated Catalogue of Acquisitions* (London: Tate Gallery, 1975), p. 96. Originally quoted in Victor Burgin, "Situational Aesthetics," *Studio International* 178, 915 (Oct. 1969): 118-121.

[40]Victor Burgin, in *The Tate Gallery* (note 39), p. 94.

A work titled *Britain* (1976), consisting of eleven black-and-white photographs, points in the direction Burgin's work was to follow. The individual photographs, taken by Burgin, include urban and suburban scenes, interiors and exteriors, with or without figures. In all cases Burgin has superimposed a printed text on a portion of the image. Acquired from existing prose found in the media, each text has a specific bearing on the photograph because of its association with it. *Today is the Tomorrow You Were Promised Yesterday* is the subtitle of one of the eleven photographs. Its text, set in the upper left-hand corner of the image, reads partially as follows: "The early-morning mist dissolves. And the sun shines on the Pacific....Wander down a winding path. Onto gentle sands. Ocean crystal clear. Sea anemones. Turquoise waters. Total immersion. Ecstasy." The message of the text, with its poetic ring, is presumably an inducement to take a costly vacation. The photograph represents a low-income housing complex and off to one side shows a pregnant woman pushing a stroller. The image thus belies the textual injunction for a promised tomorrow in a place where "pelicans splash lazily in the surf."

According to the artist, "the photographic image can carry a large number of different meanings," which generally are "controlled by its juxtaposition with a verbal text."[41] His art is motivated by the desire to declare the *misrepresentation* that "lies" beneath the surface of photographic representation, particularly in the images of the advertising media with their purely commercial objectives. Conversant from an early date with semiology (the study of signs and signification), most influentially developed by Barthes in the late 1950s and early 1960s, Burgin has articulated the theoretical premises of his work in extensive writings that complement his art. One of his main admonitions is that photographs, whose "point of view" and "frame of reference"[42] are not actually admitted within their circumscribed, two-dimensional format, have the ability to cover up "the actual material condition of the world in the service of specific vested interests"[43] because of the authority of their supposed factual presence. As Barthes affirmed, "we never encounter (at least in advertising) a literal image in a pure state."[44] With the intent of investigating the dominant ideology and its attendant social conditions, Burgin believes that the "job for the artist which no one else does is to dismantle existing communication codes and to recombine some of their elements into structures which can be used to generate new pictures of the world."[45] For Burgin, decoding photo-

graphs leads to a clearer view of the present social system.

Whereas texts and images in Burgin's work contrast with each other, in Hans Haacke's work they connect with each other. Like Burgin, Haacke seeks to penetrate realities of the contemporary social environment as these are disclosed by representation. Approaching his work from an angle slightly different from that of Burgin, he juxtaposes textual and/or photographic information so as to display assembled facts and expose dissembled images in order to reveal the contradictions within the social system.

Haacke approaches his work somewhat like a social scientist gathering empirical data.[46] Since 1969, when he began conducting polls of visitors to exhibitions, he has created works of art that depend on the acquisition of factual material and its presentation in a straightforward, matter-of-fact manner, as in his even earlier weather works that responded to the conditions of their physical environment. Haacke's poll pieces, executed over a period of several years for museum and gallery exhibitions, define an early interest in pinpointing—even quite literally—certain kinds of information. During a one-person exhibition in 1969 at the Howard Wise Gallery, New York, he tabulated the birthplaces and current residences of the visitors, having asked them to place red and blue pins, respectively, on maps of Manhattan and the five boroughs of New York.[47] The resulting accumulation of demographic data determined the form of the piece, which foregrounds its viewers' "backgrounds" within its own framework.

For a slightly later work of 1971, Haacke applied this fact-finding approach to a more elaborate and pointed inquiry into relationships between individuals, geographic location, and housing. *Shapolsky et al. Manhattan Real Estate Holdings, a Real-Time Social System, as of May 1, 1971* comprises two enlarged maps (showing the lower East Side and Harlem), in addition to one hundred forty-two black-and-white photographs of building facades or empty lots, framed above typed data sheets. The accompanying pages give the address of the piece of property concerned, its block and lot number, lot size, and building code as well as the corporation or individual holding title, with addresses and names of officers, its date of acquisition, prior owner, mortgage, and assessed tax value—all found in public records. Also included are six charts of business transactions connected with the ownership of the buildings. The work is an exhaustive, sweeping survey of one family's real estate holdings in lower-income sectors of New York. It brings together

[41]Victor Burgin, "Art, Common Sense and Photography," *Camerawork* 3 (July 1976): 2.

[42]Victor Burgin, *The End of Art Theory* (Atlantic Highlands, N.J.: Humanities Press International, Inc., 1986), p. 16.

[43]Burgin, "Art, Common Sense and Photography" (note 41), p. 1.

[44]Roland Barthes, "Rhetoric of the Image," in *Image-Music-Text* (note 38), p. 42.

[45]Burgin, *Work and Commentary* (London: Latimer New Dimensions Limited, 1973), unpag.

[46]For a specific discussion of this aspect of Haacke's work, see Howard S. Becker and John Walton, "Social Science and the Work of Hans Haacke," in Hans Haacke, *Framing and Being Framed: 7 Works 1970-75* (Halifax: The Press of the Nova Scotia College of Art and Design, and New York: New York University Press, 1975), pp. 145-53.

[47]See Brian Wallis, ed., "Catalogue of Works: 1969-1986," in *Hans Haacke: Unfinished Business* (New York: The New Museum of Contemporary Art, and Cambridge: The MIT Press, 1986) for complete, descriptive information on this and the following works discussed.

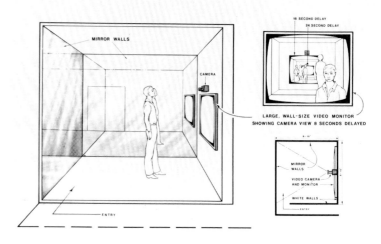

the particulars of a situation that, unless systematically compiled, would remain hidden and disregarded. Displayed on the wall and framed as an aggregate of separate but connected units, the piece opens the door to speculation, not on the value of real estate, but on the "real" value, in broader terms, of extremely limited private ownership. Facts, made visually concrete by Haacke's method of analysis, contribute to a greater understanding of the factors at work in the economic and social sphere.

Manet-PROJEKT '74 (1974) and Seurat's "Les Poseurs" (small version), 1888-1975 (1975) are works about works of art. The subject of Haacke's Manet-PROJEKT '74, Bunch of Asparagus, a painting of 1880 by Manet, is now in the Ludwig Museum, Cologne (until recently the Wallraf-Richartz-Museum); Les Poseurs (small version) by Seurat recently was bequeathed to the Philadelphia Museum of Art. Both pieces by Haacke document the provenance of the paintings in question and provide detailed biographical information on their owners, displayed within individually framed panels. Thus the history of each painting is tied in with the lives of its successive owners—nine besides Manet in the case of the former and thirteen in the latter—who have shared in the determination of its fate. The recorded events pertaining to the history of the paintings, inextricably linked with the lives and social affiliations of their possessors, express to what extent external conditions have controlled their separate destinies. Once again, researched, factual material infuses Haacke's work with its meaning. In these two works he poignantly emphasized that the intrinsic qualities of the paintings have no real bearing on, or control of, their commodity status and their value as personal property.

Haacke's two pieces make clear that the autonomy of the artwork, paradoxically, leads to its own subjugation to economic and social forces. As he affirmed in an interview, "the social forces that have an effect on the art world naturally are the same forces that affect everything else in the country, and in the world. The art world is not an isolated entity."[48] Through his work, Haacke seeks to make "direct reference to these 'outside' determinants." In so doing, he alludes to the interconnections between art and society and the interactions between institutions of power, including those devoted to art.

On Social Grease (1975), dealing with corporate sponsorship of art exhibitions, offers selected quotations by representative executives engraved in relief on a series of six metallic plaques. The words of Robert Kingsley,

representing Exxon, address Haacke's point:

> EXXON'S support of the arts serves the arts as a social lubricant.
> And if business is to continue in big cities, it needs a more lubricated environment.

As part of the work's internal content, Kingsley's quotation, along with the five others constituting the piece, brings to light the corporate machinery, requiring grease, that links the self-promoting tactics of big business with its altruistic patronage of the arts. Through his work Haacke thus exposes the covert or glossed-over economic motivations behind seemingly forthright verbal statements or visual messages.[49]

The work of Dan Graham, Daniel Buren, Marcel Broodthaers, John Knight, and Michael Asher coincides on the essential question of the object's autonomy. Each of these artists has contributed to dispelling the idea that a painting or sculpture is an isolated object disconnected from its physical, social, economic, or historical context. Within the parameters of their aesthetic production, each addresses the idea that a work of art in contemporary culture, as part of the economic system of buying and selling, is itself a commodity by definition. Although works by these artists may be purchased and owned, they cannot be detached from their supporting conditions to circulate freely, if blindly, through the established channels of commerce. Such works self-referentially analyze how they function as art by questioning their relationship to their surroundings. In so doing, they revolutionize the traditional definition of painting as a flat, separately enframed surface, and sculpture as a freestanding, three-dimensional object.

As early as 1965, Dan Graham perceived the contradictory nature of the artwork's claim to autonomy vis-à-vis its reliance on invisible, but nonetheless real, socioeconomic systems of support. From works of this date, which appeared in magazines, to his recent architectural "Pavilion/Sculptures," Graham has sought to resolve the contradictions inherited by and inherent in the socially isolated object in space. Figurative (1965), one of a number of Graham's magazine works, appeared in Harper's Bazaar in March 1968 instead of being shown in an art gallery or a museum. A section of an actual cash register receipt, with the amounts paid for numerous, inexpensive items aligned in standard, columnar fashion, endows the work with its "figurative" content. Bracketed on page ninety of the magazine between two advertisements—one for Tampax and the other for a Warner's bra—Figurative functions on several levels. For one, represen-

---

[48]Hans Haacke, "Interview by Robin White," View (Oakland, Cal.: Crown Point Press, 1978), p. 12.

[49]For an important and recent analysis of Haacke's factual approach, see Benjamin H.D. Buchloh, "Hans Haacke: Memory and Instrumental Reason," Art in America 76, 2 (Feb. 1988): 97-109, 157-59.

tational material and presentational method become inseparable since the work exists simultaneously *on* the page and *within* the timely—not timeless—context of a magazine. Furthermore, if the format of the magazine gives the work as a whole its form, the figuration on the shopping receipt, at the end of the buying process, contrasts with the two surrounding ads beckoning to the potential consumer.

Graham abandoned the magazine pieces after 1969 in order to realize his ideas through engagement with a range of other media, including performance, film, video, and architecture. His use of video as part of installation works beginning in 1974, without accounting for all of his past and present activity, illustrates some of the ways in which he has explored alternatives to the convention of sculpture as a volumetric object that is not connected with the social environment. As employed by Graham in his installation pieces, video, from the Latin "to see," serves to convey an image of a reality that is present from one time segment to another or from one place to another. *Present Continuous Past(s)* (1974) (ILL. P. 142) is the first of eight enclosed room environments. Constructed in the form of a rectangular box, the room must be entered for the work to be seen. Two adjacent walls of its interior are mirrored. A video camera, set into a third wall, records viewers and their reflections in the mirror opposite as they move about the space while a video monitor replicates the images of the viewers after eight-second intervals of delay. Viewers see themselves and others at the moment of looking in the mirrors, as part of "an infinite regress of time continuums within time continuums"[50] on the monitor screen. The work involves and is about viewing the viewing process as this takes place in time. The spectators reflected in the mirrors and video, who are simultaneously the perceiving subjects and the perceived objects, do not simply look *at* the work but are integral components *of* it.

The video medium not only enabled Graham to confront viewers with their own viewing, but it also made it possible for him, by way of strategically placed monitors, to relay information from one set of circumstances to another and to reveal contrasting or related phenomena within the social apparatus. For succeeding video works since 1974, Graham has situated monitors in a range of public spaces. As he wrote,

> *A specific architectural space tends to be institutional; it structures the needs, roles and responses that people who use it have (that is, their roles tend to be influenced by the conven-*

Daniel Buren
140 STATIONS DU MÉTRO PARISIEN (SEGUR), 1970
Photographic documentation of installation in 140 Paris Métro stations, from LEGEND I
Courtesy the artist

> *tions, history and present function of the space). Likewise the space serves a function in the larger social order.*[51]

A piece titled *Yesterday/Today* (1975) linked the activities of one room of an art gallery such as its office space with its exhibition area. Ongoing routine and daily activities as they occurred in the former were displayed on the monitor placed on view. An audio recording of the sounds and conversations taped in the same room during the same time period, but on the day before, played over the visual imagery. This work, in effect, succeeded in "documenting what is normally not expressed...in front of the artwork,"[52] that is, "the functional, social and economic realities of the art gallery,"[53] here divided between visual and aural modes of representation. These two different modes of delivering information yielded only minor discrepancies in the parallel narratives that unfolded when the work was shown. Other video pieces by Graham, similarly based on video as a conductor of existing information, expose realities behind the facades of office buildings, shopping arcades, urban malls, or suburban homes by making them visible.

For the last ten years, Graham has turned his attention to outdoor "Pavilion/Sculptures," as he terms these freestanding structures made of transparent, reflective, and mirrored glass. Grafting onto sculpture a reference to specific

[50]Dan Graham, "Present continuous past(s) (1974)," in Benjamin H.D. Buchloh, ed., *Dan Graham: Video-Architecture-Television: Writings on Video and Video Works 1970-1978* (Halifax: The Press of the Nova Scotia College of Art and Design, and New York: New York University Press, 1979), p. 7.

[51]Ibid., p. 45.
[52]Ibid., p. 46.
[53]Ibid., p. 45.

Daniel Buren
140 Stations du Métro Parisien (Place Clichy), *1970*
Photographic documentation of installation in 140 Paris Métro stations, from Legend I
Courtesy the artist

have to paint them himself, but could purchase canvas used for awnings or outdoor furniture or order mechanically printed material to suit his particular needs.

Commercially obtained, prefabricated material with vertical stripes—intended to be as neutral a (de)sign as possible—serves Buren in an aesthetic practice that frees the work from the framing edge of the canvas and from the allotted exhibition space. Since 1968 Buren has directed his concerns away from the canvas field in order to examine and expose the work of art's affiliation with its external surroundings. The placement of striped material governs the form and meaning of each of Buren's works. Having dispensed with the canvas as an arena for exclusive activity, he explores and visually highlights its contextual frame of reference. "Right from the start," Buren has asserted, "I have always tried to show that indeed a thing never exists in itself...."[54]

For a group exhibition in Paris in 1970, Buren did not install his work in the provided exhibition space, but instead installed it in the Paris Métro stations. For this work, *140 Stations du Métro Parisien* (installed again in 1973 and open to future installations), Buren glued vertically striped blue-and-white rectangles in the upper right-hand corner of 140 large billboards at each of 140 Métro stations. Typically found at every station platform, the billboards provide a backdrop for passengers entering, exiting, or waiting for the train. The available space at the upper right-hand corner of all of the billboards determined the location and size of the striped, rectangular units, which Buren pasted uniformly throughout the stations.

140 Stations dramatically inverted prior assumptions concerning the definition and province of art. With reference to the signs of expression and style deliberately eliminated from them, the vertically striped rectangles functioned like generic paintings. They took their place among the commercial messages already occupying the billboards where they mediated between the cultural domain of art and the commercial realm of mass-media advertising. Commenting on the shared features of these normally separate systems of display, the blue-and-white striped rectangles pointed to the fact that the Métro billboards—ironically, framed like enormous paintings—supplied an alternative and equally viable support for the work. However, although each striped rectangle aligned itself with products of mass-media propaganda, the work as an open-ended whole, encompassing the entire series of Métro station billboards, escaped the consolidated, material form of a commodity. Unlike a solitary, precious

yet generic architectural forms such as the bus shelter or glass skyscraper, he imparts the potential for their social use. Possessing similarities with his earlier video rooms, the "pavilions" are meant to be viewed from within as well as from without. The distinction between interior and exterior points of view is irrelevant insofar as images of spectator and setting, mutually fragmented, merge and are united within the material body of the sculpture. Visually assimilated into their surroundings, Graham's works dispense with the traditional object's outer shell in order to blend with, while reflecting (on), the nature of their physical and social environment.

Whereas Graham's work pertains to sculpture, the work of Daniel Buren has evolved from issues related to painting. For over twenty years, Buren has been working *in situ*, that is, in direct relationship to a given location or situation. Perhaps the first artist to adopt this Latin phrase, now used extensively to describe pieces done on site, Buren associates it with all of his works, whether executed in museums, art galleries, private collections, or outdoor public spaces. Initially desiring to strip painting of any and all illusionistic reference or expressive characteristics so that it might function purely as a sign of itself, Buren arrived at the decision in 1965 to reduce the pictorial content of his work to the repetition of alternating white and colored vertical bands 8.7 cm in width (about 3½ in.). He realized, moreover, that he did not

[54]Daniel Buren, "On the Autonomy of the Work of Art," in *Daniel Buren: around "Ponctuations"* (Lyon: Nouveau Musée, 1980), unpag.

MUSEUM

Kunstmuseum Basel Kupferstichkabinett

Staatliche Museen Stiftung Preußischer Kulturbesitz Berlin (West)

Antikenabteilung, Kunstbibliothek, Kunstgewerbemuseum

Kupferstichkabinett, Museum für Islamische Kunst

Nationalgalerie, Skulpturenabteilung, Museum für Völkerkunde

Abt. Amerikanische Archäologie

Staatliche Museen zu Berlin (Ost) Vorderasiatisches Museum

Akademisches Kunstmuseum der Universität Bonn

Musées Royaux d'Art et d'Histoire Brüssel

Département d'Antiquités Précolombiennes, Département de
Céramique, Département de Folklore, Département de Tapisserie

Musée Royal d'Armes et d'Armures Brüssel

Musée Wiertz Brüssel

Hetjensmuseum Düsseldorf

MUSEUM

ow and elongated, differing from the heavier, broader form of living

FIG. 1.—Skull of *Palaeoplancus sternbergi*, natural size. The cranial portion, shown by dotted lines, is crushed and distorted in the specimen.

Kunstmuseum Basel Kupferstichkabinett

Staatliche Museen Stiftung Preußischer Kulturbesitz Berlin (West)

Antikenabteilung, Kunstbibliothek, Kunstgewerbemuseum

Kupferstichkabinett, Museum für Islamische Kunst

Nationalgalerie, Skulpturenabteilung, Museum für Völkerkunde

Abt. Amerikanische Archäologie

Staatliche Museen zu Berlin (Ost) Vorderasiatisches Museum

Akademisches Kunstmuseum der Universität Bonn

Musées Royaux d'Art et d'Histoire Brüssel

Département d'Antiquités Précolombiennes, Département de
Céramique, Département de Folklore, Département de Tapisserie

Musée Royal d'Armes et d'Armures Brüssel

Musée Wiertz Brüssel

Hetjensmuseum Düsseldorf

object, exhibited in (splendid) isolation, the work had to be seen at multiple spatial and temporal intervals, as a matter of course during daily or routine travel and in conjunction with the surrounding reality.

Works by Buren participate in the given, nonart reality while concurrently commenting on the authority of the museum or gallery whose delegated exhibition spaces they often circumvent. "Where the empty canvas was once both the authority and the obstacle as a medium for experiment, today the authority of the institution is the only medium available for the artist,"[55] according to Buren. *Voile/Toile, Toile/Voile (Sail/Canvas, Canvas/Sail)* (1975-76), a work in two phases, exemplifies how existing reality may give visible shape and form to a work and how the art institution sanctions it. For the first phase of this piece, Buren organized a sailboat race on the Wannsee in Berlin. Nine boats were rigged with sails striped a different color—white with yellow, blue, red, green, orange, etc. Steered by children, they could be observed from the shore as the wind propelled them through the water. For the second phase of the work some months later, Buren hung the sails like paintings on a wall in the Berlin Akademie der Künste in the sequence of each boat's arrival at the finish line of the race. As the double-entendre of the work's French title suggests, canvas sails and sails as paintings became one and the same. In this work as in others, Buren fused form and function. He also revealed—and bridged—the gap between an art and nonart context, while connecting the museum with the reality outside its "hallowed" halls. By thus unveiling the museum's authority in the process of circumventing it, Buren's work dialectically inquires as to whether or not the institution *of* art can exist separately from society's institutions *for* it.

During a short but influential career, the late Marcel Broodthaers (1924-1976) produced works of major importance that also were directed toward a consideration of the museum. *Der Adler vom Oligozän bis heute* titles a work that was conceived as a temporary exhibition at the Städtische Kunsthalle Düsseldorf, May 16-July 9, 1972. It belongs to a larger enterprise undertaken by Broodthaers during 1968-72 under the general heading of "Musée d'Art Moderne, Département des Aigles" (Museum of Modern Art, Department of Eagles). The subheading for the Düsseldorf exhibition is the "Section des Figures" (Figure Section).[56] Although only a part of his total production, the Düsseldorf "Section des Figures" indicates the essential nature of Broodthaers's aesthetic investigation.

Hoping "to provoke critical thought about how art is represented in public,"[57] Broodthaers reversed the normal practice of participating in a museum exhibition by actually organizing one himself. Rather than simply placing examples of his "own" work on display in the museum, as is customary, he followed the curatorial procedure of borrowing objects from elsewhere and grouping them to illustrate a particular theme or subject. The subject of his exhibition was the eagle as it has been known or represented from prehistoric times to the present.

For the purpose of presenting what essentially appears to have been an exhaustive survey exhibition, Broodthaers secured the loan of 266 objects from museums and collections in Europe and America. A two-volume catalogue conceived and designed by the artist records the broad range of items bearing the image of the eagle, from its existence as a geological fossil to its rendering as a mythological creature or ideological symbol. Broodthaers included all manner of eagles in the exhibition, from the bird's depiction in the story of Ganymede in a painting by Rubens in the Museo del Prado, Madrid (reproduced in a photograph), to its heraldic function as a coat of arms on a sixteenth-century tapestry from the Kunsthistorisches Museum, Vienna, to its use as a brand name on a 1910 typewriter from a private collection in Düsseldorf. The exhibited works belonged to all categories of media and included painting, sculpture, drawings, prints, and decorative arts from ancient to modern times, as well as representations of the eagle in nonart contexts—on cigar boxes or wine bottle labels, in the comics, or on national emblems. Ironically, a number, but not all, of these items from contemporary popular or commercial culture belonged to the artist's own "Sammlung Département des Aigles" (Collection of the Department of Eagles), not to an officially established public or private collection. The image of the eagle unified the vast array of material hung on the walls of the museum or placed in glass vitrines. In treating objects of all kinds as if they had the same aesthetic, historical, or functional importance, Broodthaers did not submit them to any discernible system of hierarchical ordering.[58] He catalogued each one in the standard manner, but organized the checklist alphabetically—from Basel to Zurich—according to the city from which each piece was borrowed.

Most significantly, all exhibited items in Broodthaers's exhibition received an accompanying plastic label with the catalogue number above and a qualifying statement below that alleged in French, German, or English, "Ceci n'est

[55]Daniel Buren, "On the Institutions of the Art System," in ibid.
[56]For a more detailed discussion of this work, see Rainer Borgemeister, "*Section des Figures*: The Eagle from the Oligocene to the Present," *October* 42 (Fall 1987): 135-44.

[57]Marcel Broodthaers, "Section des Figures," in *Der Adler vom Oligozän bis heute* (Düsseldorf: Städtische Kunsthalle, 1972), vol. 2, p. 18. Translated from the German for the author by Angela Greiner.
[58]Borgemeister (note 56), p. 139.

pas un object d'art'' / ''Dies ist kein Kunstwerk'' / ''This is not a work of art.'' With this unrelenting and ubiquitous statement—based on René Magritte's famous painting *La Trahison des Images* (The Treason of Images) (1929), that represents the image of a pipe and the painted words ''Ceci n'est pas une Pipe'' (This is not a Pipe)—he paradoxically opened to question the viewing of the assembled objects as a whole. If objects long acknowledged to be art were not, then what were they doing in a museum, whether in Broodthaers's fictional museum or in those that owned them? One had to wonder if, and deny that, the artist in fact possessed the power to determine whether these were or were not works of art and whether language alone could support such an edict. In 1917 Marcel Duchamp had raised a common, nonart urinal to the status of sculpture by entering it into an art exhibition as an object of *his* authorial choice. Broodthaers, explicitly indebted to Duchamp[59] but using exactly the opposite tactics, demonstrated by means of his exhibition that what sustained Duchamp's original move was the authority of the museum or exhibition context, not simply the artist's own prerogative.

Der Adler vom Oligozän bis heute, in the form of an exhibition instead of an object *in* an exhibition, exemplified, while commenting on, the authority of the museum. It demonstrated the way in which the museum is able to accord a deceptive wholeness to works, and actual fragments, from other periods and cultures that perforce have been taken from their original historical and physical settings. By amassing a cross-section of objects unrelated to each other except through the image of the eagle, Broodthaers succeeded in relocating and reclassifying works already relocated and reclassified within the respective museums or collections that owned them. He thus subordinated a broad range of objects to a further process of decontextualization and reassembly so as to re-view the process itself. Mixing works from art and nonart contexts, moreover, he crossed the line automatically dividing the two, permitting both within the confines of his museum display. Since the myriad examples of eagles, in the end, did not actually yield a single, universal statement about this bird, but only specific manifestations of it in many different contexts, they posited the way in which the museum is able nonetheless to subsume its contents into a seemingly unified ensemble.

By means of his explicitly fictional museum, Broodthaers examined the unspoken fictions surrounding art that empower the museum to sanctify its contents. Just as he subjected the eagle—who ''is even scared of a bicycle''[60]—to scrutiny, bringing him down from his lofty heights and emblematic position of power through a process of leveling, Broodthaers pointed to the mythic proportions that art can assume when divorced from the original conditions of its creation. Representing an amalgamation of objects in the possession of others, the ''Section des Figures'' defied its own relocation and commodification since it could not be disassociated from the institutional support it simultaneously acknowledged and subverted.

Broodthaers's work called the museum into question insofar as such institutions bestow autonomous value on artworks, emphasizing qualities such as uniqueness, antiquity, originality, or authenticity, but obscure the socioeconomic realities that account for their ''worth'' in the contemporary culture. Attentive to the potential of art's fossilization—like that of the fossil eagle exhibited—and the threat of its ''failing social relevance,''[61] Broodthaers pitted the fictions of his museum against the mythical stance of art, as distinct from artifact, in isolation from its social framework. He thereby sought to reinvest art with power in place of unfounded mystique so that it might survive in a social system dominated by commercial goals. But, without illusion as to his success in light of contemporary reality, he reminded the catalogue reader that the eagle, whose wings he has clipped within the work, nonetheless still ''remains unhurt in advertising.''[62]

The work of John Knight, like that of Graham, Buren, and Broodthaers, poses questions about the reciprocal interdependence of artistic content and context. The *Journals Series*, an ongoing work begun by Knight in 1978, explores the relationship between art and nonart representation and the underlying systems of belief dividing one from the other. During the last decade, Knight has sporadically mailed nearly a hundred one-year or six-month gift subscriptions of high-gloss journals to selected recipients who are involved in the arts—artists, collectors, curators, art dealers, architects, etc. Journals that may be found on any newsstand are chosen by Knight, who with ironic intent matches the magazine to the recipient's interests or life-style. For example, he had *1001 Home Decorating Ideas* mailed to someone in cramped, disorderly living quarters, and *Town and Country* to another as a complement to the sumptuousness of that person's apartment.

Cuisine, Portfolio, Interior Design, or *Arizona Highways*, to name but a few, number among the many maga-

[59]See Broodthaers, ''Methode,'' in *Der Adler vom Oligozän bis heute* (note 57), vol. 1, p. 13. For a discussion of Duchamp's work in relation to institutional and cultural contexts, and as background for Broodthaers, see Benjamin H.D. Buchloh, ''The Museum Fictions of Marcel Broodthaers,'' in A.A. Bronson and Peggy Gale, eds., *Museums by Artists* (Toronto: Art Metropole, 1983), pp. 45-56.

[60]Broodthaers, ''Sections des Figures,'' in *Der Adler vom Oligozän bis heute* (note 57), p. 18.
[61]Ibid.
[62]Ibid., p. 19.

zines that Knight has sent to appropriate recipients. Whatever the journal's focus happens to be—cooking, fashion, interior design, nature, or art—it personifies the "realities" that are romanticized and standardized by the mass media. The magazines present visions of personal glamor, luxurious homes, spectacular "natural" views in "living color," or endless series of desirable possibilities related to indoor or outdoor life. Knight relies on the fact that although magazines have no value as art, they are subject to some of the same conditions and pitfalls. Like sculptural objects that enhance an interior decor, they sit on coffee tables and simply with the passage of time become collectors' items. Moreover, despite their dependence on and repetition of stock visual solutions and design conventions, with each new issue they superficially vary their cover image.

The *Journals Series* reflects on the value systems at work in the culture that separately govern art and nonart areas. The subscriptions sent by Knight attain art status as a result of how they are "read" by the recipient—either as the magazine that they are or as the work of an artist to be "handled with care," or both—and by how they are, or are not, assigned value by the culture. Knight's work opens the determining factors to question so that individual ownership or temporary public installation, which subjects the loaned magazine to the conventions of institutional display as defined by the borrower, ultimately completes the work and invests it with its meaning. Denuded of the traditional, material attributes of art and in the guise of nonart, the *Journals Series* reveals the mechanisms that allow the work to circulate on different levels once the artist has set it in motion. At the same time, the work as a whole embraces within its own construct as art the illusions and fantasies that the magazines uncritically proffer as real.

During the last two decades, Michael Asher has sought to develop methods of redefining the established rela-

tionship between an art object and its context. Two works of 1969 are seminal. Created for "Anti-illusion: Procedures/ Materials" at the Whitney Museum of American Art and for "Spaces" at The Museum of Modern Art in New York, they assumed the form of environmental installations that relied on controlled perceptual conditions. The work for the Whitney exhibition consisted of an invisible plane of air, produced by an airblower concealed in the ceiling; barely detectable to the touch, it was installed in the passageway between two exhibition rooms. It satisfied the theme of the exhibition by taking physical form without visibly intruding on the exhibition space. Similarly, the work for The Museum of Modern Art took its surroundings into account. In accordance with the exhibition's title, "Spaces," Asher created a room to be entered and experienced acoustically and visually in relationship to the noise and light levels outside of its walls. As the walls were built especially to absorb sound, the distance of the visitors from the exit and entry doors proportionally regulated the degree of exterior sound heard inside. By thus defining the interior space of the work in accordance with its exterior, Asher pointed to the fact that the piece, a hollow container, was not self-contained, but linked with the ambient sounds and lighting in the museum.

Two slightly later works, one in 1973 for the Galleria Toselli in Milan, the other in 1974 for the Claire Copley Galley in Los Angeles, opened up the entire exhibition space as an area for consideration. In order to realize the Toselli piece, Asher requested that all of the many layers of white paint covering the walls and ceiling of the gallery be removed. Four days of sandblasting yielded a rich brown surface, visually uniting the walls and ceiling with the brown color of the unpainted floor. Thus Asher succeeded in putting the exhibition space itself on view as an object of study and the subject of the work, having literally penetrated the superficial surface of the given exhibition space and of the work's support. In essence, he therefore fused the work with its container since content and context became one and the same.

For his exhibition at the Claire Copley Gallery, Asher followed a similar procedure when he took away the internal, freestanding partition of the gallery, which the owner had built to divide the exhibition space from the business area. During the course of the exhibition, both the owner at her desk and the gallery's storage area were in full view. Asher thereby disclosed the inner "works" of the exhibition space by exposing its behind-the-scenes operations. Through

MICHAEL ASHER
74th American Exhibition June 12–August 1, 1982

The work for this exhibition has been conceived for the Art Institute of Chicago in relation to its existing permanent collection. It comprises two separate groups of viewers each consisting of three people who are viewing two different works of art for one half hour each day. The two works viewed are located in Gallery 226 within sight of each other. These works are Nude Seated in a Bathtub, *1910, by Marcel Duchamp and* Daniel-Henry Kahnweiler, *1910, by Pablo Picasso. These particular paintings have been selected on the basis of the comparative degree to which they have been illustrated in the public domain, the Picasso having been reproduced extensively and the Duchamp hardly at all. Supposedly conveying knowledge of artistic production, reproduction paradoxically tends to color or interfere with the first-hand experience of the original work of art. With reference to the full cycle of aesthetic production and cultural reception, the viewers serve to demonstrate the museum visitor's role at the point of presentation. The viewers in front of the Duchamp and the Picasso are paradigmatic of museum visitors, who activate the museum's function. When my work is on view museum visitors are able to witness the completion of the viewing process while actively being engaged in this process themselves.*

Michael Asher
74TH AMERICAN EXHIBITION, THE ART
INSTITUTE OF CHICAGO, JUNE 12 -
AUGUST 12, 1982, *1982*
Detail of exhibition handout

Michael Asher
74TH AMERICAN EXHIBITION, THE ART
INSTITUTE OF CHICAGO, JUNE 12 -
AUGUST 12, 1982, *1982*
*Detail of installation with viewers in front
of Marcel Duchamp's* NUDE IN THE BATHTUB,
1910

Michael Asher
74TH AMERICAN EXHIBITION, THE ART
INSTITUTE OF CHICAGO, JUNE 12 -
AUGUST 12, 1982, *1982*
*Detail of installation with viewers in front
of Pablo Picasso's* PORTRAIT OF KAHNWEILER,
1910

the picture window separating the gallery from the street, viewers could see the contents of the gallery as the content of the work. From inside the work/space, they could observe the external reality outside.

Ensuing works by Asher have remained contingent on existing reality and the conditions of their presentation. A relatively recent work, for the "74th American Exhibition" at The Art Institute of Chicago in 1982, expressed the vital function of the museum as an institution for exhibiting art. For this work—initially proposed for the institute's permanent collection—he engaged two groups of viewers to stand at a designated time (one-half hour each day for practical purposes only) in front of two different paintings in the permanent collection galleries: specifically, *Nude in a Bathtub* (1910) by Marcel Duchamp and *Portrait of Kahnweiler* (1910) by Pablo Picasso. Asher selected these two particular paintings because of the disparate degree to which they had been reproduced in books, on posters, or on postcards, etc.—the Duchamp hardly at all and the Picasso extensively—and disseminated in the public domain as secondhand images. He explained the rationale behind his choice of works on printed handouts that also referred visitors to the location of the piece. On the verso of the handouts he listed fifty books in which the Picasso has been illustrated and nine in which the Duchamp could be found.

Asher took cognizance of the fact that the same institutions that provide original works of art are also those that make available photographs and reproductions. His "model" viewers, installed at normal viewing distance in front of two paintings in the same room and paradigmatic of museum visitors, demonstrated the point at which the museum's primary role to present, and the visitors' to perceive, intersect. Seeking to dismantle the barriers to direct perception engendered by reproduction, with its capacity to substitute for, and dull, the experience of the original, Asher's work reproduced as a concrete actuality the process of viewing that takes place in a museum. Rather than being a work, however, that is physically and conceptually independent of its institutional context—yet nonetheless dependent on it for its display—it could not be disengaged from the existing situation it sought to consider critically. Having abandoned the convention of sculpture in the round, the work revolved around the viewing process by materially and thematically embodying it. With coterminous reference to both art and reality, the Chicago piece serves as a quintessential example of the desire to destroy illusion—including that of the work

itself—through the removal of obstacles hindering perception.

The current exhibition indicates the course that artists of the 1980s have followed along the ground broken by artists of the 1970s while illuminating at what point their paths diverge. The art historian and critic Douglas Crimp anticipated the crucial concerns of the recent decade when he organized the exhibition "Pictures" in 1977 at Artists Space, New York. As he articulated with foresight in the catalogue:

> To an ever greater extent our experience is governed by pictures, pictures in newspapers and magazines, on television and in the cinema. Next to these pictures firsthand experience begins to retreat, to seem more and more trivial. While it once seemed that pictures had the function of interpreting reality, it now seems that they have usurped it. It therefore becomes imperative to understand the picture itself, not in order to uncover a lost reality, but to determine how a picture becomes a signifying structure of its own accord.[63]

With direct thematic relation to the contemporary social context, representation itself, no longer maintaining its role as catalyst between the work of art and the given reality, as in the 1970s, has proven in the 1980s to be the subject of inquiry instead.

Freed in the 1970s for independent formal and material use, photography and language in the 1980s have presented themselves as areas for investigation in their own right, as works in the exhibition suggest. James Welling, Troy Brauntuch, and Christopher Williams, for example, deliberately obscure their imagery or leave their original referent indeterminate. Making their represented subject matter opaque or difficult to interpret definitively, they seek to focus on the nature of the photographic medium rather than using the photograph as a transparent window on nature. Their works aim at "seeing through" photography's methods and devices, with its potentially social bias, in order to question the supposed neutrality of its representational presence. Only the signs of the photographic process—its tonal gradations and textured grain—are evident in Welling's work, while in Brauntuch's work the mere fact of rendition replaces the clear and unquestioned image. In *Angola to Vietnam** (1989) (CAT. NO. 140; SEE ILL. P. 125), Williams examined the interconnections between the aspect of photographic representa- and the external, social, and political factors that can contrib-

---

[63]Douglas Crimp, "Pictures," in *Pictures* (New York: Artists Space, 1977), p. 3.

ute to its visual "make up."

In a comparable manner to photography, language in the art of the 1980s not only speaks for itself, as in works of the 1970s, but also speaks *of* itself in relation to the ways it permeates the social system. These works have no one descriptive, concrete referential anchor, but carry ideologically weighted meanings in the delivery of their message. Works by Jenny Holzer speak with a voice of authority about the voices of authority that barrage the contemporary environment. Her assertive and sometimes virulent statements, possessing no proven basis in reality, point to the way in which language dominates the social atmosphere by bombarding it from many different directions.

Barbara Kruger, Larry Johnson, Mitchell Syrop, and Stephen Prina similarly contend with language as it operates in contemporary culture. Kruger's statements turn the persuasions of the media into phrases of accusation or resistance by employing language as a verbal weapon. Seeking to undermine the power of those who wield them, she illustrates how words often function as forceful instruments of control. Johnson and Syrop communicate the clichés, banalities, and stereotypical aspects of language as mass-media verbiage. If the former speaks about the verbal standardization that characterizes the communication of personal experience via the media, the latter highlights the deadening familiarity of certain expressions or slogans that issue from corporate or media vocabulary and suffuse society with a domineering life of their own. *Upon the Occasion of Receivership* (1989) (CAT. NO. 78; ILLS. PP. 110-111) by Prina demonstrates how language is a ubiquitous element of the culture. By carrying out Lawrence Weiner's work A TRANSLATION FROM ONE LANGUAGE TO ANOTHER (1969) through the exhibition of some sixty typed and framed translations from different languages, he succeeds in illustrating the way in which words as material entities infiltrate and occupy physical and social space.

Whereas certain artists re-present photography and language in order to show how they function in contemporary society, others directly re-present the imagery of the mass media. Their work essentially deals with the myths and ideologies propagated by the media that, fed by and feeding upon consumer culture, pervade all areas of life. Many of the works in the present exhibition are united by their analyses of the ways in which experience is "pictured" in the media-dominated society of today with its omnipresent systems of representation. Barbara Bloom has maintained that she would like her works "to 'look like' normal media imagery" so

that they might "comment upon the medium in which they are placed and upon cultural images (clichés) in general."[64] She has since extended her initial involvement with the media to an examination of different representational mediums and kinds of presentation with reference to the act of seeing. Imagery in the work of Richard Prince and Sarah Charlesworth is "drawn" directly from the printed media through the re-photography of selected aspects or details that exist within it. While Prince has analyzed the strategems that are used by advertising to create a sought-after "image," Charlesworth in parallel manner deals with the "patterns" of response elicited by the media's presentation of newsworthy events.

Dara Birnbaum, Gretchen Bender, and Richard Baim replicate the effects of television, film, or the corporate slide presentation. Splicing together excerpts from existing televised programs and advertisements, Birnbaum stresses the allure of their artificiality. Bender, who has incorporated television imagery into a number of works as it appears on the set, seeks to clarify how "the culture accepts the present through special effects: theatrical special effects, and optical special effects."[65] Her piece in the exhibition consisting of an undulating mass of celluloid specifically refers to its own disposability in the wake of ongoing media consumption. Baim's slide-show installations also confront the omnipotence of the media, but suggest the point at which its awe-inspiring aspects intersect with the overbearing nature of convincing "projections" geared to marketing and sales. Although "redemption is offered through consumption," he maintains that "after a certain lapse of time... the attendee must withdraw into his/her own inefficient world."[66]

Works by Ericka Beckman and Judith Barry similarly rely on the mediums of the media. In different ways they thematically revolve around the fictional character of contemporary social existence. While Beckman's film *Cinderella* (1986) (CAT. NO. 3; ILL. P. 25) weaves its own allegorical tale about the fashioning of, and conformity to, social norms, *Echo* (1986) (CAT. NO. 2; ILLS. PP. 68-69) by Barry centers on the representational role played by architecture. Slides projected on a two-sided, freestanding screen and an accompanying sound track convey the experience of personal fragmentation and disorientation that corporate buildings conceal behind their imposing facades.

Whereas a number of artists in the exhibition employ the mediums of the media, others contend with the media in terms of its social impact. The photographs of Cindy Sherman and Laurie Simmons, for example, elucidate the

[64]Barbara Bloom, in *T. V. Generations* (Los Angeles: Los Angeles Contemporary Exhibitions, 1986), p. 14.

[65]Gretchen Bender, "The Perversion of the Visual," in *Damaged Goods: Desire and the Economy of the Object* (New York: The New Museum of Contemporary Art, 1986), p. 9.

[66]Richard Baim, quoted in William Olander, "Richard Baim: Installation," *On View at the New Museum* (New York: The New Museum of Contemporary Art, 1987), unpag.

media's influence on the representation of the female self as a fictional construct. Working within a two-dimensional format as well, Jack Goldstein, Robert Longo, and Thomas Lawson, respectively, depict the overpowering unnaturalness of natural phenomena when reproduced from media sources, the theatrical authority of urban images, and the essential powerlessness of society's victims portrayed in the news media.

Less involved with the media per se, Peter Nagy, Mike Kelley, Haim Steinbach, and Jeff Koons represent the confluence of artistic and economic enterprise. Nagy's recent present-day culture while *Pay For Your Pleasure* (1988) (CAT. NO. 25; ILLS. PP. 90-91) by Kelley speculates on the realities of contemporary art practices in relation to the ideals of pure realities of contemporary art practices in relation to the ideals of pure artistic pursuit. The sculptures of Steinbach and Koons deal explicitly with the art form as commodity, drawing attention to themselves as indices of the all-encompassing marketing system that fosters consumerism and mass production.

Since works in the exhibition point beyond their literal presence to the broader social system, for artists such as Ronald Jones and Matt Mullican, abstract form does not in itself possess an independent purpose. In Jones's case, form embodies political import while Mullican's forms are symbols that refer to the attempt to codify all experience.

Allan McCollum, Sherrie Levine, and Louise Lawler specifically investigate the factors that determine how art receives its definition within the culture. McCollum's works obviate their connection with function and foreground the object of art as an object of possession and desire, not simply as a conveyor of unique forms or images. Deliberately suppressing her potential as image-maker, Levine recycles existing images as her own. In this way she is able to rule out personal style or expression and activate the cultural mechanisms that permit a work to be a copy and an original at the same time. Thus she establishes the idea that a work, first and foremost, may exist purely as an authorial sign, that is, as "a Levine." Lawler derives the content of her work from an exploration of the nature of art display and exhibition rather than from the creation of original imagery as such. By means of the camera, she isolates relationships between works of art and their particular institutional or domestic settings. She thereby succeeds in re-presenting modes of presenting the art of others within the framework of her art.

Works by artists of the 1980s as defined by the present exhibition are distinguished from those by artists of the preceding decade in their approach to representation. Referring simultaneously to their own material formation and to physical or social reality as firsthand experience, works by artists of the 1970s integrate the object of art with external actuality. With the intention of dispelling illusion, these artists have called into question the Modernist interpretation of art as an entity unto itself that timelessly transcends the conditions of its existence. Through their endeavor to eliminate the autonomy of material and form by the use of photography or language or by investigations into the role of context, they have succeeded in the transformation of previous concepts of art.

In their use of photography and language and in their thematic exploration of the current social environment, artists of the 1980s benefit from the methodological and theoretical innovations of their predecessors. These artists have, however, redefined their predecessors' essential concern with reality as direct experience since their work denies an immediate point of contact with existing reality and declares its own reality as representation. Under the assumption that the work of art is cut from the same cloth as the rest of the social fabric, works of the 1980s take on society's falsifying aspects in order to express them. In lieu of attempting to penetrate illusion as if it were a veil that might be pierced or drawn aside, the artists of the 1980s examine the unrealities of contemporary reality, seeking to locate meaning through a multiplicity of representational signs.

*I am indebted
to Howard Singerman for his critical insights
and to Ann Goldstein for generously sharing her ideas
on the works in the exhibition.
I would also like to thank Cora Rosevear
for her thoughtful comments on the manuscript.*

IN the TEXT

By Howard Singerman

TWENTY-FIVE YEARS AGO, in her now famous essay "Against Interpretation," Susan Sontag rode to the defense of the work of art against what she held was the numbing and displacing power of criticism.[1] Interpretation, she wrote, is "the revenge of the intellect upon art," and more, "a wish to replace it by something else." Sontag mounted her defense on two fronts; she insisted that criticism "serve the work of art" (and, in her final demand for "an erotics of art," even love it); at the same time, she wrote of a work of art that would elude its replacement, an "art whose surface is so unified and clean, whose momentum is so rapid, whose address is so direct that the work can be...just what it is."

That equation of identity—the work that is, and is allowed to be, just what it is—is crucial to Sontag's call for an erotics of art, for an art we love for itself. And what must be uncovered and then dismissed in order to secure the identity of the work is not just interpretation but the prejudice that underlies such hermeneutical endeavors: the belief that art is always representational. Opening her essay with the formulation of this belief in ancient Greece, Sontag unearthed the assumption of mimesis not only beneath centuries of figurative art but in our own century and beneath our approach to abstract art as well. "The fact is, all Western consciousness of and reflection upon art have remained within the confines staked out by the Greek theory of art as mimesis or representation." That is, we continue to see the work of art, as though through Plato's eyes, as having necessarily an absent model, and, therefore, as having its measure and its truth—its content—elsewhere.

This assumption that the work is always pointing outside itself gives birth to what Sontag termed "the odd vision" by which "something we have learned to call 'form' is separated off from something we have learned to call 'content.'" The terms of this division are far from equal; under interpretation the work not only points to its source, it is made redundant, even obviated, by it. "Whether we conceive of the work of art on the model of a picture (art as a picture of reality) or on the model of a statement (art as the statement of the artist), content still comes first... a work of art *is* its content."

For the interpretive critic, who is armed not only with the dictionary of Freud or Marx but also with the assumption of representation and the habitual, weighted division between form and content that necessarily follows from it, what the work of art "says"—and all works of art must "say"—is both its essence and that which it cannot say on its own. If, as the word suggests, content is the fullness of the work, it is also precisely what the work is not—for it can be only a representation. The critic then serves as a translator or, in this metaphysics, a medium: "'What X is saying is...,' 'What X is trying to say is....'" As the work of art is plumbed for its content, form and physicality are displaced. What is more, they are distrusted as merely surface, as a cover. It is as an antidote to the representational vision, to "the odd vision" that every work of art wants to provide us a picture, or nowadays a statement, of something that is precisely that which is not it, that Sontag insists on the primacy of form. The value of form now is not as the unfortunate if necessary house for content, but as itself, as a palpable reality, as the rare and unfamiliar opportunity for a specific, immediate, sensual experience "of things being what they are."

Sontag's combative, oppositional title makes "Against Interpretation" an emblematic work; her insistence on an art that is "just what it is" characterizes, as Sontag herself pointed out, much of Modernism. "A great deal of today's art may be understood as motivated by a flight from interpretation." Having noted that this flight "seems particularly a feature of modern painting," she constructed abstraction as one of its strategies. "Abstract painting is the attempt to have, in the ordinary sense, no content; since there is no content, there can be no interpretation." One can, in fact, argue that the roots of abstraction are formed in a flight from a constellation of forces, all of which lie, like interpretation, in the realm of written language, or more to the point, in the realm of useful, communicative, "everyday" language. (Among Sontag's complaints about interpretation are that it "assimilate[s] Art into Thought" and in so doing "makes art into an article for use.")

One can assemble a convincing number of quotations by artists of this century and the end of the last that speak against the idea of art as mere picturing, against its indebtedness to literature's narratives or to the world's appearances. In positive terms that suggest not so much a flight from but a return to, they herald the rediscovered power of the senses and of form's direct access through them to our deepest emotions. "Why does it disgust you to touch a rat and many other such things?" asked Paul Gauguin. "It is not reason behind these feelings. All five of our senses arrive *directly at the brain*, conditioned by an infinity of things which no education can destroy. I conclude that there are lines which are noble, false, etc. The straight line indicates the infinite, the curve limits creation...."[2] For Gauguin, form itself, precisely because it is physical (and precisely because its "natural" origins elude education and reason), has the power to touch us, to speak to us, yet without reference. The curved and straight lines work without what they describe, without or beyond picturing.

Gauguin's best-known aphorism, "Some advice: do not paint too much after nature," continues

---

[1] Susan Sontag, "Against Interpretation," in *A Susan Sontag Reader* (New York: Farrar, Strauss, Giroux, 1982), pp. 95-104. All Sontag quotations are from this essay.

[2] Paul Gauguin, quoted in Herschel B. Chipp, *Theories of Modern Art* (Berkeley, Los Angeles, and London: University of California Press, 1968), p. 59.

a sentence later: "Creating like our Divine Master is the only way of rising toward God."[3] The advice suggests not only the metaphysics behind Gauguin's discussion of lines and colors but also what the power of form allows: the work of art as an unindebted creation, a sovereign thing in the world. Despite this declaration of independence (Albert Aurier credited him with having secured an "art which is complete, perfect, absolute…at last"[4]), Gauguin's symbolism is consciously and markedly Platonic. (Aurier, again, characterized Gauguin's work as "Plato interpreted visually by a genial savage."[5]) The work indeed approximates and answers to another truth, but location of that truth is not necessarily other than within the work itself. Symbolism attempts to banish the transaction of representation, the replacement of one thing by another, by eliding the space in which one compares the form and its reference. In place of a model that understands the visible world as the measure of reality and the work of art as its cover, Symbolism offers a model in which the world is mere copy; it is the artist who pulls from beneath its cover its content, the essence of things. The work itself is the "materialized expression of some conjunction" of artist and nature;[6] it is the ground on which essences are revealed and condensed. And, as something of a trump card, form—the mood of lines, the harmony of colors—turns out to be the indigenous and untranslatable language in which both nature and painting naturally speak.

The urge toward an art that is "complete, perfect, absolute" has received clearer and more secular voices than those of Gauguin or Aurier—Georges Braque's, for example: "The goal is not to be concerned with the reconstitution of an anecdotal fact but with the constitution of a pictorial fact."[7] Braque's assertion that the work is made and that it is—and,

moreover, that before it was made it had not been—echoes in "Against Interpretation," but the quotations that lie closest to Sontag's essay are those of American postwar art. Their authors, in particular Clement Greenberg and Harold Rosenberg, formulated what Sontag announced: an art outside representation.

Sontag's admonition to critics that the best criticism "is of this sort that dissolves considerations of content into those of form" restates exactly Greenberg's encapsulation of the avant-garde's goal in this century: "Content is to be dissolved so completely into form that the work of art or literature cannot be reduced in whole or in part to anything not itself."[8] Absolutes being what they are, Greenberg explained, it turns out that the artists of the avant-garde were imitating, "not God," as Gauguin would have it, "but the disciplines and processes of art and literature themselves." In an equation that addresses the issue—and the unavoidability—of representation and then dismisses it, Greenberg wrote, "If, to continue with Aristotle, all art and literature are imitation, then what we have here is the imitation of imitating." Greenberg's construction at once posits a model ("some worthy constraint or original") and resecures, after this acknowledgment of representation, the reflexive identity of the work of art.

Sontag's clearest statements of identity, of "the work [that] can be…just what it is" and of "things being what they are," repeat not Greenberg's rather complex, hedged ones, but Harold Rosenberg's round-up of studio talk in "The American Action Painters":[9] "It's not a picture of a thing; it's the thing itself." "It doesn't reproduce nature; it is nature." "Art is not, not not not not…." What it is not, Rosenberg explained elsewhere, is anything else; the canvas is "an arena in which to act—rather than…a space in which to reproduce, re-design, analyze or 'express' an

object actual or imagined."

To stress the idea of action, Rosenberg warned us that language, and particularly the language of artists, is still unaccustomed to the idea of the act itself as the object. "Lacking verbal flexibility, the painters speak of what they are doing in a jargon still involved in the metaphysics of *things*." But it is just this idea of a *thing*—whose thingness is secured by virtue of being, and being indebted to, no other thing—that provides the language with which the Abstract Expressionists differentiated their project from that of European Modernism, and with which American artists at the beginning of the 1960s would differentiate theirs from both the Europeans and the preceding generation.

Two or three times in "The American Action Painters," Rosenberg offered lists of what had been voided from painting to arrive at that moment "when it was decided to paint…just TO PAINT." The writings of the artists themselves, particularly those of Barnett Newman, too, are filled with lists of what needs to be emptied from painting in order for painting to achieve images "whose reality is self-evident."[10] Tellingly, Newman's lists, like Rosenberg's, include most often the processes of reference. To Rosenberg's insistence that the canvas is not the "space in which to reproduce, re-design, analyze or 'express'"—all verbs that take an object, and, in the exaggeration of the prefix *re*, clearly a preexisting one—one could add Newman's rejection of the "props and crutches that evoke associations" and of "the impediments of memory, association, nostalgia, legend, myth, or what have you, that have been the devices of Western European painting." To cleave American art from the European tradition, Newman introduced Edmund Burke's eighteenth-century distinction between the sublime and the beautiful. Against an image of the sublime that

[3] Ibid., p. 60.
[4] Ibid., p. 93.
[5] Albert Aurier, quoted in Robert Goldwater, *Symbolism* (New York: Harper and Row, 1979), p. 185.
[6] Ibid., p. 184.
[7] Georges Braque, quoted in Chipp (note 2), p. 260.
[8] Clement Greenberg, "Avant-Garde and Kitsch," in John O'Brian, ed., *Clement Greenberg: The Collected Essays and Criticism*, vol. 1 (Chicago and London: University of Chicago Press, 1986), pp. 5-22. All Greenberg quotations are from this essay.
[9] Harold Rosenberg, *The Tradition of the New* (Chicago and London: University of Chicago Press, 1982), pp. 23-39. All Rosenberg quotations are from this source.
[10] Barnett Newman, "The Sublime Is Now," in Chipp (note 2), pp. 552-53. All Newman quotations are from this essay.

comes to resemble a mythic American landscape—boundless, uncharted, blank—the beautiful is reduced to the small, picturesque (picture*like*) clutter of the old country. The failure of modern European art, Newman asserted, is that it is incapable of moving away "from the Renaissance imagery of figures and objects." Despite their makers' struggles against the hegemony of beauty, the art of Mondrian and Picasso, like that of the Renaissance, continued to open onto a pictorial and conceptual interior, onto the reasoned shapes and internal adjustments of a picture. Against that interior and its adjudicated—and pictured—population, Newman insisted he was offering the self-evident, the "real and concrete."

Abstract Expressionism was to be an art that did not refer, that did not read out toward the subjects of culture or in toward the rational truths of a compositional logic. Its objects were to be not signs but "vehicles," the necessary, revelatory embodiments of meaning. In linguistic terms—terms that suggest that Newman did not finally escape the conventions of representation—what Newman was striving for in his paintings was a true symbol, the sign that had to, by nature rather than by convention, mean the meaning to which it referred. Indeed, it needed to do more than refer to some meaning that could be spoken otherwise, it had to be the same as that meaning, which could not become meaning without this sign. The image Newman attempted was not only self-evident, but "the self-evident one of revelation." Revelation, of course, continues to imply depth, and that it is depth of representation is signaled in the mirroring, repeating prefix *self*. "Presence," as Jacques Derrida, one of the primary excavators or, more to the point, flatteners, of such depths, wrote, "in order to be presence and self-presence, has always already begun to represent itself, has always already been penetrated."[11]

When Frank Stella rephrased Newman's offer of "images whose reality is self-evident" in the simple statement "what you see is what you see,"[12] he flattened not only Newman's language but the residual depth that the older artist could still secure, the sense that something was revealed underneath when everything else was removed. Against the fullness of the Abstract Expressionist sign, which in its depth referred to that stressed *self* that is at once the self of the artist and the self of the object, its significant presence, Stella's equation suggested only that what was evident was evident, a tautology that secured for the object a much more mundane concreteness. In his insistence on seeing, and on the equivalence of the object's identity with what is seen on, and as, its surface, Stella made clear the work's address: it is made not to reveal the unseen but precisely to be seen. Stella's description of this onliness—"If the painting were lean enough, accurate enough or right enough, you would just be able to look at it"—echoes Sontag's work of art "whose surface is so unified and clean, whose momentum is so rapid, whose address is so direct." The work of art they each describe as just what we see (Stella again: "My painting is based on the fact that only what can be seen there *is* there") is not the "natural" sign, rather it approaches straight nature: it is to be given, a fact.

The art that is most strongly influenced by that of Newman (and Clyfford Still, Mark Rothko, and Ad Reinhardt, as opposed to that by Willem de Kooning or Franz Kline) in the early 1960s—Modernist painting on the one hand and Minimal Art on the other—casts its precursor's lessons as formal or as tactical ones; in each case they take its revelations to be about the work of art. In this refolding of the revelatory depths of art back to the surface, and from there out toward the very condition of seeing, that is, in works

such as Stella's, Modernism's dream of an art without translation comes momentarily true. Much of the art of the 1960s, I would argue, operates finally and completely outside an idea of itself as representational, consciously substituting for any representational model a fully experiential one—and one that finally sees the real it strives for as secular and, as it were, uninhabited. And yet the "truth" it comes to is only partial; it is divided and contested on the nature of the real and on the nature of our experience of it: with what organs we experience it, to what or whom we credit the singularity of the experience, and even if the nature of experience is, in fact, singular. And it is necessarily contested on what any of these terms might mean when defined within the category of objects or experiences we already call art.

The debate between Modernist painting as it was theorized by Clement Greenberg and by Michael Fried and Minimal Art as it was presented, if not named, by Robert Morris and Donald Judd, can be most schematically drawn as a debate between painting and sculpture as they represent the virtual and the literal. But that distinction carries with it others, strung along the same axes: the question of whether art is an essential category, a separate realm of experience given within the objects themselves, or whether it is a conventional one, a function of naming or context. In other words, whether art's experience—and thus art itself—is essentially different from any other experience, a real that is real by virtue of its singularity, or whether its experience is of the same order as other experience, perceived with the same senses and continuous with the same real. And, perhaps as a corollary, there arises the question of whether the field within which the experience of art is defined is the diachrony of painting or sculpture as historied media or the synchrony of objects in the world. The art and

[11] Jacques Derrida, "The Theater of Cruelty and the Closure of Representation," in *Writing and Difference*, trans. Alan Bass (Chicago: University of Chicago Press, 1978), p. 249.

[12] Frank Stella, quoted in Bruce Glaser, "Questions to Stella and Judd," in Gregory Battcock, ed., *Minimal Art* (New York: E.P. Dutton, 1968), pp. 148-64. All Stella quotations are from this source.

criticism that constructed this categorical debate—for both approaches necessarily define the category inside which experience will be used or transferred or understood—mark both the culmination and the unraveling of the work without representation.

It is in this moment and within this debate, as a number of authors have convincingly argued, that what could be characterized as the necessarily representational nature of art practice is uncovered; certainly each side is caught out as representational—unavoidably and unconsciously—by the other. Minimalism's critique of Modernist painting—indeed of any painting—is that it is inherently and unavoidably illusionistic, that in order to be painting it must deny the literalness of its condition as a thing on the wall. "The main thing wrong with painting is that it is a rectangular plane placed flat against the wall. A rectangle is a shape itself; it is obviously the whole shape."[13] Before any individual painting is done, the painting is already complete, a thing in three dimensions. As Judd put it: "Three dimensions are real space. That gets rid of the problem of illusionism and of literal space, space in and around marks and colors—which is riddance of one of the salient and most objectionable features of European art."[14] What secures the concreteness of an object for Judd, and what directs it into that space he terms "real," is a refusal of interior relationships, of detail and composition—additions that would direct us into the interior of an object as another space with a different set of orders and rules. It is the sense we have, or that we are given, of the object as whole, complete, separate, and bounded, that, in Mel Bochner's words, renders three-dimensional objects as "things … as they probably are—autonomous and indifferent."[15]

That a painting is already only a thing is a risk Michael Fried assumed for Modernist painting.

It is the task of advanced painting to "defeat literalism," at once to acknowledge the material limitations of surface and edge and enfold them, to coerce them into being the picture, to make them virtual and pictorial, open to vision alone.[16] This idea of a space open to vision alone is central to Modernist painting, for it allows for the construction of an order of experience intrinsic to painting alone. Inside the term "opticality," the experience of painting—and painting itself—is cast (in words that should recall Bochner's) as singular, irreducible, autonomous. At the same time, this separate experience enfolds the experience of each specific picture into the experience of other pictures, and even into others' experiences of them. It secures the value—the point beyond individual experience—of a purely experiential art, and indeed, as Greenberg had suggested, it fully conflates form and content.

In *Three American Painters*, Fried offered the terms of this unification: in the passage from Manet to Cubism to the Abstract Expressionists, it has become increasingly clear that a certain line of artists have addressed the object of painting with increasing consciousness as a series of formal problems, problems that have been made pressing and compelling by the art of the preceding moment. This line and this consciousness form the canon and the progress of Modernism in painting, and the artist in our moment—or the moment of the 1960s—now takes it as his obligation to work through consciously the problems "thrown up by the art of the recent past."[17] Fried made it clear that it is a moral obligation, and that Modernist painting is, and is the outcome of, a moral act: "the result of this forced passage will be his art." It is this morality that is the work's content, and it is the passage as an act of sublimation, a measure of responsibility, that imbeds the artist in the work—that,

if we can push it, hollows again a space at least metaphorically tactile in which, in lieu of figuration, the artist as figure dwells. Thus Fried can say of Kenneth Noland, even as he describes his pictures as remarkably open and optical, that he is "a tense, critical, almost hurting presence in his work."[18]

Ironically, Fried's case against Minimal Art, which he calls literalist art, is based in no small part on that art's hollowed centers; as befits his label, of course, they are literally hollow. Specifically, his accusation is that because of Minimalism's hollow—and hidden—center, it "is almost blatantly anthropomorphic."[19] This "latent or hidden naturalism" is doubled by the fact that Minimal sculpture is scaled to the viewer, scaled specifically to be a physical presence that approximates or at least answers to the viewer's own; the Minimalist object is, Fried suggested, "a kind of *statue*." Still, he insisted that it is not Minimalism's anthropomorphism that he found "wrong," but its hiddenness. Hollow at its center and excessive in its presence, the Minimalist work exceeds its shape both inwardly and outwardly, despite the fact that shape is, according to Morris and Judd, sculpture's key term—its definition as an object in space. Fried set on this conjunction of hiddenness and presence the term theatrical, which he defined to a great extent by what it is not: it is not any medium, it is not any history of conventions and experiences that would obligate from its practitioners the action he referred to as Modernism or provide for its beholders "that worthy constraint" that is the test of Modernist objects. What the theatrical is instead is an effect; what is most damning in Minimalism is that its objects strive for the effects of nature.

For Fried, Minimalism as theater is a genuine threat; it threatens the work of art as a singular experience, unraveling its singularity in both time

---

[13] Donald Judd, "Specific Objects," in *Complete Writings 1959-1975* (Halifax: The Press of the Nova Scotia College of Art and Design, and New York: New York University Press, 1975), pp. 181-82.

[14] Ibid., p. 184.

[15] Mel Bochner, "Serial Art, Systems, Solipsism," in Battcock (note 12), p. 102.

[16] Michael Fried, "Art and Objecthood," in Battcock (note 12), pp. 116-47.

[17] Michael Fried, *Three American Painters* (Cambridge, Mass.: Fogg Art Museum, 1965), p. 9.

[18] Ibid., p. 33.

[19] Fried, "Art and Objecthood" (note 16). All subsequent Fried quotations are from this essay.

and space. Because effects, presences, experiences are what it strives for—or strives to imitate—Minimal sculpture can work only in situation with the viewer, whose experience must necessarily include the situation. As Morris himself wrote, "The better new work takes relationships out of the work and makes them a function of space, light and the viewer's field of vision. The object is just one of the terms in the newer aesthetic."[20] The aggressive, specific presence secured by Minimalism's constant, known shapes and its deployment of materials "as such" gives way to a shifting and infinitely adjustable experience—one that must necessarily unfold over time, in a time controlled by the viewer.

Morris's quotation above, like his insistence at the end of "Notes on Sculpture" that "a beam on its end is not the same as the same beam on its side,"[21] touches the key terms Fried linked under the heading theater: duration and situation, or, in their more dramatic forms, endlessness and dependency. With these terms, Fried suggested that theater is not only the condition of Minimalism but, reading Minimalism's objects as though representations, its subject matter as well. It signs its refusal of the unity and completion offered by a set of relationships internal and specific to a separate, self-sufficient object with Judd's famous "one thing after another."[22] The as-though-endless repetition of identical, uninflected units physically reenacts the work's exaggerated entreaty to the viewer in his space; it illustrates the displacement of relationships from the work to "the viewer's field of vision," and it pictures the duration of the viewer's experience, as well. Finally, as the Minimal work needs the viewer to complete it, it encodes its endlessness as dramatic narrative, as Fried said, "it *has* been waiting for him." Against this presence, or better, this prescience, he offers the term presentness, the sense that in the successful Modernist work "*at every moment the work itself is wholly manifest.*" "I want to claim that it is by virtue of their presentness and instantaneousness that modernist painting and sculpture defeat theater."

In a short essay on Postmodernism as it was formulated by Rosalind Krauss, Douglas Crimp, and Craig Owens in the pages of *October* at the very end of the 1970s and in the early 1980s, Hal Foster noted the centrality of Michael Fried's defense of Modernism and his critique of Minimalism to their constructions.[23] Posed as late Modernism's "classic text," Fried's "Art and Objecthood" offered not only the terms with which Modernism could be summarized as a code of laws, but also those—or I should say that—by which it had been exceeded: theater. Theater's attributes are divided among the authors. While Fried is not cited by name in Krauss's "Sculpture in the Expanded Field," he is present in (or as) "the modernist category *sculpture*" and in its suspension.[24]

Owens in "Earthwords" and Crimp in "Pictures" addressed Fried by name. Owens cited Fried's diagnoses of "the invasion of the static art of sculpture by duration, temporality," but only to correct it.[25] "What his postmortem actually discloses, however, is the emergence of *discourse.*" "Earthwords" is a book review, a review of Robert Smithson's writings, and it is artists' writings, specifically the writings of the Minimalists—Judd, Morris, Smithson, et al.—that Owens credited for "the eruption of language" that has "disrupted the stability of a modernist partitioning of the aesthetic field." It is language, that is, that lies between the arts. Crimp's "Pictures" is the most specific reading of Fried and it is the text most formed by him.[26] As proof of the erosion of Modernism's authority as well as of its categories, Crimp, like Krauss, began by pointing to the array of aesthetic activities that, since Minimalism, have staked a shifting, open position outside the historied arts. But it is the theatricality introduced by Minimalism's "preoccupation with time—more precisely with the *duration of experience*" that Crimp posed as the real threat to Fried's Modernism. "Fried's fears were well founded. For if temporality was implicit in the way minimal sculpture was experienced, then it would be made thoroughly explicit—in fact the only possible manner of experience—for much of the art that followed."[27]

Thus, as Foster suggested in a footnote, Minimalism, as it contains both "the modernist impulse to the thing in itself and the postmodernist impulse toward 'theatricality' or 'perversity'" is "the scene of a shift in sensibility, the very *brisure* of (post) modernism."[28] For Minimalism to appear as the breakthrough of Postmodernism, Fried must have been more right, or at least more "perspicacious," to use Foster's word, than the authors of Minimalism. For Minimalism becomes Postmodernism emergent as it stages its theater, as it is anthropomorphic and, worse, as it exceeds

[20] Robert Morris, "Notes on Sculpture," in Battcock (note 12), p. 232.

[21] Ibid., p. 235.

[22] Judd (note 13), p. 184.

[23] Hal Foster, "Re: Post," in Brian Wallis, ed., *Art after Modernism* (New York: The New Museum of Contemporary Art, and Boston: David R. Godine, Publisher, Inc., 1984), pp. 189-201. The article first appeared in 1982 and appears in *Art after Modernism* with a postscript that lists what the author believes are the essay's shortcomings, among them that it is "too specific—a local riposte to a local advocacy." I do not think that is a fault and, moreover, I do not think it is local enough. That is, Foster stayed in the texts of his authors rather than opening them to their writers' actual social and political relations in the art world. He is too quick to attach author and essay to Barthes's "historical chain of discourses, the progress (progressus) of discursivity"—the quotation with which he ends the article—and he is too hasty as he rescues them thereby from "the immobility of prattle." The art world is small enough that it is often the politics of lower Manhattan that perform the strongest readings on both works and texts, as Foster's recent *Discussions in Contemporary Culture* (Seattle: Bay Press, 1987) bears witness. Having complained, I will admit that my text, too, is one that stays comfortably within the pages, that seems to believe in the progress of discursivity.

[24] Rosalind Krauss, "Sculpture in the Expanded Field," in Hal Foster, ed., *The Anti-Aesthetic* (Port Townsend, Wash.: Bay Press, 1983), pp. 31-42.

[25] Craig Owens, "Earthwords," *October* 10 (Fall 1979): 121-30.

[26] Douglas Crimp, "Pictures," in Wallis (note 23), pp. 175-87. As Crimp explained in a short preface to the essay, "Pictures" was first the title of an exhibition he had organized at Artists Space in New York in 1977. It is curious and interesting that while the essay published in *October* ends with the positing of Postmodernism—and of the work discussed as Postmodernist—the essay included in the Artists Space catalogue ends with a reaffirmation of Modernism, albeit a sort of prodigal Modernism, one marked by symbolism and radicalism. The politics of the essays are different in other ways, as well; certainly Minimalism's function changes from one essay to the next. In the earlier essay, it is the example offered for an unwitting, accidental illusionism; in the later it becomes the historical instance of its discovery. Minimalism's role change marks a larger difference between the essays, and is a function of it. The *October* essay was written at a specific target: Modernism as written by Fried.

[27] Ibid., p. 176.

[28] Foster, "Re: Post" (note 23), p. 193.

its object and becomes at once "hidden" and readable—that is, as it falls within the web of representation. Indeed, representation is the term Crimp later introduced to hold all of the attributes of the theatrical, to explain its hollowness and its presence, to include its repetitions and its endlessness. Not coincidentally, the term includes Owens's eruption of language, as well, not as separate from the work but of it.

In "Pictures" and later in "The Photographic Activity of Postmodernism," Crimp traced Minimalist theatricality—which he extended to 1970s Performance Art and explained as the necessarily temporal experience of the work of art in its specific situation—as it became, in the work of a group of artists working in New York at the end of the 1970s, "that kind of presence that is possible only through the absence that we know to be a condition of representation."[29] Those artists—Jack Goldstein, Cindy Sherman, Robert Longo, Troy Brauntuch, and Sherrie Levine—have, Crimp suggested, transformed Minimalism's "theatrical dimension...and, quite unexpectedly, reinvested [it] in the pictorial image."[30] There, "presence and temporality are utterly psychologized";[31] they are no longer inscribed in a bodily relationship with a specific object but in a psychological one with its image. Thus, particularly in his discussion of Goldstein, but elsewhere through the essays as well, Crimp recast Fried's "duration of experience" as though the experience was being had by someone and as though what was being experienced was significant— was being construed as the sign of something. Specifically, Crimp recast temporality in the language of representation, in the terms and promises of narrative. As "foreboding, premonition, suspicion, anxiety,"[32] it exceeds itself; it is not this time but this time as it forecasts, yet cannot be closed by, something else. It has, one could say, a presence; indeed, this excess

defines the presence Crimp credited as Postmodern. It is, as he put it, an additive, "a kind of increment to being there...its excess, its supplement."[33] But what is added, what is layered over and strung between viewer and object, is absence, the unfolding of the object as its image. Or, to recall Derrida, it is the object as "it has always already begun to represent itself," and, therefore, as it marks its entrance into a flow of representations and repetitions, of "copies and copies of copies."[34]

It is perhaps parenthetical, but curious that Fried already performed this transformation, that from the beginning he read Minimalism as Crimp did its successors. (He had also, as Owens would do, already read Minimalism as a function of its texts: "It seeks to declare and occupy a position—one that can be formulated in words, and in fact has been formulated by some of its leading practitioners.") He already fashioned its presence as a function of absence—of the hollowness at the sculptures' center—and he cast that presence as other than material, as, in fact, "a *stage* presence." Moreover, from the outset, he psychologized the terms of duration and read Minimalism as a narrative. He expanded and dramatized duration with exaggerated, exasperated italics: *ad infinitum* and *endlessness*, and certainly with his comment that Minimalism's objects have even been waiting for us. Finally, in a longish reading of Tony Smith's narrative of a revelatory nighttime drive on the not-yet-completed New Jersey Turnpike, Fried located the psychologization of presence at the core of Minimalism, and he located as well at that core "that absence we know to be a condition of representation" and its enfolding into a field of continuous repetitions:

> It is as though the turnpike, airstrips, and drill ground reveal the theatrical character of literalist art, only without

the object, that is, without the art itself—*as though the object is needed only within a room.... In each of the above cases the object is, so to speak,* replaced *by something: for example, on the turnpike by the constant onrush of the road, the simultaneous recession of new reaches of dark pavement illumined by the onrushing headlights, the sense of the turnpike itself as something enormous, abandoned, derelict, existing for Smith alone.... This last point is important. On the one hand, the turnpike, airstrips, and drill ground belong to no one; on the other, the situation established by Smith's presence is in each case felt by him to be his. Moreover, in each case being able to go on and on indefinitely is of the essence. What replaces the object— what does the same job of distancing or isolating the beholder, of making him a subject, that the object did in the closed room—is above all the endlessness, or objectlessness, of approach or onrush or perspective.*

Again as befits the art, the distances and replacements Fried located in Smith's narrative are literal, and yet it is not only Fried's choice of words—his italicized *replaced*, for example—that is telling. It is also that in each case the object is replaced by an experience that is at once pointed at Smith—organized by him in a way that it organizes him as its subject—and slipping immediately away from him to be replaced by another whose function is precisely the same.

What Fried did was, as I have suggested, to read Minimalism against itself as unavoidably representational. And of course that is what Crimp did, as

[29] Douglas Crimp, "The Photographic Activity of Postmodernism," *October* 15 (Winter 1980): 92.
[30] Crimp, "Pictures" (note 26), p. 177.
[31] Ibid.
[32] Ibid., p. 180.
[33] Crimp, "The Photographic Activity of Postmodernism" (note 29), p. 92.
[34] Ibid., p. 94.

well, if on the other side. Crimp wrote from a position within what Rosalind Krauss called "the discourse of reproductions without originals, that discourse which could only operate in Mondrian's work as the inevitable subversion of his purpose, the residue of representationality that he could not sufficiently purge from the domain of his painting."[35] As Krauss insisted a number of times in the article from which that quotation is taken, "The Originality of the Avant-Garde," that discourse forms "*our* perspective" and "this perspective," "a strange new perspective" from which "we look back on the modernist origin and watch it splintering into endless replication."

To read Minimalism through that discourse—from *our* perspective—is not only to read it as representational, but to read it as a model of representation. In this linguistic analogy, Minimalism's constant, regular unit is always in repetition, always a reproduction. Whether it is Tony Smith's single cube or Judd's multiple ones, there is always an image—the instant, already-known image that Morris described with the word *gestalt*, perhaps—that preexists and determines its usage. Even Carl Andre's fire bricks and styrofoam blocks—things that are obviously, palpably, real things—are caught up as reproductions, just some of the myriad, undifferentiated copies produced in the insistent repetition of mass production—objects whose originals could also only be image, if that. Minimalism's repeated, uninflected units are, like the objects of manufacture—and like the units of language—differentiated not internally and thus positively as they embody meaning but negatively, that is, only by not being any other one within the order "one thing after another." Their meaning is always extrinsic to them; constructed in their situation, their context, and their reader, it is a function of their being read, being consumed as a sign. The theoretical model

Minimalism-as-Postmodernism echoes is that offered by Poststructuralism, a model within which both the real and its representations are at once constructed and decentered by the functions of language itself. It is a model within which, Derrida assured us, there is nothing outside of the text,[36] an assurance that insists on the unraveling of the "real" as a function of representation, and one that insists, as well, on the unraveling of representation, not only because there has never been any real at its center to delimit and "mean" its meaning, but also because to understand the real as a function of representation is to understand representation as an apparatus of power, with meaning as its exercise. Finally, it is a model within which, as Jean Baudrillard put it, "art is constrained to signify."[37]

That last point we know. We are now well within the "return of representation" that was ushered in at the end of the 1970s. The return was visible not only in "Pictures," which, under the influence of French Structuralist and Poststructuralist theories and the writings of the German Frankfurt School, introduced the issue of representation as a critique of its functions. It was also readily evident in a much more pervasive and naive version in New Image Painting and Neo-Expressionism and even in Pattern and Decoration, which overlaid the surface of Modernist abstraction with images of quilts and beadwork and the topics of liberal left politics. Two decades after Sontag's wish for an art that is "just what it is," we can no longer see art as other than something else, as other than representational. Representation is assumed, and the terms of representation, from high theory to weak iconography, symbol-naming, and story-telling, have become, as Thomas Crow put it, the "patois," the village language of the art world.[38] Thus, Sontag's surfaces, once so unified and clean, so rapid and direct that they repelled interpretation, are now encrusted

with it, as "speed" or "nature" have become their subject matter and certainly as the personages of Greenberg and Fried have become their content. And two decades after her insistence that "what we decidedly do not need now is further to assimilate Art into Thought, or (worse yet) Art into Culture," that is all we can do. Since the return of representation, or at least within its headier critique, we cannot see art other than as evidence of The Culture, which has overseen its making and which sanctions its significations. We cannot see it as other than significant and as other than the conjunction of conventions that allow it signify. Indeed what it signifies is the working of those conventions.

As Sontag pointed out, to look at art as representational already begins its hollowing out; it at once assumes and produces "that absence we know to be a condition of representation." And it is, as Fried insisted, a threat. The concerted catching-out of representation as it would be hidden—recent theory's method against Modernism—reveals again and again exactly what, according to Fried, Tony Smith's nighttime drive did: "What seems to have been revealed to Smith that night was...one might say, the conventional nature of art." To begin to enumerate what is at stake in that revelation and what is threatened by a critique of representation,[39] I want to turn to one other text of the 1960s, E.C. Goosen's essay for his exhibition "The Art of the Real."[40]

Installed at The Museum of Modern Art in 1968, the exhibition focused not on any sort of pictorial or sculptural realism, but rather on painting and sculpture as real, that is, on Modernist abstraction and Minimal sculpture. As a reminder of the overarching ambition of this moment of the 1960s, and of its most prevalent discourse—the real, it included comfortably not only Noland and Morris Louis, Stella and

[35] Rosalind Krauss, "The Originality of the Avant-Garde: A Postmodernist Repetition," in Wallis (note 23), p. 27.

[36] Jacques Derrida, *Of Grammatology*, trans. Gayatri Chakravorty Spivak (Baltimore and London: The Johns Hopkins University Press, 1976), p. 158.

[37] Jean Baudrillard, *For a Critique of the Political Economy of the Sign*, trans. Charles Levin (St. Louis: Telos Press, 1981), p. 109.

[38] Thomas Crow, "Versions of Pastoral in Some Recent Art," in David A. Ross and Jürgen Harten, *American Art of the Late 80s: The BiNATIONAL* (Boston: The Institute of Contemporary Art and the Museum of Fine Arts, and Cologne: DuMont Buchverlag, 1988), p. 20.

[39] "The critique of representation" is a phrase that, like its substitutes—Postmodernism or Poststructuralism—is extremely overcoded, impossibly thickened, and, increasingly, the site not of openings but of prohibitions and exclusions, of academic battles and competing bibliographies. They are stupid terms simply to use.

[40] E.C. Goosen, *The Art of the Real: USA 1948-1968* (New York: The Museum of Modern Art, and Greenwich, Conn.: New York Graphic Society, 1968). All Goosen quotations are from this short text.

Larry Poons, but also Judd and Morris, Andre and Sol LeWitt. Goosen, like Newman, Stella, and Judd before him, began his demarcation of the real by separating it from any European version and, at the same time, from "metaphor, or symbolism, or any kind of metaphysics." "Today's 'real,' on the contrary...seems to have no desire at all to justify itself, but instead offers itself for whatever its uniqueness is worth—in the form of the simple, irreducible, irrefutable object." That object, which Goosen asserted "is very much like a chunk of nature, a rock, a tree, a cloud," is born of Abstract Expressionism and "the desire to find one's real self on the canvas through personal imagery and format." This desire, he repeated, "is not mystical or metaphysical; quite the opposite. It was an overriding ambition to make something so original that its reality could not be challenged." And, pointing to precisely what could not be done, he added, "their aim was not to *represent* something, but to *make* something, something which had never existed in the world before."

Goosen's text plots three locations as sites for the real: the self, the object, and the world. And he made it clear that the real that is achieved in each of these arenas is a function—a direct result—of uniqueness and originality. The real self, the real thing, the real world are each created in the crossing of not ever having been and not being like any other thing. The real thing is made anew, and the proof of its realness is its autonomy; as Goosen put it, the real work is irreducible and irrefutable, and it is these things—that is, it is real—because it is unique and original. What is striking about Goosen's prose is its repetition, some of which I have repeated here. Each of his requirements for the real and each of his proofs of it—the unique, the original, the irreducible—repeats the same central figure. Ironically, that repeated figure is oneness: the unit, the origin, that which cannot be

reduced. His topology of the real, too, is striking, for the sites he has located and linked so clearly with the language of origins—the self, the object, and the world—are precisely those that many of the key texts of Postmodernism have attempted to open up and spread out to the point where they are no longer sites. This they have done most often by pointing to the ways in which the original and the unique are effects, the products of a smuggled system of signification, always already caught up in their own representation, in re-doubling and repetition. In fact, in each of the texts I cited above as formulating Postmodernism in the late 1970s and in many of the key texts that stand behind them—or beneath them as footnotes—the singular words of Modernism—unique, original, primal, autonomous, authentic—are played against and unraveled by the double and the many, by a whole list of words that begin with the prefix *re*. In the space that remains I would like to use Goosen's map to trace this displacement of the one by the many.

Walter Benjamin's remarkably influential essay "The Work of Art in the Age of Mechanical Reproduction" is the footing beneath Crimp's "The Photographic Activity of Postmodernism" and beneath his and others' nomination of photography as Modernism's historical nemesis and, thus, as Postmodernism's major actor. Writing in 1936, only a few decades after the appearance of photomechanical reproduction and the ensuing public for its wares, Benjamin saw sweeping—indeed, historical, necessary—repercussions in the reproduction and dissemination on a broad scale of the images of works of art. He began by setting out a difference: "Even the most perfect reproduction of a work of art is lacking in one element: its presence in time and space, its unique existence at the place

where it happens to be."[41] That is, the reproduction lacks the original as a thing, as that body which has been subject to history or event or ownership. "The presence of the original is the prerequisite to the concept of authenticity," and the authenticity of a work of art—that is, the conception of its singularity—"is the essence of all that is transmissible from its beginning," from its age and to the history it has experienced. It is authenticity that grants a work of art its authority, its singular power, and it is these paired terms that Benjamin subsumed in the word "aura" in his now-famous declaration, "that which withers in the age of mechanical reproduction is the aura of the work of art."

Linked to art's prehistory in ritual and magic and described as a sense of unapproachability, aura is, Benjamin suggested, an understanding of the work's authority over us in the name of its authenticity, its "historical testimony," and the tradition within which that testimony is held. "The uniqueness of the work of art," he asserted, "is inseparable from its being imbedded in the fabric of tradition," and it is from that domain that reproduction detaches it. Substituting "a plurality of copies for a unique existence," reproduction circulates images where no original could go, to the studio or the living room. It makes the work available without its place, and, therefore, without the pilgrimage common to both shrines and great works. Reproduction makes the work available without its physical body; the printed page, hand-held, transient, and even disposable, gives material lie to the authority—the conjunction of permanence and authenticity—of the object. In each of these ways, geographically and physically, the reproduced image erases the distance and defies the unapproachability

[41] Walter Benjamin, "The Work of Art in the Age of Mechanical Reproduction," in *Illuminations*, trans. Harry Zohn (New York: Schocken Books, 1969), pp. 217-51. All Benjamin quotations are taken from this text, particularly pages 220-28. Published in 1939, Benjamin's essay is, obviously, earlier than the other works included here, most of which date from the past two decades. It is included here because its analysis of the way in which the technology of photography has placed into question the relationship of artist and work, of work and beholder, and of image and model is well understood in the texts of Postmodernism. Moreover, the essay foresees a criticism that fashions the relationship of art to society not as its reflection (a model that smuggles with it art's continued separateness) but as its product. In "The Work of Art," Benjamin insisted on the mutability of art practice, even entertained its disappearance, within the dynamics of history. Equally influential, however, has been his melancholy; while it infiltrates all his works, it appears most strongly in his writing on allegory, a literary genre that, in his reading, figures within itself the elaborate artificiality of culture—its textuality.

of the work of art. On paper in my room it can be used: it can be studied in myriad ways that would have violated its original; it can be captioned, cropped, enlarged, recombined, shuffled through another folio, compared to another image, and so on. Its value, and the value of the work of art seen with this familiarity, is what Benjamin termed "exhibition value." What is important is not that the work *is*—the original, authentic body—but that it is *seen*—the image, public and multiple. And seen with this familiarity, seen again and again, even the original becomes only another instance, another copy of its image.

Against the fullness of the work of art, the photograph and its offspring are curious objects. They cannot partake comfortably in the discourse of the original; the technology of photography includes its replication and places at its center a physical absence—the negative—which is precisely what the image is not. Moreover, without a conscious effort to contravene the technology, there is no limit and no difference to its replication; as Benjamin put it, "from a photographic negative…one can make any number of prints; to ask for the 'authentic' print makes no sense." And photography certainly cannot pretend to what he referred to as art's "semblance of autonomy." As only a copy, only one of the many that lie about in living rooms or on the pages of magazines, a work of art is no different than an image of an industrial fire or of fine furniture; reduced to their images they are reduced, as well, to the sameness of the copy. All equally useful and all readily exchangeable, they are, one could say, copies of one another. And even after that there is that scene in the world, that thing other than itself that the photograph must necessarily picture. The photograph is indebted to it, it cannot be other than that other thing, and yet, of course, it cannot be it. Against the original which testifies "I have been, I have seen, and I am here," a photograph can tell us only "this has been," which must also mean that is no longer, at least no longer here. The photograph's testimony is that the thing of its image is absent; indeed, rather than making it present, it traces and enforces its distance. Thus, there is a double absence at the photograph's center; it circulates (which is all it can do, since it can neither begin nor end) without origin or referent.

That image of the photograph is copied again in the image of language that was offered by Derrida in his essay "Structure, Sign and Play."[42] He wrote of a rupture, an event, a moment after which,

> it was necessary to begin thinking that there was no center, that the center could not be thought in the form of a present-being, that the center had no natural site, that it was not a fixed locus but a function, a sort of nonlocus in which an infinite number of sign-substitutions came into play.

Before that event, the center had been omnipresent, indeed, "an invariable presence," despite the succession of names it had worn: "*eidos, arche, telos, energia, ousia* (essence, existence, substance, subject), *aletheia*, transcendentality, consciousness, God, man, and so forth." The final referent of all the system's possibilities and the origin of all its meanings, the center as presence governed the substitutions made in its name and, at the same time, it remained reassuringly unreachable by the play of meanings it both sanctioned and limited.

Although Derrida was reticent to name or date this event within "the history of the concept of the structure," it is at least contemporaneous with what Benjamin labeled "the age of mechanical reproduction," that is, with the advent of Modernism. It took place at the end of the nineteenth century and the beginning of the twentieth in the writings of Nietzsche, Freud, and Heidegger, specifically in their critiques of the concepts of truth and being and self-presence, and even more specifically in the form those critiques take. They threaten truth and being and presence not by revamping or renaming, which would in effect only replace them with some other presence—some other absolute, some other transcendental—that would occupy the same place, but rather by "putting into question" the system in which those concepts function. It is here that, as Derrida put it,

> the structurality of structure had to begin to be thought…. Henceforth, it became necessary to think both the law which somehow governed the desire for a center in the constitution of structure, and the process of signification which orders the displacements and substitutions for this law of central presence.

To think "the structurality of structure" is to understand the center as function rather than presence, as of the system rather than separate from it, preceding and endowing it. In a centered system, language could mean the thing it named absolutely because it was backed by the power of a "transcendental signified" that took credit not only for language but for the object world it would represent. Without a central presence that would hold language and the world apart as two discrete manifestations of itself, the system is revealed as the system of language itself.

> This was the moment when language invaded the universal problematic, the moment when, in the absence of a center or origin, everything became discourse…that is to say, a system in which the central signified, the original or tran-

42 Jacques Derrida, "Structure, Sign and Play in the Discourse of the Human Sciences," in *Writing and Difference* (note 11), pp. 278-93. All subsequent Derrida quotations are taken from this essay.

scendental signified, is never absolutely present outside a system of differences. Within this system of replacements and substitutions, meanings are exchanged for one another rather than for Meaning or Truth or Being; "the substitute does not substitute itself for anything which has somehow existed before it." And, in its absence, "the domain and the play of signification [extends] indefinitely."

The rupture of which Derrida wrote is played as though in microcosm in literature. There, there is another overseer, a subcontractor named the author. Roland Barthes's description of the author recalls the "invariable presence" at Derrida's center: "To give a text an Author is to impose a limit on that text, to furnish it with a final signified, to close the writing."[43] He is, like the "absolute signified," at once everywhere in the book and always prior to it; he is both its origin and its end. For after all, the book means him; it is he, to return to Sontag's topography at the outset, who is found beneath its surface. As Barthes put it, "The *explanation* of a work is always sought in the man or woman who produced it, as if it were always in the end, through the more or less transparent allegory of fiction, the voice of single person, the *author* 'confiding' in us."

The title of Barthes's essay is "The Death of the Author." What has killed him, Barthes suggested, is the decentering of language of which Derrida wrote and, in its wake, the loosing of that language which "has no other origins than language itself, language which ceaselessly calls into question all origins. His death is recorded in a trio of births: that of the text, the writer, and the reader. "We know now," Barthes wrote, "that the text is not a line of words releasing a single 'theological' meaning (the 'message' of the Author-God) but a multi-dimensional space in which a variety of writings, none of them original,

blend and clash." Against the depth in which the author as origin dwells, "the text is a tissue of quotations." It has had myriad authors, or, better, writers, each of whom can only "imitate a gesture that is always anterior, never original."

> *Succeeding the Author, the scriptor no longer bears within him passions, humors, feelings, impressions, but rather this immense dictionary from which he draws a writing that can know no halt: life never does more than imitate the book, and the book itself is only a tissue of signs, an imitation that is lost, infinitely deferred.*

The text is plural, spreading, shot through with quotations that are "anonymous, untraceable and yet *already read*";[44] thus, its unity lies not within its multiple origins but in its destination: "The reader is the space on which all the quotations that make up a writing are inscribed." But with that inscription, language without origin displaces the reader as presence, as well. "The reader is without history, biography, psychology; he is simply that someone who holds together in a single field all the traces by which the written text is constituted."

"The birth of the reader must be at the cost of the death of the Author." But the author who controlled the meaning and limited the possibility of the book before the birth of the reader was not, of course, a biological fact, nor is he as simply done away with. Rather, he was and he remains a function, and as Michel Foucault suggested in response to Barthes, a largely ideological one. For Foucault, the author does, as Barthes suggested, limit the possibilities of signification; but where, in Barthes, the author seems little more than a habit of reading, one overthrown by the opening of language, for Foucault he is clearly a

product of "our era of industrial and bourgeois society,"[45] of "the system of property that characterizes our society,"[46] and he will be unseated by its transformation. Following Barthes, but stressing that it is not the author who limits but rather us in his name, Foucault's author is "a certain functional principle by which in our culture, one limits, excludes, and chooses; in short, by which one impedes the free circulation, the free manipulation, the free composition, decomposition, and recomposition of fiction."[47] And he made it clear that our representation of the author cannot be separated from the function it performs:

> *if we are accustomed to presenting the author as a genius, as a perpetual surging of invention, it is because, in reality, we make him function in exactly the opposite fashion. One can say that the author is an ideological product, since we represent him as the opposite of his historically real function.*[48]

Foucault made the comment that this is a world "where one is thrifty not only with one's resources and riches, but also with one's discourses and their significations. The author is the principle of thrift in the proliferation of meaning."[49] His economics appear quite different from the free play of exchanges offered by Derrida and Barthes; against Barthes's anonymous and untraceable "quotations without inverted commas,"[50] Foucault's remain credited, obligated by rights and contracts and the rules of academic discourse. If language can do nothing to stop its exchanges, if the conventions of the system of substitutes that is language can only structure and facilitate still more substitutions, there are other conventions that, like the author, are neither natural nor of the language, but rather social and institutional. They control not only the play of language, but who may use

[43] Roland Barthes, "The Death of the Author," in *Image, Music, Text*, trans. Stephen Heath (New York: Hill and Wang, 1977), pp. 142-48. All Barthes quotations are from this source, unless otherwise noted.
[44] Barthes, "From Work to Text," in ibid., p. 160.

[45] Michel Foucault, "What Is an Author?" in Josue V. Harari, ed., *Textual Strategies* (Ithaca, N.Y.: Cornell University Press, 1979), p. 159.
[46] Ibid., p. 149.
[47] Ibid., p. 159.
[48] Ibid.
[49] Ibid.
[50] Barthes, "From Work to Text" (note 43), p. 160.

it and what truths it may speak. For if, "in appearance, speech may well be of little account," it is finally "no mere verbalization of conflicts and systems of domination"; rather, "it is the very object of man's conflicts."[51] "In every society," Foucault wrote in "The Discourse of Language," "the production of discourse is at once controlled, selected, organized and redistributed according to a certain number of procedures, whose role is to avert its powers and its dangers...."[52]

Thus, alongside Derrida's assertion that there is nothing outside the text, one must place the rights of the legal system, the medical profession, the sciences, the academic disciplines, and religious and philosophical doctrines, embodied in the figure of the law and the expert and the author, to decide who is "*dans le vrai* (within the true)."[53] That is, "who, among the totality of speaking individuals, is accorded the right to use this sort of language? Who is qualified to do so?"[54] As discourse establishes interiors and exteriors, as it divides, on its terms, sense from nonsense, truth from folly, it excludes certain speakers and prohibits certain speech—indeed, its truth is a function of exclusion, of the limit to what can be said. It is, Craig Owens wrote, at this limit,

> the legislative frontier between what can be represented and what cannot that the postmodernist operation is being staged—not in order to transcend representation, but in order to expose that system of power that authorizes certain representations while blocking, prohibiting or invalidating others.[55]

Discourse's suppressions echo and, more than that, they perform society's own. To speak from the margins of society is to have one's speech marginalized. To speak as a woman, person of color, a lesbian, or a gay man is already to speak outside the truth, for it is to speak in a language that is not one's own, a language in which these names are not the names of speaking subjects but of objects or of absences. This language speaks, like Barthes's author, always as He, and He speaks always of Mankind and of Men, by which, of course, he means a certain group of men that share with him being named in the language. For whether one fashions the center of the system of language as presence or as power, it is, like God, created in His image. In the name of the center—in His name—difference is cast as opposition; against his truth difference is cast as other—as folly, as crime, as evil, as animal—and banished beyond language, where, as the mad, the criminal, the savage, or the natural, it cannot speak. To be not Him is to be defined by one's non-ness; we all know to say white and nonwhite, Western and non-Western. Thus, to speak at the margins is always to have already been an interpreter, a translator, and to have always already thought at the point where self and language are at once constructed and decentered each by the other. It is to have always already been, as Postmodernism now claims to be, the "ruin of representation."[56]

It is here that Postmodernism enters the real world, a vulgarism by which I mean an arena of orders and relationships among people inscribed in language as speakers. But what of Goosen's real world, by which I assume he meant the visible physical world; like the real thing and real self, this location, too, is shot through with language. The real world, too, as it reads matter as a literature of presence, is a representation that would be transparent, as solid and as clear as the matter to which it refers. And yet it, too, has been caught up in the procession of the copy. The world conceived as Man's or culture's or science's purview—that which he looked out on—has suffered the same fate as the work of art in the proliferation of images without centers. It has passed from Nature as presence, which, "imbedded in the fabric of tradition," converted its soil, its weather, and its matter into impermeable symbols of a greater bounty or fury or order. Now, after uncountable pictures—from paintings and postcards to National Geographic Specials—nature is no longer present in the fullness of its symbols as that "hard bottom and rocks in place, which we can call reality."[57] Rather it is dispersed in the multiplication of its images; indeed, it is only another instance of its image. Perhaps it is most clear at roadside vistas and scenic overlooks where frame and viewer are built into the earth itself, but everywhere nature presents itself to us as nature, it has always already been pictured.

This loss of the primary experience before nature, an experience that was integral to the construction of Romanticism and then Modernism, is the one written about most frequently in recent art criticism. But what of that other, or yet another, real world, the pedestrian world of objects, of the things we use. Always part of a serial chain of identical copies, clothes, cars, computers, and so on are necessarily enfolded in a rationalized and differential system of exchanges that is, according to Baudrillard, not a mirror or a replica of the exchanges of language but the same as it. "What is consumed is the object not in its materiality, but in its difference—i.e., *the object as sign*."[58] Within that system, value stems not from use as it is mirrored in the need of an individual user—that is, from what Marx posited as "use value," that autonomous, primordial, and unexchangeable truth of the object as that which is needed. The function of use value, Baudrillard pointed out, was to rescue the real world and the individual who needs its object from their mutual reduction in the repetitions of exchange. But it is no longer a question of needing clothes or a

51 Michel Foucault, *The Archeology of Knowledge*, trans. A.M. Sheridan Smith (New York: Pantheon Books, 1971), p. 216. This quotation and most of those that follow are taken from "The Discourse on Language," an appendix that follows the main text.
52 Ibid.
53 Ibid., p. 224.
54 Ibid., p. 50.
55 Craig Owens, "The Discourse of Others: Feminists and Postmodernism," in Foster, *The Anti-Aesthetic* (note 24), p. 59.
56 Michele Montrelay, quoted in ibid.
57 Henry David Thoreau, *Walden* (Salt Lake City, Utah: Gibbs M. Smith, Inc., 1981), p. 88. Even before the pond was reduced to its image on a postcard or the drive-by of a tour bus, it was already held in representation by Thoreau in the first half of the nineteenth century. Half of a binary equation whose other half was Boston, by which its attributes were read as not-Boston, the pond's realness was already caught up in the sign. And, while the pond and Thoreau's experience of it were to be unmediated and unwritten—at least until he wrote it—he would locate that hard bottom for future generations with the very image of the commensurate and the exchangeable, a measuring device, albeit a fictional one, a "realometer."
58 Jean Baudrillard, quoted in Craig Owens, "Analysis Logical and Ideological," *Art in America* 73, 5 (May 1985): 31.

car; we are never faced with that question, even if that is how we word it before heading to the mall. Rather, it is always already a question of "which" before the serial expanse of objects, each "specified by its trademark, charged with differential connotations of status, prestige and fashion."[59]

We consume clothes or computers always as differences, this one instead of that one, according to a logic of fashion, according to its signification within the code (there is a fashion and a legibility to Penney's as well as to Nordstrom's; all consumption is conspicuous, even if its audience is limited to one). It is not a question of authorship or actorship, of signing or projecting one's self through one's choice of a car or a brand of cigarettes; this much Madison Avenue will own up to, for this projection still places the consumer at the center. But as Baudrillard said: "The origin of meaning is never found in the relation between a subject (given a priori as autonomous and conscious) and an object produced for rational ends." Rather, it is to be found in "a differential structure that establishes a social relation, and not the subject as such." That is, we choose one name over another because we too are written into the system of exchanges as a repetition. Through a series of discourses—economics, sociology, demographics, psychology, politics, marketing, and so on—we are written as our social relations, as our function within the system of consumption. The system precedes us; indeed, it engenders us. But more than that, each of its instances precedes our own. Like the object of Minimalism, the trademark drawn from the racks at Bullock's "has been *waiting* for" us.

What Baudrillard described is not alienation, for, he insisted, we are not other than another function within the system of differences. Thus, here too, one might say, there is nothing outside the text.

But here the autonomous subject has not been decentered by a critique of metaphysics or by the opening of language, and he does not reappear, as he does in Derrida's and Barthes's affirmations of free play and the text, as "active interpretation"[60] or the reader. Rather, he has been displaced, ground out (by which I mean both eradicated and endlessly repeated) by the paired logics of production and signification. Baudrillard's consumer is the nightmare of Barthes's reader, who, without history or psychology or biography, is "simply that *someone*" who has read. In the act of reading, the reader is constructed as a destination, he is imagined as "a single field" and given control, even if only temporarily, of the traces of writing. Baudrillard's consumer is not destination but link; he is simply that *someone* criss-crossed by what he consumes, which does not construct him but registers him as on-line. "He can no longer produce the limits of his own being, can no longer play nor stage himself, can no longer produce himself as mirror. He is now only pure screen, a switching center for all the networks of influence."[61]

This is the background against which the work included in the exhibition "A Forest of Signs" has been made. These texts, their authors, and the language in which they are written are part of a bibliography that is familiar to—and, in most cases, read by—the artists represented here, as well as by the curators who have assembled them, other artists, critics, students, and so on across a significant section of the "fellowship of discourse" that is the art world. There are other texts, other authors, and other orderings and gatherings for an essay such as this. But they too would be marked by the same actors—first and foremost, language—and by the same processional topography from the one to the many—from the discrete center to a structured field, a field at once limitless and inscribed with losses and absences and gaps and margins.

It is from that topography, and from its texts, that the works in this exhibition take their tone—and perhaps their places. They are presented here as they are most often presented elsewhere, as critique and as mourning. Those activities suggest the margins and the absences of the field; criticism would take place outside the dominant discourse and mourning, after the center. And yet this exhibition is here in the museum and this essay here in the catalogue, a pair of institutions that suggest the centrality of this work and the criticism that surrounds it, including my own. Moreover, they suggest one of the continuing functions of the museum, to guard the canon and the center by patrolling and recuperating the margins. The work in this exhibition and its criticism is made knowing all this, as well. It understands that it fills positions that have preceded it in institutions that value, that already model, the artist precisely as critic and as mourner and that allow criticism as an official language of transgression precisely because it constructs Culture. The question is how do we signify our discomfort and our disbelief in those surroundings; how do we sign our knowing better, and is it enough?

[59] Baudrillard (note 37), p. 64. Unless otherwise noted, this and subsequent Baudrillard quotations are taken from the essay "The Ideological Genesis of Need," pp. 63-87.

[60] Derrida, "Structure, Sign and Play" (note 42), p. 292.

[61] Baudrillard, "The Ecstasy of Communication," in Foster, *The Anti-Aesthetic* (note 24), p. 133. It is perhaps only the continuous production of the world as sign and exchange value that explains how we can now conceive of strafing villages or blowing up jets as "sending a message."

CHRONOLOGY of EXHIBITIONS

The following chronology is a partial listing of shows and catalogue texts that help to provide a historical context for "A Forest of Signs: Art in the Crisis of Representation." Wherever possible, the first one-person exhibitions (in the United States and abroad) of each of the thirty artists in the present exhibition are included. Also referenced is a selection of one-person museum and related group exhibitions.

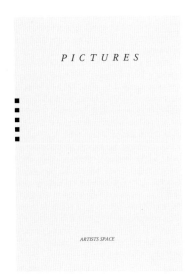

Catalogue cover,
PICTURES, 1977

Catalogue cover,
A FATAL ATTRACTION: ART AND THE MEDIA,
1982

1969
Haim Steinbach, Panoras Gallery, New York.

1971
Allan McCollum, Jack Glenn Gallery, Corona Del Mar, California.

1972
Jack Goldstein, Rico Mizuno Gallery, Los Angeles.
Jack Goldstein, Nigel Greenwood Gallery, London.

1973
Matt Mullican, Project Inc., Boston.
Richard Prince, Angus Whyte Gallery, Boston.

1974
Barbara Bloom, Byrd Hoffman Foundation, New York.
Barbara Bloom, Foundation de Appel, Amsterdam.
Barbara Kruger, Artists Space, New York.
Sherrie Levine, De Saisset Art Museum, Santa Clara, California.

1976
Robert Longo, Hallwalls, Buffalo, New York.
James Welling, Arco Center for Visual Arts, Los Angeles.

1977
Dara Birnbaum, Artists Space, New York.
Sarah Charlesworth, MTL Gallery, Brussels, Belgium.
Thomas Lawson, Artists Space, New York.
PICTURES, Artists Space, New York. Organized by Douglas Crimp. Artists exhibited: Troy Brauntuch, Jack Goldstein, Sherrie Levine, Robert Longo, and Philip Smith. Traveled to Allen Memorial Art Museum, Oberlin College, Oberlin, Ohio; Fine Arts Museum, University of Colorado, Boulder; and the Los Angeles Institute of Contemporary Art. Catalogue text by Crimp.

1978
Judith Barry, KALEIDOSCOPE, San Francisco Museum of Modern Art.
Jenny Holzer, SPECIAL PROJECT, P.S.1, New York.
Jenny Holzer, Franklin Furnace (window), New York.
MASTERS OF LOVE—SALLE, GOLDSTEIN, MULLICAN, BECKMAN, BRAUNTUCH, MCMAHON, New Langton Arts, San Francisco.
Richard Prince, Galerie Jollenbeck, Cologne, West Germany.

1979
Troy Brauntuch, The Kitchen, New York.
Sarah Charlesworth, MODERN HISTORY, New 57 Gallery, Edinburgh, Scotland. Catalogue published.
Jack Goldstein, Groninger Museum, Groningen, The Netherlands. Catalogue texts by Jan Wessel and Eddy Determeer.
Louise Lawler, A MOVIE WILL BE SHOWN WITHOUT THE PICTURES, Aero Theater, Santa Monica, California.
Robert Longo, SURRENDER, performance at Moderna Museet, Stockholm. Traveled to Amerika-Haus, Berlin; American Center, Paris; and Van Abbemuseum, Eindhoven, The Netherlands.
Cindy Sherman, Hallwalls, Buffalo, New York.
Laurie Simmons, Artists Space, New York.

1980
Barbara Bloom, Groninger Museum, Groningen, The Netherlands.
Jenny Holzer, Rüdiger Schöttle, Munich.
HORROR PLENI: PICTURES IN NEW YORK TODAY, Padiglione D'Arte Contemporanea, Milan. Curated by Zeno Birolli. Artists exhibited: Ericka Beckman, Jonathan Borofsky, Jack Goldstein, Michael Hurson, Sherrie Levine, Paul McMahon, Robert Moskowitz, Matt Mullican, Susan Rothenberg, David Salle, and James Welling. Catalogue text by Birolli.
Jeff Koons, THE NEW, The New Museum of Contemporary Art, New York.
Barbara Kruger, P.S.1, Long Island City, New York.
OPENING EXHIBITION, Metro Pictures, New York. Artists exhibited: Troy Brauntuch, Jack Goldstein, Michael Harvey, Thomas Lawson, William Leavitt, Sherrie Levine, Robert Longo, Richard Prince, Cindy Sherman, Laurie Simmons, James Welling, and Michael Zwack.
PICTURES AND PROMISES, The Kitchen, New York. Organized by Barbara Kruger. Artists exhibited included Dara Birnbaum, Jenny Holzer, Sherrie Levine, Matt Mullican, Richard Prince,

Cindy Sherman, Laurie Simmons, and James Welling.
PLEASURE & FUNCTION, David Amico Gallery, Los Angeles. Artists exhibited: Peter Fend, Colen Fitzgibbon, Jenny Holzer, Peter Nadin, Richard Prince, and Robin Winters.
Richard Prince, WAR PICTURES, Artists Space, New York. Artist's book published.

1981
Richard Baim, THE EDGE OF NIGHT, Gallery Yves Arman, New York.
BODY LANGUAGE: FIGURATIVE ASPECTS OF RECENT ART, The Hayden Gallery, Massachusettes Institute of Technology, Cambridge. Organized by Roberta Smith. Twenty artists exhibited, including Troy Brauntuch, Robert Longo, Richard Prince, Cindy Sherman, and Laurie Simmons. Traveled to Fort Worth Art Museum, Texas; University of South Florida Art Gallery, Tampa; and The Contemporary Arts Center, Cincinnati. Catalogue text by Smith.
EXHIBITION, California Institute of the Arts, Valencia, California. Curated by Helene Winer. Forty-six artists exhibited, including Ericka Beckman, Barbara Bloom, Troy Brauntuch, Jack Goldstein, Mike Kelley, Matt Mullican, and James Welling. Catalogue introduction by Winer.
Mike Kelley, Rico Mizuno Gallery, Los Angeles.
Robert Longo, EMPIRE: A PERFORMANCE TRILOGY, performance at The Corcoran Gallery of Art, Washington, D.C.
WESTKUNST—HEUTE, Museen der Stadt, Cologne, West Germany. Organized by Laszlo Glozer, Karl Ruhrberg, and Kasper Koenig. Thirty-seven artists exhibited, including Barbara Bloom, Troy Brauntuch, Jack Goldstein, and Robert Longo. Catalogue text by Koenig.
Christopher Williams, Jancar/Kuhlenschmidt Gallery, Los Angeles.

1982
74TH AMERICAN EXHIBITION, The Art Institute of Chicago. Organized by A. James Speyer and Anne Rorimer. Thirty-seven artists exhibited, including Dara Birnbaum, Jack Goldstein, Jenny Holzer, Barbara Kruger, Sherrie Levine, Stephen Prina, and Christopher Williams. Catalogue introduction by Rorimer.
Judith Barry, SPACE INVADERS OR THE FAILURE OF THE PRESENT, International Cultureel Centrum, Antwerp, Belgium. Catalogue texts by Barry and others.
DOCUMENTA 7, Museum Fridericianum, Kassel, West Germany. Organized by Rudi H. Fuchs. One hundred seventy-eight artists exhibited, including Dara Birnbaum, Troy Brauntuch, Jack Goldstein, Jenny Holzer, Barbara Kruger, Robert Longo, Matt Mullican, and Cindy Sherman. Catalogue texts by Saskia Bos, Coosje van Bruggen, Fuchs, and others.
EIGHT ARTISTS: THE ANXIOUS EDGE, Walker Art Center, Minneapolis, Minnesota. Organized by Lisa Lyons. Artists exhibited: Jonathan Borofsky, Chris Burden, Bruce Charlesworth, Robert Longo, David Salle, Italo Scanga, Cindy Sherman, and Hollis Sigler. Catalogue text by Lyons.
A FATAL ATTRACTION: ART AND THE MEDIA, The Renaissance Society at The University of Chicago. Twenty artists exhibited, including Dara Birnbaum, Barbara Bloom, Troy Brauntuch, Sarah Charlesworth, Jack Goldstein, Jeff Koons, Barbara Kruger, Thomas Lawson, Robert Longo, Matt Mullican, Richard Prince, and Cindy Sherman. Catalogue text by Thomas Lawson.
FIGURATION IN AMERICA, Milwaukee Art Museum, Wisconsin. Organized by Russell Bowman. Twenty-four artists exhibited, including Troy Brauntuch, Thomas Lawson, Robert Longo, Richard Prince, and Cindy Sherman. Catalogue texts by Bowman and Peter Schjeldahl.
(("'")) FRAMES OF REFERENCE, Whitney Museum of American Art, Downtown Branch, New York. Curated by Nora Halpern. Artists exhibited: Gretchen Bender, Michael Harvey, Barbara Kruger, Thomas Lawson, Robert Longo, Richard Prince, and Cindy Sherman. Catalogue text by Halpern.
IMAGE SCAVENGERS: PAINTING, Institute of Contemporary Art, University of Pennsylvania, Philadelphia. Organized by Janet Kardon. Artists exhibited: Richard Bosman, Nancy Dwyer, Ehry, Jack Goldstein, Thomas Lawson, Robert Longo, Judy Rifka, Walter Robinson, David Salle, Richard Seehausen, and Robin Winters. Catalogue text by Kardon.
IMAGE SCAVENGERS: PHOTOGRAPHY, Institute of Contemporary Art, University of Pennsylvania, Philadelphia. Organized by Paula Marincola. Artists exhibited: Ellen Brooks, Eileen Cowin, Jimmy de Sana, Barbara Kruger, Sherrie Levine, Richard Prince, Don Rodan, Cindy Sherman, and Laurie Simmons. Catalogue texts by Douglas Crimp and Marincola.

Catalogue cover,
THE ART OF MEMORY / THE LOSS OF HISTORY,
1985

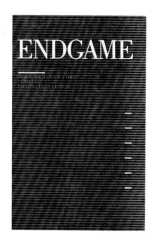

Catalogue cover,
ENDGAME: REFERENCE AND SIMULATION IN RECENT
PAINTING AND SCULPTURE, 1986

NEW NEW YORK, University Fine Arts Galleries, Florida State University, Tallahassee. Organized by Albert Stewart. Fifty-three artists exhibited, including Robert Longo, Richard Prince, Cindy Sherman, and Laurie Simmons. Traveled to the Metropolitan Museum and Art Centers, Coral Gables, Florida. Catalogue text by Stewart.

Cindy Sherman, Stedelijk Museum, Amsterdam. Traveled to Gewad, Ghent, Belgium; Watershed Gallery, Bristol, England; John Hansard Gallery, University of Southampton, England; Palais Stutterheim, Erlangen, West Germany; Haus am Waldsee, Berlin; Centre d'Art Contemporain, Geneva, Switzerland, Sonja Henie-Niels Onstadt Foundation, Copenhagen, Denmark; and Louisiana Museum, Humlebaek, Denmark. Catalogue published.

1983

ART AND SOCIAL CHANGE, U.S.A., Allen Memorial Art Museum, Oberlin College, Oberlin, Ohio. Curated by William Olander. Artists exhibited: Eric Bogosian, Nancy Buchanan, Sarah Charlesworth, John Feker, Mike Glier, Candice Hill-Montgomery, Jenny Holzer, Barbara Kruger, and Sherrie Levine. Catalogue texts by David Deitcher, Jerry Kearns, Lucy Lippard, and Craig Owens.

BACK TO THE U.S.A., Kunstmuseum Luzern, Switzerland. Organized by Klaus Honnef and Barbara Küchels. Forty-seven artists exhibited, including Troy Brauntuch, Jack Goldstein, Robert Longo, Matt Mullican, and Cindy Sherman. Traveled to Rheinisches Landesmuseum, Bonn; and Württembergischer Kunstverein, Stuttgart. Catalogue text by Robert Becker, Honnef, Deborah C. Phillips, and others.

Ericka Beckman, YOU THE BETTER, The Kitchen, New York.

Gretchen Bender, Nature Morte, New York.

1983 BIENNIAL EXHIBITION, Whitney Museum of American Art, New York. Seventy-six artists exhibited, including Ericka Beckman, Jenny Holzer, Barbara Kruger, Robert Longo, and Cindy Sherman. Catalogue published.

Troy Brauntuch, Galerie Schellmann/Klüser, Munich.

DARK ROOMS, Richard Baim and Judith Barry at Artists Space, New York. Catalogue text by John G. Hanhardt.

DIRECTIONS 1983, Hirshhorn Museum and Sculpture Garden, Smithsonian Institute, Washington, D.C. Curated by Phyllis Rosenzweig. Artists exhibited: Ida Applebroog, Siah Armajani, Jonathan Borofsky, Scott Burton, Kendall Buster, Mary Jones, Robert Longo, Elizabeth Murray, Pierre Picot, David Salle, Julian Schnabel, Judith Shea, Cindy Sherman, Alexis Smith, Anita Thatcher, Robert Wilhite, and Elyn Zimmerman. Catalogue text by Rosenzweig.

Ronald Jones, ACHIEVEMENT IS MYTH, Centro Documentazione Artein, Rome.

Barbara Kruger, WE WON'T PLAY NATURE TO YOUR CULTURE, The Institute of Contemporary Arts, London. Organized by Iwona Blazwick and Sandy Nairne. Traveled to Kunsthalle Basel, Switzerland; Nouveau Musée, Villeurbanne, France; Watershed Gallery, Bristol, England. Catalogue texts by Craig Owens and Jane Weinstock.

THE LOS ANGELES/NEW YORK EXCHANGE, Los Angeles Contemporary Exhibitions and Artists Space, New York. Organized by Marc Pally and Linda Shearer. Artists exhibited: Jill Giegerich, Victor Henderson, Kim Hubbard, Lari Pittman, Mitchell Syrop, Megan Williams, Charles Clough, Rebecca Howland, Jeff Koons, Nachume Miller, Christy Rupp, and Reese Williams. Catalogue texts by Susan C. Larson and Roberta Smith.

Richard Prince, Le Nouveau Musée, Villeurbanne, France. Catalogue text by Kate Linker.

THE REVOLUTIONARY POWER OF WOMEN'S LAUGHTER, Protetch/McNeil, New York. Organized by Joanne Isaac. Artists exhibited: Mike Glier, Jenny Holzer, Barbara Kruger, Mary Kelly, and Nancy Spero.

1984

ALIBIS, Musée National d'Art Moderne, Centre Georges Pompidou, Paris. Organized by Bernard Blistène. Artists exhibited: Richard Artschwager, Gérard Collen-Thebaut, Gérard Garouste, Luciano Fabro, Pierre Klossowski, Robert Longo, Carlo Maria Mariani, Cindy Sherman, Jan Vercruysse, Didier Vermeiren, and William Wegman. Catalogue texts by Yann Beauvais, Blistène, Pascal Bonitzer, and Jean-François Chevrier.

AUSTRALIAN BIENNALE, PRIVATE SYMBOL: SOCIAL METAPHOR, The Art Gallery of New South Wales, Sydney, Australia. Organized by Leon Paroissien. Sixty-three artists exhibited, including Jenny Holzer, Barbara Kruger, Robert Longo, and

Cindy Sherman. Catalogue texts by Colin McCahon, Stuart Morgan, Annelie Pohlen, and others.

DARA BIRNBAUM - RETROSPECTIVE SCREENING, The Institute of Contemporary Arts, London.

CONTENT: A CONTEMPORARY FOCUS 1974-1984, Hirshhorn Museum and Sculpture Garden, Smithsonian Institute, Washington, D.C. Curated by Howard N. Fox, Miranda McClintic, and Phyllis Rosenzweig. One hundred thirty-seven artists exhibited, including Dara Birnbaum, Troy Brauntuch, Jenny Holzer, Barbara Kruger, Robert Longo, and Cindy Sherman. Catalogue texts by Fox, McClintic, and Rosenzweig.

DIFFERENCE: ON REPRESENTATION AND SEXUALITY, The New Museum of Contemporary Art, New York. Curated by Kate Linker and Jane Weinstock. Twenty artists exhibited, including Judith Barry, Dara Birnbaum, Barbara Kruger, and Sherrie Levine. Traveled to The Renaissance Society at The University of Chicago and The Institute of Contemporary Arts, London. Catalogue texts by Craig Owens, Jacqueline Rose, Lisa Tickner, Jane Weinstock, and Peter Wollen.

DISARMING IMAGES: ART FOR NUCLEAR DISARMAMENT, The Contemporary Arts Center, Cincinnati. Organized by Bread & Roses, and curated by Nina Felshin. Forty-four artists exhibited, including Jenny Holzer, Barbara Kruger, Sherrie Levine, Robert Longo, and Laurie Simmons. Traveled to University Art Gallery, San Diego State University, California; Museum of Art, Washington State University, Pullman; New York State Museum, Albany; University Art Museum, University of California, Santa Barbara; Munson-Williams-Proctor Institute Museum of Art, Utica, New York; Fine Arts Gallery, University of Nevada, Las Vegas; Baxter Art Gallery, California Institute of Technology, Pasadena; Yellowstone Art Center, Billings, Montana; and Bronx Museum of the Arts, New York. Catalogue text by Felshin.

FOR PRESENTATION AND DISPLAY: IDEAL SETTINGS, Diane Brown Gallery, New York. A collaboration between Louise Lawler and Allan McCollum.

THE HEROIC FIGURE, The Contemporary Arts Museum, Houston. Organized by Linda L. Cathcart. Artists exhibited: John Ahearn, Ellen Carey, William Cozier, Nancy Dwyer, Jedd Garet, Thomas Lawson, Robert Longo, Robert Mapplethorpe, Richard Prince, David Salle, Julian Schnabel, Cindy Sherman, and Michael Zwack. Traveled to Brooks Memorial Art Gallery, Memphis, Tennessee; Alexandria Museum, Alexandria, Louisiana; and Santa Barbara Museum of Art, California. Catalogue texts by Cathcart and Craig Owens.

Jenny Holzer, PRIVATE PROPERTY CREATED CRIME, Kunsthalle Basel, Switzerland, and Le Nouveau Musée, Villeurbanne, France. Catalogue introduction by Jean-Christophe Ammann.

HOLZER, KRUGER, PRINCE, The Knight Art Gallery, Spirit Square Art Center, Charlotte, North Carolina. Catalogue text by William Olander.

AN INTERNATIONAL SURVEY OF PAINTING AND SCULPTURE, The Museum of Modern Art, New York. Organized by Kynaston McShine. One hundred sixty-six artists exhibited, including Troy Brauntuch, Jack Goldstein, and Robert Longo. Catalogue text by McShine.

JENNY HOLZER, STEPHEN PRINA, MARK STAHL, CHRISTOPHER WILLIAMS, Gewad, Ghent, Belgium, and Foundation De Appel, Amsterdam. Curated by Coosje van Bruggen. Catalogue texts by Saskia Bos and van Bruggen.

Barbara Kruger, Galerie Crousel-Hussenot, Paris.

NATURAL GENRE, Fine Arts Gallery, Florida State University, Tallahassee, Florida. Curated by Tricia Collins and Richard Milazzo. Twenty-four artists exhibited, including Ericka Beckman, Gretchen Bender, Sarah Charlesworth, Louise Lawler, Allan McCollum, Peter Nagy, and James Welling. Catalogue text by Collins and Milazzo.

NEO-YORK, The University Art Museum, University of California, Santa Barbara. Organized by Phyllis Plous and Mary Looker. Sixty-seven artists exhibited, including Gretchen Bender and Peter Nagy. Catalogue texts by Dan Cameron, Michael Kohn, Carlo McCormick, Plous, and Walter Robinson.

THE NEW CAPITAL, White Columns, New York. Curated by Tricia Collins and Richard Milazzo. Artists exhibited: Vikky Alexander, Jane Bauman, Alan Belcher, Gretchen Bender, Barry Bridgewood, Sarah Charlesworth, Peter Halley, Jeff Koons, Daniel Leavin, Frank Majore, Peter Nagy, Joseph Nechvatal, David Robbins, Tyler Turkle, Meyer Vaisman, and Oliver Wasow. Exhibition statement by Collins and Milazzo.

NEW YORK, AILLEURS ET AUTREMENT, ARC/Musée d'Art Moderne de la Ville de Paris. Organized by Suzanne Pagé and Béatrice Parent. Artists exhibited: Jenny Holzer, Barbara Kruger,

Louise Lawler, Sherrie Levine, Allan McCollum, Richard Prince, Martha Rosler, and James Welling. Catalogue text by Claude Gintz.

Cindy Sherman, The Akron Art Museum, Akron, Ohio. Traveled to the Institute of Contemporary Art, University of Pennsylvania, Philadelphia; Museum of Art, Carnegie Institute, Pittsburgh; Des Moines Art Center, Iowa; and The Baltimore Museum of Art, Maryland. Catalogue published.

Laurie Simmons, Galerie Tanja Grunert, Stuttgart.

STILL LIFE WITH TRANSACTION, International With Monument Gallery, New York. Curated by Tricia Collins and Richard Milazzo. Twenty-one artists exhibited, including Ericka Beckman, Sarah Charlesworth, Peter Nagy, Richard Prince, and Laurie Simmons. Exhibition statement by Collins and Milazzo.

Mitchell Syrop, Richard Kuhlenschmidt Gallery, Los Angeles.

1985

ACTUAL PHOTOS, Nature Morte Gallery, New York. A collaboration between Allan McCollum and Laurie Simmons. Traveled to Heath Gallery, Atlanta; Texas Gallery, Houston; Rhona Hoffman Gallery, Chicago; and Kuhlenschmidt/Simon Gallery, Los Angeles.

THE ANTICIPATED RUIN, The Kitchen, New York. Curated by Howard Halle. Artists exhibited: Joseph Beirne, Gretchen Bender, Robert Garrat, Jim Jacobs, Komar & Melamid, Louise Lawler, Sherrie Levine, Allan McCollum, Peter Nagy, Stephen Parrino, and Meyer Vaisman. Catalogue text by Halle.

THE ART OF MEMORY/THE LOSS OF HISTORY, The New Museum of Contemporary Art, New York. Curated by William Olander. Twenty-five artists exhibited, including Judith Barry, Troy Brauntuch, Sarah Charlesworth, Louise Lawler, Stephen Prina, Richard Prince, and Christopher Williams. Catalogue texts by David Deitcher, Olander, and Abigail Solomon-Godeau.

1985 BIENNIAL EXHIBITION, Whitney Museum of American Art, New York. Eighty-four artists exhibited, including Ericka Beckman, Dara Birnbaum, Sarah Charlesworth, Jack Goldstein, Jenny Holzer, Mike Kelley, Barbara Kruger, Sherrie Levine, Richard Prince, Cindy Sherman, and Laurie Simmons. Catalogue published.

A BRAVE NEW WORLD, A NEW GENERATION: FORTY NEW YORK ARTISTS, Exhibition Hall at Charlottenburg, Copenhagen, Denmark. Curated by Thomas B. Solomon. Forty artists exhibited, including Gretchen Bender and Peter Nagy. Catalogue texts by Mogens Breyen, Carlo McCormick, and Solomon.

1985 CARNEGIE INTERNATIONAL, Museum of Art, Carnegie Institute, Pittsburgh. Curated by John R. Lane and John Caldwell. Forty-two artists exhibited, including Dara Birnbaum, Jenny Holzer, and Cindy Sherman. Catalogue texts by Caldwell, Hilton Kramer, and Lane.

Sarah Charlesworth, The California Museum of Photography, Riverside. Catalogue published.

As FOUND, at The Institute of Contemporary Art, Boston. One of a series of three exhibitions comprising DISSENT: THE ISSUE OF MODERN ART IN BOSTON. Organized by David Joselit, Gillian Levine, and Elisabeth Sussman. Artists exhibited: Alan Belcher, Sarah Charlesworth, Jenny Holzer, Barbara Kruger, Louise Lawler, Sherrie Levine, Allan McCollum, Peter Nagy, and Richard Prince. Catalogue texts by Benjamin H.D. Buchloh, Serge Guillbaut, Reinhold Heller, Joselit, and Sussman.

Jack Goldstein, Städtische Galerie, Erlangen, West Germany. Traveled to Kunstverein, Ingolstadt, West Germany. Catalogue text by Jean Fisher.

INFOTAINMENT (18 ARTISTS FROM NEW YORK), Livet Reichard, New York. Artists exhibited: Alan Belcher, Gretchen Bender, Jennifer Bolande, Sarah Charlesworth, Clegg & Guttmann, Jessica Diamond, Peter Halley, Kevin Larmon, Richard Milani, Peter Nagy, Joseph Nechtval, Joel Otterson, Stephen Parrino, David Robbins, Laurie Simmons, Haim Steinbach, and Julie Wachtel. Traveled to Texas Gallery, Houston; Rhona Hoffman Gallery, Chicago; Vanguard Gallery, Philadelphia; and Aspen Art Museum, Colorado. Calatogue texts by Thomas Lawson, David Robbins, and George W.S. Trow.

Ronald Jones, The Contemporary Arts Center, New Orleans.

KUNST MIT EIGEN SINN, Museum Moderner Kunst, Vienna. One hundred eleven artists exhibited, including Ericka Beckman, Gretchen Bender, Barbara Bloom, Jenny Holzer, Barbara Kruger, and Cindy Sherman. Catalogue texts by Jean-Pierre Dubost, Gertrude Koch, Eva Meyer, and others.

Sherrie Levine, Mary and Leigh Block Gallery, Northwestern University Evanston, Illinois. Brochure text by David Deitcher.

Robert Longo, PERFORMANCE WORKS 1977-81, The Brooklyn Museum, New York.

Robert Longo, Stedelijk Museum, Amsterdam. Brochure text by Els Barents.

Peter Nagy, International With Monument Gallery, New York.

THE PUBLIC ART SHOW, Nexus Contemporary Art Center, Atlanta. Curated by Ronald Jones. Forty-four artists exhibited, including Ericka Beckman, Gretchen Bender, Dara Birnbaum, Sarah Charlesworth, Jenny Holzer, Barbara Kruger, Thomas Lawson, Allan McCollum, Peter Nagy, Stephen Prina, Richard Prince, Cindy Sherman, Laurie Simmons, and Mitchell Syrop. Catalogue text by Jones.

SIGNS, The New Museum of Contemporary Art, New York. Curated by Ned Rifkin. Artists exhibited: Gary Falk, Ken Feingold, Marian Galczenski, Jenny Holzer, John Knight, Manual, Matt Mullican, Ted Savinar, and Al Souza. Catalogue text by Rifkin.

STEPHEN PRINA, MARK STAHL, CHRISTOPHER WILLIAMS, Galerie Crousel-Hussenot, Paris.

TALKING BACK TO THE MEDIA, Stedelijk Museum, Amsterdam. Artists exhibited included Judith Barry, Dara Birnbaum, Barbara Kruger, and Peter Nagy. Catalogue texts by Rob Stolk and others.

1986

ART AND ITS DOUBLE: A NEW YORK PERSPECTIVE, Centre Cultural de la Fundació Caixa de Pensions, Barcelona, Spain. Curated by Dan Cameron. Artists exhibited: Ashley Bickerton, Sarah Charlesworth, Robert Gober, Peter Halley, Jenny Holzer, Jeff Koons, Barbara Kruger, Louise Lawler, Sherrie Levine, Matt Mullican, Tim Rollins & KOS, Peter Schuyff, Cindy Sherman, Haim Steinbach, and Philip Taaffe. Catalogue text by Cameron.

ARTS AND LEISURE, The Kitchen, New York. Curated by Group Material. Thirty-nine artists exhibited, including Barbara Kruger, Louise Lawler, Allan McCollum, Richard Prince, and Haim Steinbach. Catalogue text by Glenn O'Brien.

Richard Baim, WINDOW ON BROADWAY, The New Museum of Contemporary Art, New York. Brochure published.

A BROKERAGE OF DESIRE, The Otis Art Institute of Parsons School of Design, Exhibition Center, Los Angeles. Organized by Howard Halle and Walter Hopps. Artists exhibited: Alan Belcher, Gretchen Bender, Anne Doran, Jeff Koons, Peter Nagy, and Haim Steinbach. Catalogue texts by Halle and Hopps.

Dara Birnbaum, Kunstmuseum Bern, Switzerland.

DAMAGED GOODS: DESIRE AND THE ECONOMY OF THE OBJECT, The New Museum of Contemporary Art, New York. Curated by Brian Wallis. Artists exhibited: Judith Barry, Gretchen Bender, Barbara Bloom, Andrea Fraser, Jeff Koons, Justin Ladda, Louise Lawler, Ken Lum, Allan McCollum, and Haim Steinbach. Catalogue texts by Deborah Bershad, Hal Foster, Wallis, and others.

ENDGAME: REFERENCE AND SIMULATION IN RECENT PAINTING AND SCULPTURE, The Institute of Contemporary Art, Boston. Artists exhibited: Richard Baim, Gretchen Bender, Ross Bleckner, General Idea, Peter Halley, Perry Hoberman, Jeff Koons, Sherrie Levine, Joel Otterson, Haim Steinbach, and Philip Taaffe. Catalogue texts by Yve-Alain Bois, Thomas Crow, Elisabeth Sussman, and others.

EUROPA-AMERIKA, Museum Ludwig, Cologne, West Germany. Organized by Sigfried Gohr. One hundred twenty-five artists exhibited, including Jeff Koons, Jenny Holzer, and Sherrie Levine. Catalogue texts by Craig Adcock, Gohr, Rafael Jablonka, and others.

JENNY HOLZER/BARBARA KRUGER, Israel Museum, Jerusalem. Curated by Suzanne Landau. Catalogue text by Landau.

JENNY HOLZER & CINDY SHERMAN: PERSONAE, The Contemporary Arts Center, Cincinnati. Organized by Sarah Rogers-Lafferty. Catalogue text by Rogers-Lafferty.

JENNY HOLZER: SIGNS, Des Moines Art Center, Iowa. Curated by Joan Simon. Traveled to The Aspen Art Museum, Colorado; Artspace, San Francisco; and The Fruitmarket Gallery, Edinburgh, Scotland. Catalogue text by Simon, interview by Bruce Ferguson.

Larry Johnson, 303 Gallery, New York.

Ronald Jones, A TRIBUTE TO THE FUTURE, High Museum at Georgia Pacific Center, Atlanta. Catalogue text by John Howett.

LA MAGIE DE L'IMAGE, Musée d'Art Contemporain de Montréal, Quebec. Artists exhibited: Shelagh Alexander, Ellen Brooks, Bernard Faucon, Marvin Gasoi, Holly King, Barbara Kruger, George Legrady, Nic Nicosia, Pierre et Gilles, Richard

Catalogue cover,
ART AGAINST AIDS, 1987

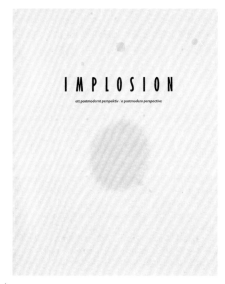

Catalogue cover,
IMPLOSION: A POSTMODERN PERSPECTIVE, 1987

Catalogue cover,
CALARTS: SKEPTICAL BELIEFS, 1987

Prince, Cindy Sherman, Laurie Simmons, Sandy Skoglund, and Boyd Webb. Catalogue text by Paulette Gagnon.

Allan McCollum, INVESTIGATIONS 18, Institute of Contemporary Art, University of Pennsylvania, Philadelphia. Curated by Judith Tannenbaum. Brochure text by Andrea Fraser.

NEW SCULPTURE, The Renaissance Society at The University of Chicago. Organized by Gary Garrels. Artists exhibited: Robert Gober, Jeff Koons, and Haim Steinbach. Catalogue text by Garrels.

PARAVISION, Margo Leavin Gallery, Los Angeles. Curated by Tricia Collins and Richard Milazzo. Twenty-five artists exhibited, including Gretchen Bender, Sarah Charlesworth, Jeff Koons, Barbara Kruger, Robert Longo, Peter Nagy, Haim Steinbach, and James Welling. Exhibition statement by Collins and Milazzo.

POETIC RESEMBLANCE, Hallwalls, Buffalo, New York. Curated by Barbara Broughel. Artists exhibited: Advent, Gary Bachman, Alan Belcher, Ashley Bickerton, Barbara Bloom, Chris Burden, Stephen Frailey, Fank Gillette, Mike Kelley, David McDermott & Peter McGough, and James Welling. Catalogue text by Broughel.

PROJECTS: JUDITH BARRY, The Museum of Modern Art, New York. Brochure text by Barbara London.

THE REAL BIG PICTURE, Queens Museum, Flushing, New York. Curated by Marvin Heiferman. Fifty artists exhibited, including Richard Baim, Sarah Charlesworth, Barbara Kruger, Louise Lawler, Allan McCollum, Richard Prince, and Laurie Simmons. Catalogue text by Heiferman.

REMEMBRANCES OF THINGS PAST, Long Beach Museum of Art, California. Curated by Connie Fitzsimmons. Artists exhibited: Marina Abramovic/Ulay, Richard Baim, Dara Birnbaum, Barbara Ess, Jochen Gerz, Douglas Huebler, Komar & Melamid, Marcel Odenbach, Laurie Simmons, Alexis Smith, and Anne Turyn. Catalogue texts by Lydia Davis, Howard Singerman, Bernard Welt, and others.

ROOTED RHETORIC, Castel dell'Ovo, Naples, Italy. Curated by Gabriele Guercio. Artists exhibited: Gregg Bordowitz, Clegg & Guttmann, Mark Dion, Hans Haacke, Peter Halley, Jenny Holzer, Joseph Kosuth, Barbara Kruger, Louise Lawler, Thomas Lawson, Allan McCollum, Peter Nagy, Stephen Prina, Richard Prince, David Robbins, Haim Steinbach, Meyer Vaisman, and Christopher Williams. Catalogue texts by Benjamin H.D. Buchloh, Guerco, Joseph Kosuth, and others.

SPIRITUAL AMERICA, CEPA Gallery, Buffalo, New York. Curated by Tricia Collins and Richard Milazzo. Forty artists exhibited, including Gretchen Bender, Sarah Charlesworth, Jeff Koons, Allan McCollum, and Peter Nagy. Exhibition statement by Collins and Milazzo.

T.V. GENERATIONS, Los Angeles Contemporary Exhibitions. Curated by John Baldessari and Bruce Yonemoto. Thirty-five artists exhibited, including Ericka Beckman, Gretchen Bender, Barbara Bloom, Stephen Prina, Richard Prince, Mitchell Syrop, and Christopher Williams. Catalogue texts by Baldessari, Peter D'Agostino, John G. Hanhardt, and Yonemoto.

UPLIFTED ATMOSPHERES, BORROWED TASTE, Hallwalls, Buffalo, New York. Organized by Howard Halle. Artists exhibited: Dennis Adams, Joe Beirne, Anne Doran, Larry Johnson, Peter Nagy, Stephen Parrino, David Robbins, Anthony Silvestrini, and Robin Weglinski. Catalogue text by Halle.

1987

ART AGAINST AIDS, New York. A series of sales exhibitions at seventy-two New York galleries for the benefit of the American Foundation for AIDS Research. Organized by Levit Reichard. Seven hundred twenty-one artists exhibited, including Ericka Beckman, Gretchen Bender, Sarah Charlesworth, Jack Goldstein, Jenny Holzer, Larry Johnson, Ronald Jones, Mike Kelley, Jeff Koons, Barbara Kruger, Louise Lawler, Thomas Lawson, Sherrie Levine, Robert Longo, Allan McCollum, Matt Mullican, Peter Nagy, Richard Prince, Cindy Sherman, Laurie Simmons, Haim Steinbach, and James Welling. Catalogue text by Robert Rosenblum and others.

THE ARTS FOR TELEVISION, The Museum of Contemporary Art, Los Angeles, and Stedelijk Museum, Amsterdam. Curated by Kathy Rae Huffman and Dorine Mignot. One hundred two artists exhibited, including Dara Birnbaum and Robert Longo. Traveled to The Institute of Contemporary Art, Boston; Kölnischer Kunstverein, Cologne, West Germany; Kunsthaus Zurich; Centro Videoarte, Palazzo di Diamante, Ferrara, Italy; Centro de Arte Reina Sofia, Madrid; Museum Moderner Kunst, Vienna; San Francisco Museum of Modern Art; Museum voor Hedendaagse Kunst, Ghent, Belgium; The Museum of Modern

Art, New York; Musée National d'Art Moderne, Centre Georges Pompidou, Paris; and Tate Gallery, London. Catalogue texts by Rosetta Brooks, Anne- Marie Duguet, Huffman, and others.

AVANT-GARDE IN THE EIGHTIES, Los Angeles County Museum of Art. Organized by Howard N. Fox. One hundred seven artists exhibited, including Gretchen Bender, Troy Brauntuch, Jenny Holzer, Mike Kelley, Jeff Koons, Barbara Kruger, Sherrie Levine, Robert Longo, Allan McCollum, Matt Mullican, Haim Steinbach, and Mitchell Syrop. Catalogue text by Fox.

1987 BIENNIAL EXHIBITION, Whitney Museum of American Art, New York. Seventy-two artists exhibited, including Judith Barry, Ericka Beckman, Jeff Koons, Barbara Kruger, and Richard Prince. Catalogue published.

Barbara Bloom, Gemeentemuseum, Arnhem, The Netherlands. Catalogue text by Saskia Bos.

CALARTS: SKEPTICAL BELIEFS, The Renaissance Society at The University of Chicago. Curated by Suzanne Ghez. Fifty-three artists exhibited, including Ericka Beckman, Barbara Bloom, Troy Brauntuch, Jack Goldstein, Larry Johnson, Mike Kelley, Matt Mullican, Stephen Prina, Mitchell Syrop, James Welling, and Christopher Williams. Traveled to Newport Harbor Art Museum, Newport Beach, California. Catalogue texts by Susan A. Davis, Catherine Lord, Howard Singerman, and others.

CONSTITUTION, The Temple Gallery, Philadelphia. Organized by Group Material. Forty-one artists exhibited, including Gretchen Bender, Jenny Holzer, Barbara Kruger, Thomas Lawson, and Sherrie Levine. Catalogue texts by Donald Kuspit, Michael Ratner, Margaret Ratner, and Bruce McM. Wright.

CURRENTS 12: SIMULATION, NEW AMERICAN CONCEPTUALISM, Milwaukee Art Museum, Wisconsin. Curated by Dean Sobel. Artists exhibited: Ashley Bickerton, Jeff Koons, Annette Lemieux, Sherrie Levine, Allan McCollum, Haim Steinbach, and Meyer Vaisman. Brochure text by Sobel.

DOCUMENTA 8, Museum Fridericianum, Kassel, West Germany. Four hundred three artists exhibited, including Dara Birnbaum, Jack Goldstein, Jenny Holzer, Barbara Kruger, and Robert Longo. Group Material's installation included works by forty-seven artists, including Gretchen Bender, Jenny Holzer, Larry Johnson, Ronald Jones, Barbara Kruger, Louise Lawler, Thomas Lawson, Allan McCollum, Peter Nagy, Haim Steinbach, and Christopher Williams. Catalogue texts by Bazon Brock, Vittorio Fagone, Edward F. Fry, and others.

IMPLOSION: A POSTMODERN PERSPECTIVE, Moderna Museet, Stockholm. Organized by Lars Nittve. Twenty-eight artists exhibited, including Gretchen Bender, Dara Birnbaum, Barbara Kruger, Louise Lawler, Sherrie Levine, Robert Longo, Allan McCollum, Cindy Sherman, Laurie Simmons, and James Welling. Catalogue texts by Germano Celant, Kate Linker, Nittve, and Craig Owens.

Larry Johnson, Isabella Kacprzak Gallery, Stuttgart.

LA: HOT AND COOL, Albert and Vera List Visual Arts Center, Massachusettes Institute of Technology, Cambridge. Organized by Dana Friis-Hansen. Twenty-three artists exhibited, including Mike Kelley, Stephen Prina, Mitchell Syrop, and Christopher Williams. Catalogue texts by Dennis Cooper, Friis-Hansen, Rita Valencia, Benjamin Weissman, and a conversation between Christopher Knight and Howard Singerman.

Thomas Lawson, La Jolla Museum of Contemporary Art, California.

L'EPOQUE, LA MODE, LA MORALE, LA PASSION (1977-1987), Musée National d'Art Moderne, Centre Georges Pompidou, Paris. One hundred twenty-seven artists exhibited, including Dara Birnbaum, Jack Goldstein, Jenny Holzer, Barbara Kruger, Robert Longo, Matt Mullican, and Cindy Sherman. Catalogue texts by Christine Van Assche, Jean-François Chevrier, Serge Daney, Philippe Dubois, and Johannes Gachnang.

Matt Mullican, CONCENTRATION 15, The Dallas Museum of Art. Brochure text by Sue Graze.

Peter Nagy, Galleria Pinta, Genoa, Italy.

NEW YORK ART NOW, The Israel Museum, Jerusalem. Curated by Suzanne Landau. Artists exhibited: Peter Halley, Jeff Koons, Sherrie Levine, Allan McCollum, Peter Nagy, and Haim Steinbach. Catalogue text by Brian Wallis.

THE NEW WHO'S WHO, Hoffman/Borman Gallery, Santa Monica, California. Organized by Marvin Heifferman. Fifty artists exhibited, including Jenny Holzer, Larry Johnson, Jeff Koons, Barbara Kruger, Louise Lawler, Allan McCollum, Richard Prince, Cindy Sherman, Laurie Simmons, and Mitchell Syrop. Brochure text by Heiferman.

NON IN CODICE, Galleria Pieroni, Rome. Artists exhibited: Ju-

Catalogue cover,
SCHLAF DER VERNUNFT, 1988

Catalogue cover,
MEDIA POST MEDIA, 1988

Catalogue cover,
HORN OF PLENTY: SIXTEEN ARTISTS FROM NYC,
1989

dith Barry, Dara Birnbaum, Barbara Ess, Dan Graham, Rodney Graham, and John Knight. Catalogue texts by Benjamin H.D. Buchloh, Jean Fisher, Ken Saylor, and others.

NOTHING SACRED, Margo Leavin Gallery, Los Angeles. Curated by Cindy Bernard and Brad Dunning. Artists exhibited: Gary Bachman, Glen Baxter, Clegg & Guttman, Mike Kelley, Liz Larner, Louise Lawler, Peter Nagy, Terry Pendlebury, Stephen Prina, Susan Silas, Julie Wachtel, and Christopher Williams.

PERVERTED BY LANGUAGE, Hillwood Art Gallery, Long Island University, Greenvale, New York. Curated by Robert Nickas. Thirty-three artists exhibited, including Jenny Holzer, Larry Johnson, Ronald Jones, Louise Lawler, Peter Nagy, Richard Prince, and Haim Steinbach. Catalogue text by Nickas.

PHOTOGRAPHY AND ART: INTERACTIONS SINCE 1946, Los Angeles County Museum of Art. Curated by Andy Grundberg and Kathleen McCarthy-Gauss. One hundred ten artists exhibited, including Barbara Kruger, Louise Lawler, Sherrie Levine, Allan McCollum, Richard Prince, Cindy Sherman, Laurie Simmons, and James Welling. Traveled to The Museum of Art, Ft. Lauderdale, Florida; Queens Museum, Flushing, New York; and Des Moines Art Center, Iowa. Catalogue texts by Grundberg and McCarthy-Gauss.

POST-ABSTRACT ABSTRACTION, Aldrich Museum of Contemporary Art, Ridgefield, Connecticut. Twenty-three artists exhibited, including Jeff Koons, Sherrie Levine, Robert Longo, and Haim Steinbach. Catalogue text by Eugene Schwartz.

PROJECTS: LOUISE LAWLER, The Museum of Modern Art, New York. Brochure text by Cora Rosevear.

Cindy Sherman, Whitney Museum of American Art, New York. Traveled to The Institute of Contemporary Art, Boston, and the Dallas Museum of Art. Catalogue texts by Peter Schjeldahl and Lisa Phillips.

Haim Steinbach, Lia Rumma Gallery, Naples, Italy.

THIS IS NOT A PHOTOGRAPH: TWENTY YEARS OF LARGE-SCALE PHOTOGRAPHY, 1966-1986, The John and Mable Ringling Museum of Art, Sarasota, Florida. Curated by Joseph Jacobs. Fifty-nine artists exhibited, including Sarah Charlesworth, Jeff Koons, Barbara Kruger, Louise Lawler, Allan McCollum, Richard Prince, Cindy Sherman, and Laurie Simmons. Traveled to the Akron Art Museum, Akron, Ohio; and The Crysler Museum, Norfolk, Virginia. Catalogue texts by Marvin Heiferman and Jacobs.

James Welling, Samia Saouma, Paris.

1988

ART AT THE EDGE: SHERRIE LEVINE, High Museum of Art, Atlanta, and Hirshhorn Museum and Sculpture Garden, Smithsonian Institute, Washington, D.C. Organized by Susan Krane and Phyllis Rosenzweig. Catalogue texts by Krane and Rosenzweig.

AUSTRALIAN BIENNALE, FROM THE SOUTHERN CROSS: A VIEW OF WORLD ART C. 1940-88, Art Gallery of New South Wales, Sydney, Australia. One hundred eight artists exhibited, including Sarah Charlesworth, Jenny Holzer, and Barbara Kruger. Traveled to the National Gallery of Victoria, Melbourne, Australia. Catalogue texts by Nick Waterloo, Frances Lindsay, Daniel Thomas, and others.

Richard Baim, (C)OVERT: A SERIES OF EXHIBITIONS, P.S.1, New York. Curated by Tom Smith. Catalogue text by Smith and others.

Gretchen Bender, The Museum of Fine Arts, Houston. Brochure published.

THE BINATIONAL: AMERICAN ART OF THE LATE 80S, The Institute of Contemporary Art, Boston. Twenty-six artists exhibited, including Mike Kelley, Jeff Koons, Stephen Prina, Richard Prince, Haim Steinbach, and James Welling. Traveled to Städtische Kunsthalle, Kunstsammlung Nordrhein-Westfalen, Kunstverein für die Rheinlande und Westfalen, Dusseldorf; Kunsthalle Bremen, West Germany; and Württembergischer Kunstverein, Stuttgart. Catalogue texts by Thomas Crow and Lynne Tillman; interviews by Trevor Fairbrother, David Joselit, David Ross, and Elisabeth Sussman.

CARNEGIE INTERNATIONAL, Museum of Art, Carnegie Institute, Pittsburgh. Curated by John Caldwell. Thirty-nine artists exhibited, including Jeff Koons and Sherrie Levine. Catalogue texts by Caldwell, Vicky A. Clark, Thomas McEvilley, Lynne Cooke, and Milena Kalinovska.

Jack Goldstein, The Fruitmarket Gallery, Edinburgh, Scotland. Catalogue text by Gordon Lebredt.

HOVER CULTURE, Metro Pictures, New York. Organized by Ronald Jones. Artists exhibited: Jennifer Bolande, Jiri Georg Dokoupil, Peter Halley, Sherrie Levine, Richard Prince, and Haim Steinbach.

INFORMATION AS ORNAMENT, Feature and Rezac, Chicago. Thirty-one artists exhibited, including Jenny Holzer, Larry Johnson, Allan McCollum, and Richard Prince. Catalogue texts by Kevin Maginnis and David Robbins.

Mike Kelley, THREE PROJECTS: HALF A MAN, FROM MY INSTITUTION TO YOURS, PAY FOR YOUR PLEASURE, The Renaissance Society at The University of Chicago. Catalogue texts by Howard Singerman and John Miller.

Jeff Koons, Museum of Contemporary Art, Chicago. Organized by Michael Danoff. Catalogue text by Danoff.

Barbara Kruger, National Art Gallery, New Zealand. Curated by Jenny Harper. Catalogue texts by Harper and Lita Barrie.

LA BIENNALE DI VENEZIA, APERTO 88, Venice, Italy. Two hundred twenty-five artists exhibited, including Judith Barry, Barbara Bloom, Larry Johnson, Mike Kelley, and Allan McCollum. Catalogue texts by Guido Ballo, Achille Bonito Oliva, Giovanni Carandente, and others.

L'OBJECT DE L'EXPOSITION, Centre National des Arts Plastiques, Paris. Artists exhibited: John Armleder, IFP, Jeff Koons, Bertrand Lavier, Louise Lawler, Ange Leccia, Sherrie Levine, and Richard Prince. Catalogue texts by Jean-Michel Foray and Jean-Pierre Criqui.

Allan McCollum, Portikus, Frankfurt, West Germany. Traveled to Foundation De Appel, Amsterdam. Catalogue texts by Andrea Fraser and Ulrich Wilmes.

Matt Mullican, 39th Bath International Festival, Bath, England. Catalogue text by Denys Zacharopoulos and interview by Dan Cameron.

MEDIA POST MEDIA, Scott Hanson Gallery, New York. Curated by Tricia Collins and Richard Milazzo. Nineteen artists exhibited, including Gretchen Bender, Sarah Charlesworth, Jenny Holzer, Barbara Kruger, Sherrie Levine, Cindy Sherman, and Laurie Simmons. Catalogue text by Collins and Milazzo.

NOSTALGIA AS RESISTANCE, The Clocktower, New York. Curated by Thomas Lawson. Artists exhibited: Jennifer Bolande, Jessica Diamond, Mark Dion, Richard Prince, David Robbins, Cindy Sherman, and Haim Steinbach.

Stephen Prina, Luhring, Augustine and Hodes Gallery, New York.

Stephen Prina, University Art Museum, University of California, Santa Barbara.

PUBLIC DISCOURSE, Real Art Ways, Hartford, Connecticut. Curated by Leslie Tonkonow. Artists exhibited: Dennis Adams, Richard Baim, Judith Barry, Kate Ericson & Mel Ziegler, Peter Fend, General Idea, Alfredo Jaar, and Krzysztof Wodiczko. Catalogue texts by Tonkonow and Theresa Lichtenstein.

SCHLAF DER VERNUFT, Museum Fridericianum, Kassel, West Germany. Twenty-nine artists exhibited, including Jeff Koons, Haim Steinbach, and James Welling. Catalogue texts by Markus Brüderlin, Veit Loers, and Lucius Burckhardt.

SEXUAL DIFFERENCE: BOTH SIDES OF THE CAMERA, The Miriam and Ira D. Wallach Art Gallery, Columbia University, New York. Curated by Abigail Solomon-Godeau. Eighteen artists exhibited, including Richard Baim, Sarah Charlesworth, Louise Lawler, Richard Prince, and Cindy Sherman. Catalogue text by Solomon-Godeau.

Haim Steinbach, CAPC/Musée d'Art Contemporain, Bordeaux, France. Catalogue texts by Jean-Louis Froment, Germano Celant, Elisabeth Lebovici, and John Miller.

UTOPIA POST UTOPIA: CONFIGURATIONS OF NATURE AND CULTURE IN RECENT SCULPTURE AND PHOTOGRAPHY, The Institute of Contemporary Art, Boston. Curated by Elisabeth Sussman and David Joselit. Artists exhibited: Dorit Cypis, Robert Gober, Larry Johnson, Richard Prince, Lorna Simpson, Jeff Wall, Oliver Wasow, Meg Webster, and James Welling. Catalogue texts by Frederic Jameson, Eric Michaud, Sussman, and others.

1989 (through January)

HORN OF PLENTY: SIXTEEN ARTISTS FROM NYC, Stedelijk Museum, Amsterdam. Curated by Gosse Oosterhof. Artists exhibited: Ashley Bickerton, Saint Clair Cemin, Anne Doran, Carroll Dunham, Christian Eckart, Kate Ericson & Mel Ziegler, Robert Gober, Peter Halley, Jon Kessler, Jeff Koons, Jonathan Lasker, Richard Prince, Tim Rollins & KOS, Haim Steinbach, Christopher Wool, and Robert Yarber. Catalogue text by Dan Cameron.

Christopher Williams, Galerie Crousel-Robelin, Bama, Paris.

RICHARD BAIM
Born 1952 in Los Angeles
Lives in Brooklyn, New York

1. TURN OF THE CENTURY, 1989
   Mixed-media installation with black-and-white and color photographs and slide projections
   Two rooms: 25 x 40 ft. overall
   Courtesy the artist

JUDITH BARRY
Born 1949 in Columbus, Ohio
Lives in New York

2. ECHO, 1986
   Installation of slides, video transferred to Super-8 film, and audiotape, 25 x 40 ft. overall
   Collection of the artist

ERICKA BECKMAN
Born 1951 in Hempstead, New York
Lives in New York

3. Selection of films
   TRILOGY WORKS:
   WE IMITATE; WE BREAK UP, 1978
   Super-8 film, 30 min.
   THE BROKEN RULE, 1979
   Super-8 film, 24 min.
   OUT OF HAND, 1981
   Super-8 film, 25 min.
   Courtesy the artist
   YOU THE BETTER, 1983
   16mm film, 35 min.
   Courtesy the artist
   CINDERELLA, 1986
   16mm film, 27 min.
   Courtesy the artist
   BLIND COUNTRY, 1989
   3/4 in. color video with two-track sound, 15 min.
   Written and performed by Mike Kelley
   Produced and directed by Ericka Beckman
   Courtesy the artist
4. BOUNDARY FIGURES, 1989
   Three framed Type-C prints, sequenced lighting, and audiotape
   Prints: 60 x 72 in. each
   Courtesy the artist

GRETCHEN BENDER
Born 1951 in Seaford, Delaware
Lives in New York

5. PEOPLE IN PAIN, 1988
   Silkscreen and paint on heat-set vinyl and neon, 84 x 560 x 11 in.
   Collection of the artist
   Courtesy Metro Pictures, New York
6. Installation of 13 in. television sets, silkscreen on acetate, and metal shelves, 1989
   Televisions: 15 x 20 x 15 in. each
   Courtesy Metro Pictures, New York

DARA BIRNBAUM
Born 1946 in New York
Lives in New York

7. PM MAGAZINE, 1982/89
   Five-channel color video with six-channel sound, two black-and-white photographic enlargements, and painted walls
   Dimensions variable

Courtesy the artist, Josh Baer Gallery, New York, and Rhona Hoffman Gallery, Chicago

BARBARA BLOOM
Born 1951 in Los Angeles
Lives in New York

8. THE REIGN OF NARCISSISM, 1988-89
   Mixed-media installation
   Hexagonal room: 20 x 20 x 12 ft.
   Courtesy Jay Gorney Modern Art, New York, and Isabella Kacprzak, Cologne

TROY BRAUNTUCH
Born 1954 in Jersey City, New Jersey
Lives in Jersey City, New Jersey

9. UNTITLED, 1978
   Type-C prints
   Three panels: 48 x 96 in.; 48 x 48 in.; and 48 x 48 in.
   Lannan Foundation
10. UNTITLED, 1980
    Type-C print, 97 x 165 in.
    Lannan Foundation
11. UNTITLED, 1981
    White pencil on paper, 82-1/2 x 30 in.
    Collection of Kent Fine Art, New York
12. UNTITLED, 1981
    White pencil on black construction paper
    Three panels: 53-1/8 x 29 in.; 28-5/8 x 100 in.; and 53-1/4 x 28-5/8 in.
    The Museum of Modern Art, New York
    Gift of Mr. and Mrs. Eugene Schwartz

SARAH CHARLESWORTH
Born 1947 in East Orange, New Jersey
Lives in New York

13. APRIL 21, 1978, 1978
    Forty-five black-and-white photographs
    Approx. 20 x 24 in. each
    Collection of the artist
    Courtesy Jay Gorney Modern Art, New York, and Margo Leavin Gallery, Los Angeles

JACK GOLDSTEIN
Born 1945 in Montreal, Canada
Lives in New York

14. Selection of 16mm films, 1971-78
    Courtesy the artist
15. UNTITLED, 1983
    Acrylic on canvas, 96 x 96 in.
    Collection of Doris and Robert Hillman, New York
16. UNTITLED, 1983
    Acrylic on canvas, 96 x 168 in.
    The Oliver-Hoffmann Collection, Chicago
17. UNTITLED, 1983
    Acrylic on canvas, 84 x 132 in.
    Collection of B.Z. and Michael Schwartz, New York

JENNY HOLZER
Born 1950 in Gallipolis, Ohio
Lives in Hoosik Falls, New York

18. Selections from "Inflammatory Essays," 1979-82
    Offset paper posters
    17 x 17 in. each; installation dimensions variable
    Courtesy Barbara Gladstone Gallery, New York

LARRY JOHNSON
Born 1959 in Los Angeles
Lives in Los Angeles

19. UNTITLED (I HAD NEVER SEEN ANYTHING LIKE IT), 1988
    Type-C print, 45-1/2 x 90 in.
    Collection of Richard Prince, New York
    Courtesy 303 Gallery, New York
20. UNTITLED (JOHN-JOHN AND BOBBY), 1988
    Type-C prints
    Two panels: 90 x 48-3/4 in. each
    Courtesy 303 Gallery, New York
21. UNTITLED (Q. & A.), 1988
    Type-C print, 88-1/4 x 41-3/4 in.
    Courtesy 303 Gallery, New York
22. UNTITLED (THE FRIENDS YOU KEEP AND THE BOOKS YOU READ), 1988
    Type-C print, 47-3/4 x 89-1/2 in.
    Collection of Thomas M. Lyons, Chicago
    Courtesy 303 Gallery, New York
23. UNTITLED (THE L FACTOR), 1988
    Type-C print, 90 x 43 in.
    Courtesy First Bank System, Incorporated, Minneapolis, Minnesota, and 303 Gallery, New York

RONALD JONES
Born 1952 in Falls Church, Virginia
Lives in New York

24. UNTITLED (SITE FOR THE DEBARKATION OF JAPANESE AMERICANS TO RELOCATION CENTERS, CENTRAL AVENUE AT 1ST STREET, LOS ANGELES, CALIFORNIA, 1942.), 1988
    UNTITLED (DEPARTMENT OF BLOCKPRINTING, BUILDING 15, BLOCK 60, 11TH STREET BETWEEN G AND H STREETS, POSTON-UNIT I AREA, POSTON RELOCATION CENTER, POSTON, ARIZONA, WAR RELOCATION PROJECT, COLORADO RIVER RELOCATION PROJECT, 1942.), 1988
    UNTITLED (JAPANESE POETRY DEPARTMENT, BUILDING 13, BLOCK 310, 2ND STREET BETWEEN C AND D STREETS, POSTON-UNIT III AREA, POSTON RELOCATION CENTER, POSTON, ARIZONA, WAR RELOCATION PROJECT, COLORADO RIVER RELOCATION PROJECT, 1942.), 1988
    UNTITLED (MUSIC DEPARTMENT, BUILDING 15, BLOCK 44, 8TH STREET BETWEEN G AND H STREETS, POSTON-UNIT I AREA, POSTON RELOCATION CENTER, POSTON, ARIZONA, WAR RELOCATION PROJECT, COLORADO RIVER RELOCATION PROJECT, 1942.), 1988
    Marble, granite, and slate floor inlays
    Commissioned for the exhibition

MIKE KELLEY
Born 1954 in Detroit, Michigan
Lives in Los Angeles

25. PAY FOR YOUR PLEASURE, 1988
    Pastel on paper by William Bonin and forty-two painted Tyvek banners
    Drawing: 16 x 13-3/4 in.; banners: approx. 96 x 48 in. each
    Collection of Timothy and Suzette Flood, Chicago
    Promised gift to The Museum of Contemporary Art, Los Angeles

JEFF KOONS
Born 1955 in York, Pennsylvania
Lives in New York

26. BEAR AND POLICEMAN, 1988
    Polychromed wood, 85 x 43 x 37 in.
    Courtesy Sonnabend Gallery, New York
27. BUSTER KEATON, 1988
    Polychromed wood, 65-3/4 x 50 x 26-1/2 in.
    Collection of the artist
    Courtesy Sonnabend Gallery, New York

28. STRING OF PUPPIES, *1988*
    Polychromed wood, 42 x 62 x 37 in.
    Collection of Phoebe Chason, Harrison, New York
29. USHERING IN BANALITY, *1988*
    Polychromed wood, 38 x 62 x 30 in.
    Collection of the artist
    Courtesy Sonnabend Gallery, New York
30. WOMAN IN TUB, *1988*
    Porcelain, 24-3/4 x 36 x 27 in.
    The Mottahedan Collection

BARBARA KRUGER
Born 1945 in Newark, New Jersey
Lives in New York

31. UNTITLED (PLEDGE), *1989*
    Painted wall mural
    Courtesy the artist and Mary Boone Gallery, New York
    Commissioned for the exhibition

LOUISE LAWLER
Born 1947 in Bronxville, New York
Lives in New York

32. "STANDING BEFORE YOU, RATHER BEHIND YOU, TO TELL
    YOU OF SOMETHING I KNOW NOTHING ABOUT", *1989*
    Installation of photographs, labels, printed cards,
    paperweights, and pedestals
    Courtesy the artist and Metro Pictures, New York
    Commissioned for the exhibition

THOMAS LAWSON
Born 1951 in Glasgow, Scotland
Lives in Brooklyn, New York

33. DEATH AT THE DINER, *1980*
    Oil on canvas, 51-1/2 x 41 in.
    Courtesy the artist and Metro Pictures, New York
34. HE DIED LIKE MANY OF HIS INNOCENT VICTIMS, *1980*
    Oil on canvas, 51-1/2 x 41 in.
    The Rivendell Collection
35. WILD IN THE STREET, HANGED IN THE PARK, *1980*
    Oil on canvas, 51-1/2 x 41 in.
    Courtesy the artist and Metro Pictures, New York
36. BEATEN TO DEATH, *1981*
    Oil on canvas, 48 x 48 in.
    Courtesy the artist and Metro Pictures, New York
37. BOY SHOT FOR A BIKE, *1981*
    Oil on canvas, 48 x 48 in.
    Collection of the artist
38. DON'T HIT HER AGAIN, *1981*
    Oil on canvas, 48 x 48 in.
    Collection of Raymond J. Learsy, Sharon, Connecticut
39. INCHES FROM DEATH, *1981*
    Oil on canvas, 48 x 48 in.
    Courtesy the artist and Metro Pictures, New York
40. SHOT BY THE FATHERS, *1981*
    Oil on canvas, 51-1/2 x 41 in.
    Collection of the artist
41. FORTY-FIVE SECONDS OF BILLIE HOLIDAY, *1982*
    Audiotape, 45 sec.
    Courtesy the artist
42. DECLINE AND FALL, *1989*
    Color and black-and-white photographs mounted on
    masonite, acrylic, and fluorescent fixtures,
    112 x 67 x 3-1/2 in.
    Courtesy the artist and Metro Pictures, New York

SHERRIE LEVINE
Born 1947 in Hazleton, Pennsylvania
Lives in New York

43. UNTITLED (IGNATZ: 1), *1988*
    Casein on wood, 24 x 20 in.
    Courtesy Mary Boone Gallery, New York
44. UNTITLED (IGNATZ: 2), *1988*
    Casein on wood, 24 x 20 in.
    Collection of the Kroyer Corporation, New York
    Courtesy Mary Boone Gallery, New York

45. UNTITLED (IGNATZ: 3), *1988*
    Casein on wood, 24 x 20 in.
    Courtesy Mary Boone Gallery, New York
46. UNTITLED (IGNATZ: 4), *1988*
    Casein on wood, 24 x 20 in.
    Courtesy Mary Boone Gallery, New York
47. UNTITLED (IGNATZ: 5), *1988*
    Casein on wood, 24 x 20 in.
    Courtesy Mary Boone Gallery, New York
48. UNTITLED (IGNATZ: 6), *1988*
    Casein on wood, 24 x 20 in.
    Courtesy Mary Boone Gallery, New York
49. UNTITLED (KRAZY KAT: 1), *1988*
    Casein on wood, 18 x 15-1/2 in.
    Collection of Emily Fisher Landau, New York
    Courtesy Mary Boone Gallery, New York
50. UNTITLED (KRAZY KAT: 2), *1988*
    Casein on wood, 18 x 15-1/2 in.
    Courtesy Donald Young Gallery, Chicago
51. UNTITLED (KRAZY KAT: 3), *1988*
    Casein on wood, 18 x 15-1/2 in.
    Private Collection
    Courtesy Thea Westreich Associates
    and Mary Boone Gallery, New York
52. UNTITLED (KRAZY KAT: 4), *1988*
    Casein on wood, 18 x 15-1/2 in.
    Courtesy Mary Boone Gallery, New York
53. UNTITLED (KRAZY KAT: 5), *1988*
    Casein on wood, 18 x 15-1/2 in.
    Collection of the Kroyer Corporation, New York
    Courtesy Mary Boone Gallery, New York
54. UNTITLED (KRAZY KAT: 6), *1988*
    Casein on wood, 18 x 15-1/2 in.
    Courtesy Mary Boone Gallery, New York

ROBERT LONGO
Born 1953 in Brooklyn, New York
Lives in New York

55. UNTITLED, *1981-87*
    Charcoal, graphite, and ink on paper, 96 x 60 in.
    Collection of the artist
    Courtesy Metro Pictures, New York
56. UNTITLED, *1981-87*
    Charcoal, graphite, and ink on paper, 96 x 60 in.
    Collection of the artist
    Courtesy Metro Pictures, New York
57. UNTITLED, *1981-87*
    Charcoal, graphite, and ink on paper, 96 x 60 in.
    Collection of Neil and Barbara Bluhm, Chicago
58. UNTITLED, *1981-88*
    Charcoal, graphite, and ink on paper, 96 x 60 in.
    Collection of the artist
    Courtesy Metro Pictures, New York
59. UNTITLED, *1981-88*
    Charcoal, graphite, and ink on paper, 96 x 60 in.
    Collection of the artist
    Courtesy Metro Pictures, New York
60. UNTITLED, *1982-85*
    Charcoal, graphite, and ink on paper, 96 x 48 in.
    Collection of Richard Price, New York
61. UNTITLED, *1983-84*
    Lacquer on wood, 96 x 88 x 36 in.
    Private Collection, New York

ALLAN McCOLLUM
Born 1944 in Los Angeles
Lives in New York

62. INDIVIDUAL WORKS, *1987/89*
    Approx. 10,000 enamel on cast Hydrocal objects, approx.
    2 x 5 in. each
    Courtesy the artist and John Weber Gallery, New York

MATT MULLICAN
Born 1951 in Santa Monica, California
Lives in New York

63. UNTITLED *(bulletin board), 1979-present*
    Mixed media on board, 96 x 48 in.
    Courtesy Michael Klein, Inc., New York
64. UNTITLED *(bulletin board), 1979-present*
    Mixed media on board, 96 x 48 in.
    Courtesy Michael Klein, Inc., New York
65. UNTITLED *(bulletin board), 1979-present*
    Mixed media on board, 96 x 48 in.
    Courtesy Michael Klein, Inc., New York
66. UNTITLED *(bulletin board), 1979-present*
    Mixed media on board, 96 x 48 in.
    Courtesy Michael Klein, Inc., New York
67. UNTITLED *(bulletin board), 1979-present*
    Mixed media on board, 96 x 48 in.
    Courtesy Michael Klein, Inc., New York
68. UNTITLED *(bulletin board), 1979-present*
    Mixed media on board, 96 x 48 in.
    Courtesy Michael Klein, Inc., New York
69. UNTITLED, *1984*
    Cotton appliqué, 24 x 14 ft.
    Courtesy Michael Klein, Inc., New York
70. UNTITLED (MACHINES), *1988*
    Mixed media, 44 x 47 x 94 in.
    Courtesy Michael Klein, Inc., New York
71. UNTITLED (WORKING MODEL FOR A CITY), *1988*
    Mixed media, 4-1/4 x 41-3/4 x 90 in.
    Courtesy Michael Klein, Inc., New York

PETER NAGY
Born 1959 in Bridgeport, Connecticut
Lives in New York

72. AMERICA INVENTED EVERYTHING, *1986*
    Acrylic on canvas, 72 x 72 in.
    Collection of William S. Ehrlich, New York
73. LEGER, *1986*
    Acrylic on canvas, 72 x 72 in.
    Collection of Alice and Marvin Kosmin, New York
74. MONDO CANE, *1986*
    Acrylic on canvas, 72 x 72 in.
    Collection of Max Holtzman Inc., Rockville, Maryland
75. BELIEF IN STYLE, *1988*
    Acrylic on canvas, 72 x 72 in.
    Collection of John L. Stewart, New York
76. KIBOUGAOKA, *1988*
    Acrylic on canvas, 72 x 48 in.
    The Oliver-Hoffmann Collection, Chicago
77. L'AGE D'OR, *1988*
    Acrylic on canvas, 72 x 72 in.
    Collection of Ellyn and Saul Dennison, Bernardsville,
    New Jersey

STEPHEN PRINA
Born 1954 in Galesburg, Illinois
Lives in Los Angeles

78. UPON THE OCCASION OF RECEIVERSHIP, *1989*
    LANGUAGE TYPE A:
    1. ENGLISH*
    2. FRENCH
    3. GERMAN
    4. ITALIAN
    5. SPANISH*
    LANGUAGE TYPE B:
    6. DANISH
    7. DUTCH
    8. FLEMISH
    9. LATIN
    10. NORWEGIAN
    11. PORTUGUESE
    12. RUMANIAN
    13. SWEDISH
    LANGUAGE TYPE C:
    14. AFRIKAANS
    15. ALBANIAN
    16. ARABIC
    17. ARMENIAN
    18. BULGARIAN
    19. CANTONESE
    20. CZECH
    21. ESTONIAN
    22. FARSI
    23. FINNISH
    24. GREEK
    25. HEBREW
    26. HINDI
    27. HUNGARIAN
    28. ICELANDIC
    29. INDONESIAN
    30. JAPANESE*
    31. KOREAN
    32. LATVIAN
    33. LITHUANIAN
    34. MANDARIN
    35. POLISH
    36. RUSSIAN
    37. SERBO-CROATIAN
    38. SLOVAK
    39. SLOVENIAN
    40. TAGALOG
    41. THAI
    42. TURKISH

43. UKRAINIAN	52. LAOTIAN
44. URDU	53. NEPALI
45. VIETNAMESE	54. PASHTO
46. YIDDISH	55. PROVENÇALE
LANGUAGE TYPE D:	56. PUNJABI
47. BENGALI	57. SINHALESE
48. BURMESE	58. SWAHILI
49. GUJURATI	59. TAHITIAN
50. HAWAIIAN	60. TAMIL
51. KHMER	61. UZBEK

*Not in the exhibition
Lawrence Weiner, A TRANSLATION FROM ONE
LANGUAGE TO ANOTHER, Amsterdam, 1969
Laserprinting on letterhead stationery
Sixty-one units: 18-5/16 x 15-5/8 in. each (framed)
Courtesy the artist
and Luhring Augustine Gallery, New York

RICHARD PRINCE
Born 1949 in Panama Canal Zone
Lives in New York

79. ALL I'VE HEARD, 1988
Acrylic and silkscreen on canvas, 56 x 48 in.
Courtesy Barbara Gladstone Gallery, New York
80. CAN YOU IMAGINE, 1988
Acrylic and silkscreen on canvas, 56 x 48 in.
Courtesy Barbara Gladstone Gallery, New York
81. GOOD NEWS BAD NEWS, 1988
Acrylic and silkscreen on canvas, 56 x 48 in.
Courtesy Barbara Gladstone Gallery, New York
82. GOOD NEWS BAD NEWS, 1988
Acrylic and silkscreen on canvas, 56 x 48 in.
Courtesy Barbara Gladstone Gallery, New York
83. MY USUAL PROCEDURE, 1988
Acrylic and silkscreen on canvas, 56 x 48 in.
Courtesy Barbara Gladstone Gallery, New York
84. SO WHAT ELSE IS NEW, 1988
Acrylic and silkscreen on canvas, 56 x 48 in.
Courtesy Barbara Gladstone Gallery, New York
85. WHAT A KID I WAS, 1988
Acrylic and silkscreen on canvas, 56 x 48 in.
Courtesy Barbara Gladstone Gallery, New York
86. WHAT A KID I WAS, 1988-89
Acrylic and silkscreen on canvas, 75 x 116 in.
Courtesy Barbara Gladstone Gallery, New York
87. THE WRONG JOKE, 1989
Acrylic and silkscreen on canvas, 56 x 48 in.
Courtesy Barbara Gladstone Gallery, New York

CINDY SHERMAN
Born 1954 in Glen Ridge, New Jersey
Lives in New York

88. UNTITLED FILM STILL (#4), 1977
Black-and-white photograph, ed. 1/3, 30 x 40 in.
Private Collection
89. UNTITLED FILM STILL (#13), 1978
Black-and-white photograph, ed. 1/3, 40 x 30 in.
Collection of Doris and Robert Hillman, New York
90. UNTITLED FILM STILL (#14), 1978
Black-and-white photograph, ed. 1/3, 40 x 30 in.
Collection of Richard L. Sandor, Chicago
91. UNTITLED FILM STILL (#15), 1978
Black-and-white photograph, ed. 1/3, 40 x 30 in.
Collection of Joyce Eliason, Los Angeles
92. UNTITLED FILM STILL (#21), 1978
Black-and-white photograph, ed. 1/3, 30 x 40 in.
Collection of Linda Cathcart, Venice, California
93. UNTITLED FILM STILL (#37), 1979
Black-and-white photograph, ed. 1/3, 40 x 30 in.
Collection of Douglas Crimp, New York
94. UNTITLED FILM STILL (#38), 1979
Black-and-white photograph, ed. 1/3, 40 x 30 in.
Private Collection, New York
95. UNTITLED FILM STILL (#40), 1979
Black-and-white photograph, ed. 1/3, 30 x 40 in.
Collection of Eileen and Matthew Cohen, New York

96. UNTITLED FILM STILL (#46), 1979
Black-and-white photograph, ed. 1/3, 30 x 40 in.
Collection of Rosalind E. Krauss, New York
97. UNTITLED FILM STILL (#50), 1979
Black-and-white photograph, ed. 1/3, 30 x 40 in.
Fried, Frank, Harris, Shriver and Jacobson Art Collection,
New York

LAURIE SIMMONS
Born 1949 in Far Rockaway, New York
Lives in New York

98. WALKING CAMERA (JIMMY THE CAMERA), 1987
Black-and-white photograph, 83-1/4 x 47-1/4 in.
The Saint Louis Art Museum, Missouri
Funds provided by Mrs. Ada J. Kling, Mr. and Mrs. Jack P.
Freund, Jr., the John R. Goodall Trust, Mrs. Robert R.
Imse, and Station List Publishing Company through the
1987 Annual Appeal
99. WALKING CAKE, 1989
Black-and-white photograph, 83-1/4 x 47-1/4 in.
Courtesy Metro Pictures, New York
100. WALKING COMMODE, 1989
Black-and-white photograph, 83-1/4 x 47-1/4 in.
Courtesy Metro Pictures, New York
101. WALKING HOURGLASS, 1989
Black-and-white photograph, 83-1/4 x 47-1/4 in.
Courtesy Metro Pictures, New York
102. WALKING HOUSE, 1989
Black-and-white photograph, 83-1/4 x 47-1/4 in.
Courtesy Metro Pictures, New York
103. WALKING PURSE, 1989
Black-and-white photograph, 83-1/4 x 47-1/4 in.
Courtesy Metro Pictures, New York

HAIM STEINBACH
Born 1944 in Israel
Lives in Brooklyn, New York

104. Mixed-media installation including:
UNTITLED (WAKAMBA GOURDS), 1989
Formica-laminate shelf with gourds, 49 x 80 x 22 in.
Courtesy Jay Gorney Modern Art, New York, Margo
Leavin Gallery, Los Angeles, and Sonnabend Gallery,
New York

MITCHELL SYROP
Born 1953 in Yonkers, New York
Lives in Los Angeles

105. ALL MEN ARE CREATED EQUAL, 1982
Black-and-white photograph, 40 x 30 in.
Collection of Consiline and Tony Antoville, Rancho Palos
Verdes, California
106. ALL MEN ARE CREATED EQUAL, 1982
Black-and-white photograph, 24 x 20 in.
Collection of Shaunna and Joe Garlington, La Crescenta,
California
107. CAESAR'S PALACE, 1982
Black-and-white photograph, 30 x 40 in.
Collection of Isabel Brones, Los Angeles
108. SIT IN JUDGEMENT, 1982
Photo silkscreen, 48 x 66 in.
Collection of Dr. Joel Weisman, Beverly Hills, California
109. ALL GOD'S CHILLUN' GOT WINGS, 1984
Gouache on paper, 29 x 20 in.
Collection of Lee Kaplan, Los Angeles
110. ALL SYSTEMS GO!, 1984
Sixteen pieces of cast soap in individual boxes (from an
edition of thirty), 3-5/8 x 4-1/2 x 1-1/4 in. each
Courtesy the artist
and Richard Kuhlenschmidt Gallery, Santa Monica,
California (thirteen pieces)
Collection of Nora Halpern Brougher and Kerry Brougher,
Los Angeles (two pieces)
Collection of Harry Stein, Los Angeles (one piece)
111. BETTER TO SHINE THAN TO REFLECT, 1984
Black-and-white photograph mounted on board,
40 x 30 in.
Collection of Andrew Schwartz, Los Angeles

112. LIFT AND SEPARATE, 1984
Black-and-white photographs mounted on board
Nine panels: 24 x 20 in. each
Collection of Gregory Linn, Los Angeles
113. LIFT AND SEPARATE, 1984
Black-and-white photographs mounted on board
Three panels: 50 x 40 in. each; 50 x 120 in. overall
Courtesy the artist and
Richard Kuhlenschmidt Gallery, Santa Monica, California
114. Porcelain object, 1984
7 x 7 x 5 in.
Collection of Dorit Cypis, Minneapolis, Minnesota
115. Porcelain object, 1984
7 x 7 x 5 in.
Collection of Hunter Drohojowska, Venice, California
116. Porcelain object, 1984
7 x 7 x 5 in.
Collection of Richard Kuhlenschmidt, Santa Monica,
California
117. STOOP TO CONQUER, 1984
Black-and-white photograph mounted on board,
36 x 66 in.
Collection of Ann and Aaron Nisenson, Santa Barbara,
California
118. THE GIFT THAT KEEPS ON GIVING, 1984-86
Lacquer on canvas
Two panels: 120 x 76 in. overall
Newport Harbor Art Museum, Newport Beach,
California
Purchased with funds provided by the Acquisition
Committee

JAMES WELLING
Born 1951 in Hartford, Connecticut
Lives in New York

119. UNTITLED, 1977-80
Silver print, 17 x 14 in.
Courtesy the artist and Jay Gorney Modern Art,
New York
120. UNTITLED, 1977-80
Silver print, 17 x 14 in.
Courtesy the artist and Jay Gorney Modern Art,
New York
121. UNTITLED, 1977-80
Silver print, 17 x 14 in.
Courtesy the artist and Jay Gorney Modern Art,
New York
122. UNTITLED, 1977-80
Silver print, 17 x 14 in.
Courtesy the artist and Jay Gorney Modern Art,
New York
123. UNTITLED, 1977-80
Silver print, 17 x 14 in.
Courtesy the artist and Jay Gorney Modern Art,
New York
124. UNTITLED, 1977-80
Silver print, 17 x 14 in.
Courtesy the artist and Jay Gorney Modern Art,
New York
125. UNTITLED, 1977-80
Silver print, 17 x 14 in.
Courtesy the artist and Jay Gorney Modern Art,
New York
126. UNTITLED, 1977-80
Silver print, 17 x 14 in.
Courtesy the artist and Jay Gorney Modern Art,
New York
127. UNTITLED, 1977-80
Silver print, 17 x 14 in.
Courtesy the artist and Jay Gorney Modern Art,
New York
128. UNTITLED, 1977-80
Silver print, 17 x 14 in.
Courtesy the artist and Jay Gorney Modern Art,
New York
129. UNTITLED, 1977-80
Silver print, 17 x 14 in.
Courtesy the artist and Jay Gorney Modern Art,
New York
130. UNTITLED, 1977-80
Silver print, 17 x 14 in.

Courtesy the artist and Jay Gorney Modern Art,
New York
131. AMES MEMORIAL HALL LOGGIA, NORTH EASTON, MA;
1879-81, 1988
Dye transfer photograph, 18 x 22 in.
Collection of Alain Clairet, New York
Courtesy Thea Westreich Associates, New York
132. BIGELOW HOUSE, NEWTON, MA; 1886-87, 1988
Silver print, 18 x 22 in.
Courtesy the artist and Jay Gorney Modern Art,
New York
133. CITY HALL, ALBANY, NY; 1880-83, 1988
Silver print, 22 x 18 in.
Collection of Alain Clairet, New York
Courtesy Thea Westreich Associates, New York
134. CORNERSTONE, IMMANUAL BAPTIST CHURCH, NEWTON,
MA; 1884-86, 1988
Silver print, 22 x 18 in.
Collection of Art & Knowledge Workshop, Inc., Bronx,
New York
135. GLESSNER HOUSE, CHICAGO, IL; 1885-87, 1988
Silver print, 18 x 22 in.
Collection of Alain Clairet, New York
Courtesy Thea Westreich Associates, New York
136. LAW SCHOOL, CAMBRIDGE, MA; 1881-83, 1988
Silver print, 18 x 22 in.
Collection of Alain Clairet, New York
Courtesy Thea Westreich Associates, New York
137. STACK WING, AMES FREE LIBRARY, NORTH EASTON, MA;
1877-79, 1988
Silver print, 18 x 22 in.
Collection of Alain Clairet, New York
Courtesy Thea Westreich Associates, New York
138. STOUGHTON HOUSE, CAMBRIDGE, MA; 1882-83, 1988
Silver print, 18 x 22 in.
Collection of Alain Clairet, New York
Courtesy Thea Westreich Associates, New York
139. WINN MEMORIAL PUBLIC LIBRARY, WOBURN, MA;
1876-79, 1988
Silver print, 18 x 22 in.
Collection of Alain Clairet, New York
Courtesy Thea Westreich Associates, New York

CHRISTOPHER WILLIAMS

Born 1956 in Los Angeles
Lives in Los Angeles

140. ANGOLA TO VIETNAM*, 1989
Twenty-seven gelatin silver prints, ed. 2/5, each
accompanied by a 2 x 3-1/2 in. silkscreen on Plexiglas
label card
Courtesy Galerie Crousel-Robelin, Bama, Paris
ANGOLA
Blaschka Model 439, 1894
Genus no. 5091
Family, Sterculiaceae
Cola acuminata (Beauv.) Schott and Endl.
Cola Nut, Goora Nut
14 x 11 in.
ARGENTINA
Blaschka Model 289, 1892
Genus no. 7438
Family, Solanaceae
Nierembergia gracilis Hook.
Nierembergia calycina Hook.
14 x 11 in.
BOLIVIA
Blaschka Model 268, 1892
Genus no. 5397
Family, Begoniaceae
Begonia boliviensis A.DC.
14 x 11 in.
BRAZIL
Blaschka Model 104, 1889
Genus no. 3870
Family Leguminosae
Erythrina Crista-galli Linn.
Coral-tree, Coral-plant, Cocksomb
11 x 14 in.
CENTRAL AFRICAN REPUBLIC
Blaschka Model 783, 1923

Genus no. 5112
Family Ochnaceae
Ochna mulitflora DC.
11 x 14 in.
CHILE
Blaschka Model 180, 1890
Genus no. 7474
Family, Scrophulariaceae
Calceolaria scabiosaefolia Roem and Schult.
14 x 11 in.
COLOMBIA
Blaschka Moderl 158, 1890
Genus no. 8642
Family, Cucurbitaceae
Cylanthera pedata Schrad.
Pepino de Comer
11 x 14 in.
DOMINICAN REPUBLIC
Blaschka Model 601, 1896
Genus no. 4493
Family, Euphorbiaceae
Hura crepitans Linn.
Sandbox tree
11 x 14 in.
EL SALVADOR
Blaschka Model 639, 1898
Genus no. 7158
Family, Verbenceae
Petrea volubilis Jacq.
Purple Wreath
11 x 14 in.
ETHIOPIA
Blaschka Model 478, 1894
Genus no. 8381
Family, Rubiaceae
Coffea arabica Linn.
Coffee, "Coffa"
11 x 14 in.
GUATEMALA
Blaschka Model 227, 1891
Genus no. 1660
Family, Orchidaceae
Lycaste Skinneri (Batem.) Lindl.
14 x 11 in.
HAITI
Blaschka Model 601, 1896
Genus no. 4493
Family, Euphorbiaceae
Hura crepitans Linn.
Sandbox tree
11 x 14 in.
HONDURAS
Blaschka Model 469, 1894
Genus no. 4155
Family, Meliaceae
Cedrela odorata Linn.
West Indian Cedar, Jamaica Cedar, Spanish Cedar
14 x 11 in.
INDONESIA
Blaschka Moderl 693, 1903
Genus no. 1318
Family, Musaceae
Musa paradisiaca Linn.
subsp. sapientum (Linn.) Ktze.
Banana
11 x 14 in.
LEBANON
Blaschka Model 770, 1906
Genus no. 1961
Family, Moraceae
Ficus Carica Linn.
The Fig
11 x 14 in.
MEXICO
Blaschka Model 160, 1890
Genus no. 9228
Family, Compositae
Dahlia pinnata Cav.
Dahlia variabilis (Willd.) Desf.
Dahlia
11 x 14 in.

NAMIBIA
Blaschka Model 95, 1889
Genus no. 3164
Family, Crassulaceae
Cotyledon orbiculata Linn.
14 x 11 in.
NICARAGUA
Blaschka Model 424, 1894
Genus no. 4546
Family, Anacardiaceae
Anacardium occidentale Linn.
Cashew Acajou
11 x 14 in.
PARAGUAY
Blaschka Model 494, 1894
Genus no. 663d
Family, Palmae
Arecastrum Romanzoffianum (Cham.) Becc.
var. australe (Mart.) Becc.
cocos australis Mart.
Pindo Palm
14 x 11 in.
PERU
Blaschka Model 180, 1890
Genus no. 7474
Family, Scrophulariaceae
Calceolaria scabiosaefolia Roem and Schult.
11 x 14 in.
PHILIPPINES
Blaschka Model 387, 1893
Genus no. 5020
Family, Malvaceae
Gossypium herbaceum Linn.
Gossypium Nanking Meyen
Nanking Cotton
11 x 14 in.
SOUTH AFRICA
Blaschka Model 95, 1889
Genus no. 3164
Family, Crassulaceae
Cotyledon orbiculata Linn.
14 x 11 in.
SRI LANKA
Blaschka Model 694, 1903
Genus no. 1318
Family, Musaceae
Musa rosacea Jacq.
11 x 14 in.
TOGO
Blaschka Model 439, 1894
Genus no. 5091
Family, Sterculiaceae
Cola acuminata (Beauv.) Schott and Endl.
Cola Nut, Goora Nut
14 x 11 in.
UGANDA
Blaschka Model 482, 1894
Genus no. 3892
Family, Leguminosae
Cajanus Cajan (Linn.) Druce
Cajanus indicus Spreng.
Pigeon Pea
14 x 11 in.
URUGUAY
Blaschka Model 175, 1890
Genus no. 7447
Family, Solanaceae
Browallia viscosa HBK
11 x 14 in.
VIETNAM
Blaschka Model 272, 1892
Genus no. 8594
Family, Cucurbitaceae
Luffa cylindrica (Linn.) Roem.
11 x 14 in.

INDEX

Note: Numbers in italics refer to illustrations.

Photography Credits

Most of the photographs reproduced in A Forest of Signs: Art in the Crisis of Representation *have been provided by the artists or by the collections indicated in the accompanying captions. We thank them for their generosity and would like to acknowledge the following for their contributions as well: Rudolph Burkhardt, courtesy Leo Castelli Gallery, New York: p. 131; Michel Cenet: pp. 144, 145; Geoffrey Clements Inc., New York: p. 138; Donald Young Gallery: p. 136; Susan Einstein: p. 111; James Franklin: pp. 120, 121; Gamma One Conversions, New York: pp. 122, 123; Greg Gorman: pp. 92, 93; Michael Kreizer: pp. 68, 69; Daniel J. Martinez: p. 130; Charles Mayer: p. 74 (center); Luis Medina: p. 150; Bill Orcutt: p. 107; Douglas M. Parker: p. 38; Kira Perov: p. 75 (center); The Press of the Nova Scotia College of Art and Design, Halifax: p. 142; Ken Schles: pp. 29, 52; F. Scruton: pp. 135, 190; Oren Slor: p. 40; Squidds & Nunns: p. 42; Tom Vinetz: p. 129; John Weber Gallery: p. 140; Alice Z. Weiner: p. 138; Dorothy Zeidman: p. 139; Zindman/Fremont: p. 46, 100.*